50 cycles to Country Pubs

Cycle routes researched and written by Neil Coates, David Foster, John Gillham, Paul Grogan, David Hancock, Dennis Kelsall, Tim Locke, Richard Love, Terry Marsh, Jon Sparks and Sue Viccars

Produced by AA Publishing

Published by AA Publishing (a trading name of Automobile Association Developments Limited, whose registered office is Fanum House, Basing View, Basingstoke, Hampshire RG21 4EA; registered number 1878835).

A02779

Ordnance Survey® This product includes mapping data licensed from Ordnance Survey® with the permission of the Controller of Her Majesty's Stationery Office. © Crown copyright 2005. All rights reserved. Licence number 399221.

ISBN-10: 0-7495-4812-6
ISBN-13: 978-0-7495-4812-4

A CIP catalogue record for this book is available from the British Library.

The contents of this book are believed correct at the time of printing. Nevertheless, the publishers cannot be held responsible for any errors or omissions or for changes in the details given in this book or for the consequences of any reliance on the information it provides. We have tried to ensure accuracy in this book, but things do change and we would be grateful if readers would advise us of any inaccuracies they may encounter. This does not affect your statutory rights.

We have taken all reasonable steps to ensure that these cycle rides are safe and achievable by people with a realistic level of fitness. However, all outdoor activities involve a degree of risk and the publishers accept no responsibility for any injuries caused to readers whilst following these cycle rides. For advice on cycling in safety, see page 6.

Visit AA Publishing's website www.theAA.com/bookshop

Colour reproduction by M.R.M. Graphics Ltd
Printed in Slovenia by MKT PRINT d.d.

AA

50 Cycles to
Country Pubs

Contents

Locator map

Cycling in safety

Cycling is a fun activity which all the family can enjoy, and teaching your child to ride a bike, and going on family cycling trips, are rewarding experiences. Not only is cycling a great way to travel, but as a regular form of exercise it can make an invaluable contribution to your health and fitness.

The growth of motor traffic has made Britain's roads increasingly dangerous and unattractive to cyclists. Cycling with children is an added responsibility and, as with everything, there is a risk when taking them out for a day's cycling. However, in recent years measures have been taken to address this, including the on-going development of the National Cycle Network (8,000 miles utilising quiet lanes and traffic-free paths) and off-road routes for families, such as converted railway lines, canal tow paths and forest tracks.

In devising these cycles, every effort has been made to use cycle paths, or to link them with quiet lanes and waymarked byways. Unavoidably, in a few cases, some relatively busy B-roads have been used to link quieter, more attractive routes.

Rules of the road

- Ride in single file on narrow and busy roads.
- Be alert, look and listen for traffic, especially on narrow lanes and blind bends and be extra careful when descending steep hills, as loose gravel can lead to an accident.
- In rain make sure you keep a good distance between you and other riders.
- Indicate your intentions clearly.
- Brush up on *The Highway Code* before venturing out on to the road.

Off-road safety code of conduct

- Only ride where you know it is legal to do so. It is forbidden to cycle on public footpaths, marked in yellow. The only 'rights of way' open to cyclists are bridleways (blue markers) and unsurfaced tracks, known as byways, which are open to all traffic and waymarked in red.
- Canal tow paths: you need a permit to cycle on some stretches of tow path (www.waterscape.com). Remember that access paths can be steep and slippery and always get off and push your bike under low bridges and by locks.
- Always yield to walkers and horses, giving adequate warning of your approach.
- Don't expect to cycle at high speeds.
- Keep to the main trail to avoid any unnecessary erosion to the area beside the trail and to prevent skidding, especially if it is wet.
- Remember the Country Code.

Preparing your bicycle

A basic routine includes checking the wheels for broken spokes or excess play in the bearings, and checking the tyres for punctures, undue wear and the correct tyre pressures. Ensure that the brake blocks are firmly in place and not worn, and that cables are not frayed or too slack. Lubricate hubs, pedals, gear mechanisms and cables. Make sure you have a pump, a bell, a rear rack to carry panniers and, if cycling at night, a set of working lights.

Preparing yourself

Comfort is key when considering what to wear. Essentials are padded cycling shorts or warm stretch leggings (avoid tight-fitting trousers like jeans or baggy tracksuit trousers), stiff-soled training shoes, and a wind/waterproof jacket. Fingerless gloves will add to your comfort. A cycling helmet provides essential protection if you fall off your bike, so they are recommended for young children who are still learning.

About the pub

Generally, all the pubs are on the cycle route. Some are close to the start/finish point, others are at the midway point, and occasionally, the recommended pub is a short drive from the start/finish point.

The description of the pub is intended to convey its history and character and in the 'food' section we list a selection of dishes, which indicate the style of food available. Under 'family facilities', we say if the pub offers a children's menu or smaller portions of adult dishes, and whether the pub has a family room, highchairs, baby-changing facilities, or toys. There is detail on the garden, terrace, and any play area.

DIRECTIONS: If the pub is very close to the start point we state see Getting to the Start. If the pub is on the route the relevant direction/map location number is given, in addition to general directions. In some cases the pub is a short drive away from the finish point, so we give detailed directions to the pub from the end of the route.

PARKING: The number of parking spaces is given. All but a few of the walks and rides start away from the pub. If the pub car park is the parking/start point, then we have been given permission by the landlord to print the fact. You should always let the landlord or a member of staff know that you are using the car park before setting off.

OPEN: If the pub is open all week we state 'daily' and if it's open throughout the day we say 'all day', otherwise we just give the days/sessions the pub is closed.

FOOD: If the pub serves food all week we state 'daily' and if food is served throughout the day we say 'all day', otherwise we just give the days/sessions when food is not served.

BREWERY/COMPANY: This is the name of the brewery to which the pub is tied or the pub company that owns it. 'Free house' means that the pub is independently owned and run.

REAL ALE: We list the regular real ales available on handpump. 'Guest beers' indicates that the pub rotates beers from a number of microbreweries.

DOGS: We say if dogs are allowed in pubs on walk routes and detail any restrictions.

ROOMS: We list the number of bedrooms and how many are en suite. For prices please call the pub.

Please note that pubs change hands frequently and new chefs are employed, so menu details and facilities may change at short notice. Not all the pubs featured in this guide are listed in the *AA Pub Guide*. For information on those that are, including AA-rated accommodation, and for a comprehensive selection of pubs across Britain, please refer to the *AA Pub Guide* or see the AA's website www.theAA.com

Alternative refreshment stops

At a glance you will see if there are other pubs or cafés along the route. If there are no other places on the route, we list the nearest village or town where you can find somewhere else to eat and drink.

☞ Where to go from here

Many of the routes are short and may only take a few hours. You may wish to explore the surrounding area after lunch or before tackling the route, so we have selected a few attractions with children in mind.

Marazion to Penzance

Marazion CORNWALL

Enjoy an easy ride along one of south Cornwall's most beautiful bays.

St Michael's Mount

Marazion – and the whole of Mount's Bay – is dominated by the rocky bulk of St Michael's Mount, accessible by foot via the 600yd (549m) causeway at low tide, and by ferry from the beach when the tide is up (weather permitting). This extraordinary granite outcrop is topped by a medieval castle, dating from the 12th century and now mainly in the care of the National Trust. Originally the site of a Benedictine priory, it has been the home of the St Aubyn family for over 300 years. There is also a 14th-century church on the rock, as well as a pub, restaurant and shops round the little harbour, and a private garden with limited opening times. Marazion Marsh, passed on the right of the road near the start of the ride, is the largest reedbed in Cornwall. An RSPB nature reserve, this area of reedbeds, open water and willow carr attracts overwintering bitterns, sedge, Cetti's and reed warblers, butterflies and damselflies. There is a hide from which the birds can be watched (including the rare, spotted crake) and good access via boardwalks.

the ride

1 This ride is part of the First and Last Trail, the first stretch of the Cornish Way long-distance cycle route, which starts at Land's End and runs for 180 miles (288km) through the county. Marazion, where this ride starts, is Cornwall's oldest charter town, dating from 1257. Its unusual name comes from the Cornish 'marghas yow' – Thursday market. Marazion was the main trading port in Mount's Bay until Penzance overtook it in the 16th century. It's worth having a look around this attractive village before you set off.

From the pub car park cycle uphill (away from the beach) onto West End. (The Godolphin Arms can be found by turning right.) Turn left along **West End** and cycle out of the village. There is a parking area on the left along much of this road, so look out for people opening their car doors suddenly. **Marazion Marsh** lies to the right.

2 Where the road bears right to cross the Penzance to Exeter main railway line, keep straight ahead through a **parking area**, with the Pizza Shack (and toilets behind) on the right. Again, take care cycling through the car park.

St Michael's Mount seen from across the river

1h30	5 MILES	8 KM	LEVEL 1 2 3

MAP: OS Explorer 102 Land's End
START/FINISH: The Godolphin Arms car park, Marazion, grid ref: SW 516306
TRAILS/TRACKS: short stretch of road, track generally level, rough and bumpy in places
LANDSCAPE: village, beach, seaside, townscape
PUBLIC TOILETS: on Points 2 and 3 of the route, and in the car park at Penzance
TOURIST INFORMATION: Penzance, tel 01736 362207
CYCLE HIRE: The Cycle Centre, Penzance, tel 01736 351671
THE PUB: The Godolphin Arms, Marazion
🛑 Short stretch of road at start and finish, one car park to be negotiated

Getting to the start

From Penzance, take the A30 past the heliport. At the second roundabout turn right, signed Marazion. The Godolphin Arms car park is signed right (towards the beach).

Why do this cycle ride?

This level, easy, there-and-back route along the edge of Mount's Bay, with spectacular views over St Michael's Mount, is an ideal option for families with young children. With just a short road stretch at the start and finish, the ride runs along the back of the huge expanse of sands between Marazion and Penzance, originally a tiny fishing community, today popular with tourists.

Researched and written by: Sue Viccars

3 Keep ahead and leave the car park to the left of the old station (now the **Station pub**), to join a level track that runs along the back of the beach. Follow this track, passing more public toilets on the right.

St Michael's Mount seen from Marazion

Marazion CORNWALL

9

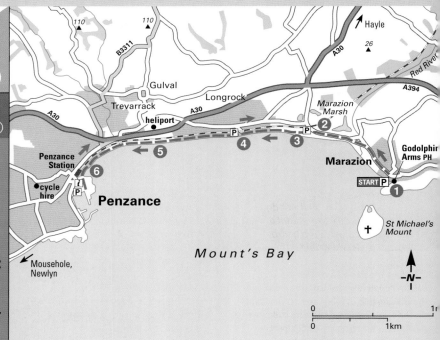

4 Take care where the track drops to meet an entrance road to a **beachside car park** (there are warning notices 'Give way to traffic'). Pass through the parking area and continue along the track, with the railway close by on the right.

5 Pass the **heliport**, from which helicopters fly regularly to the Isles of Scilly, which lie more than 17 miles (28 km) southwest of Land's End (day trips are available). Good views open up ahead towards Penzance.

6 On approaching the station the track narrows into a concrete walkway and becomes busier, so look out for pedestrians. Follow the track into the car park by Penzance railway and bus station, with the **tourist information centre** to the right. This is where you should turn round and return to Marazion. The First and Last

Trail actually runs along the road to Newlyn and beyond, but is pretty busy in terms of traffic and is not recommended for families with young children.

There is a lot to see in Penzance, however, which developed as in important pilchard fishing centre in medieval times. Penzance, Newlyn and Mousehole (along the coast to the west) were all destroyed by Spanish raiders in 1595, but by the early 17th century Penzance's fortunes had revived on account of the export of tin from local mines, and it became a fashionable place to live. The coming of the Great Western Railway in Victorian times gave the town another boost and it is now the main centre in Penwith (the far western part of Cornwall). The harbour is always full of interest, and it is from here that the RMV *Scillonian* makes regular sailings to the Isles of Scilly.

The Godolphin Arms

Located right at the water's edge opposite St Michael's Mount, The Godolphin Arms affords superb views across the bay. It's so close that the sea splashes at the windows in the winter and you can watch the movement of seals, dolphins, ferries and fishing boats. From the traditional wood-floored bar and beer terrace to the light and airy restaurant and most of the bedrooms, the Mount is clearly visible.

Food

The bar menu offers a choice of salads, sandwiches, light bites such as pan-fried sardines and spicy meatballs, and seafood tagliatelle, or ham, egg and chips. Seafood features prominently on the dinner menu, perhaps line-caught whole sea bass stuffed with thyme and lemon.

Family facilities

Children of all ages are allowed in the pub. There's an area set aside for families, and high chairs and baby-changing facilities for young children. Smaller portions from the main menu, a children's menu and two family bedrooms are also available. The beach is just below the pub's rear terrace.

about the pub

The Godolphin Arms
West End, Marazion
Penzance, Cornwall TR17 0EN
Tel 01736 710202
www.godolphinarms.co.uk

DIRECTIONS: see Getting to the start
PARKING: 70
OPEN: daily; all day
FOOD: daily; all day in summer
BREWERY/COMPANY: free house
REAL ALE: Sharp's Special and Eden Ale, Skinner's Spriggan
ROOMS: 10 en suite

Alternative refreshment stops

There are plenty of pubs, cafés and restaurants in both Marazion and Penzance.

☛ Where to go from here

Head for Newlyn where you will find Britain's only working salt pilchard factory, the Pilchard Works, where you can experience at first hand a Cornish factory that has continued producing salt pilchards for over 90 years (www.pilchardworks.co.uk). Art lovers should visit the Penlee House Gallery and Museum in Penzance (www.penleehouse.org.uk) to learn more about the Newlyn School of Artists and view one of the regular exhibitions. Kids will enjoy a visit to the Lighthouse Centre in Penzance or to the Wild Bird Hospital and Sanctuary in Mousehole. For information about St Michael's Mount see www.nationaltrust.org.uk.

The Camel Trail – Dunmere to Wadebridge

Enjoy a quiet and easy section of the Camel Trail along the lovely wooded banks of the River Camel.

Bodmin Moor

The River Camel rises on Bodmin Moor. Like Dartmoor, over the county boundary in Devon, it is a raised granite plateaux, part of the same huge belt of ancient rock that outcrops to form Penwith in west Cornwall and the Isles of Scilly off Land's End.

Bodmin and Dartmoor are characterised by the presence of tors, heavily weathered outcrops of granite: Bodmin's most famous is the Cheesewring. The highest point on the moors is Brown Willy (1,368ft/417m) and many of Cornwall's beautiful rivers rise on the boggy moorland heights. An old name for this upland tract was 'Fowey Moor' – the source of the River Fowey lies just below Brown Willy. There is evidence of extensive Bronze Age occupation, in the form of megalithic chambered tombs, standing stones and stone circles dating back over 4,000 years. Tin and copper were mined on the moor from the mid 18th century, and china clay – one of

Cornwall's most important sources of wealth – was mined from 1862 until 2001. Bodmin Moor is also recorded for posterity in Daphne du Maurier's classic novel *Jamaica Inn*.

the ride

1 The Camel Trail is clearly accessed from the car park. Push your bike down the steep ramp to join the **old railway track**. A granite block displays a map of the 17-mile (27.4km) trail from Poley's Bridge to Padstow. The railway line from Wadebridge to Dunmere Junction, and then to Bodmin is the third in the country, and the first steam-hauled railway in Cornwall (others used horse power). The Wadebridge to Padstow line opened in 1889 and closed in 1967. Turn left, soon crossing the **River Camel**, which reaches the sea at Padstow.

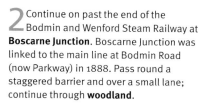
2 Continue on past the end of the Bodmin and Wenford Steam Railway at **Boscarne Junction**. Boscarne Junction was linked to the main line at Bodmin Road (now Parkway) in 1888. Pass round a staggered barrier and over a small lane; continue through **woodland**.

3 Cross the next lane via a gate (a left turn here will take you to **Nanstallon**, site of a Roman fort); you'll see the Camel Trail Tea Garden on the right. Cycle past access to the **Camel Valley Vineyard** (right) and continue through pretty, mixed woodland – oak, ash, beech, spindle, hazel and holly – with glimpses of the River Camel through the trees left. Pass **Grogley Halt**, where there are picnic tables and access to the river (popular with salmon fishermen here) on the left.

Below: Taking a break on The Camel Trail

MAP: OS Explorer 109 Bodmin Moor and 106 Newquay & Padstow
START/FINISH: Camel Trail car park at Dunmere, grid ref: SX 047675
TRAILS/TRACKS: well-surfaced former railway track
LANDSCAPE: wooded river valley
PUBLIC TOILETS: The Platt, Wadebridge
TOURIST INFORMATION: Wadebridge, tel 08701 223337
CYCLE HIRE: Bodmin Cycle Hire, General Station, Bodmin, tel 01208 73555
THE PUB: The Borough Arms, Dunmere
🚲 Busy road through centre of Wadebridge to rejoin the Camel Trail

Getting to the start

Bodmin lies just off the A30. From the centre of town follow signs for Wadebridge, along the A389 (Dunmere Road). After about 1 mile (1.6km) the road drops downhill. The Borough Arms will be seen on the left. Turn left through the car park into the official Camel Trail car park.

Why do this cycle ride?

This is an easy ride along a pretty, wooded section of the old Bodmin to Wadebridge railway line – now the Camel Trail – and you'll be in Wadebridge before you know it. You can extend the ride by passing through the town and rejoining the Camel Trail along the beautiful Camel estuary to Padstow.

Researched and written by: Sue Viccars

Wadebridge CORNWALL

4 Pass through a cutting and then by beautiful stone and slate cottages at **Polbrock**. Pass under a bridge and look left for access to the riverbank (note cycle racks on the side of the trail). Pass the grass-covered **Shooting Range Platform** on the left. Cross the Camel again: look ahead right to see the edge of Egloshayle, on the west bank of the Camel. The name means 'church on the estuary', and the church tower soon comes into view across the river meadows and reedbeds.

5 Pass under a small bridge to reach **Guineaport Road**. Follow this quiet residential road towards Wadebridge, passing the **old station** on the left (now the John Betjeman Centre – Sir John Betjeman is buried at St Enodoc Church, near Brea Hill on the Camel Estuary). Follow the road as it bears left to reach a roundabout, with the cinema opposite. Turn right down **The Platt** (once regularly flooded so boats were

drawn up here in the 19th century). **Wadebridge**, dating back to the early 14th century and situated at the lowest crossing point of the Camel, makes a good focus for the ride. There are plenty of pubs and cafés, and it's worth taking a look at the much-altered medieval bridge across the Camel, believed by some to have been built on sacks of wool.

6 If you want to keep going on the Camel Trail keep straight ahead at the next roundabout along **Eddystone Road** passing the tourist information (and various cafés) on the right. Granite for the rebuilding of the Eddystone lighthouse, off Plymouth, was shipped from Wadebridge Town Quay. At the next roundabout take the **third exit** (by the bike hire shops) and you'll be back on the Camel Trail again. Return along the trail to the car park and The Borough Arms at Dunmere.

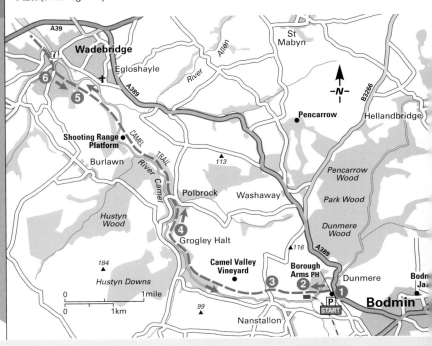

The Borough Arms

Situated in glorious countryside close to Bodmin Moor, this popular pub stands on the route of the Camel Trail and welcomes walkers and cyclists exploring this traffic-free route between Bodmin and Padstow. Much extended over recent years it makes a great spot to rest weary legs and refuel with a pint of Cornish ale and some hearty pub food. There are bike racks in the car park and children, who are really welcome, can explore the adventure playground on fine days.

Food

Traditional pub fare includes a light menu of sandwiches, ploughman's and jacket potatoes. More substantial dishes include steak and ale pie, beer battered cod and chips and lasagne, plus daily specials and a fill-your-own-plate carvery.

Family facilities

Children are allowed in the areas away from the bar and notices inform parents that children must be accompanied at all times. In addition to the family areas, there's a kid's menu, smaller portions of adult meals, high chairs and baby-changing facilities.

Alternative refreshment stops

The Camel Trail Tea Garden at Point 3 and various pubs and cafés in Wadebridge.

☛ Where to go from here

Restored steam locomotives at the Bodmin & Wenford Railway take you back to the glory days of the Great Western Railway when holidaymakers travelled the route to the sun (www.bodminandwenfordrailway.co.uk).

about the pub

The Borough Arms
Dunmere, Bodmin
Cornwall PL31 2RD
Tel 01208 73118
www.borougharms.ukpub.net

DIRECTIONS: see Getting to the start
PARKING: 30
OPEN: daily; all day
FOOD: daily
BREWERY/COMPANY: Spirit Group
REAL ALE: Sharp's Own and Doom Bar, Skinner's beers

Bodmin Gaol is a former country prison, built in 1778, with spooky underground passages where the Crown Jewels were stored during the First World War. There's plenty to keep children amused at Dobwalls Family Adventure Park, with stretches of miniature American railroads to ride, and action-packed areas filled with indoor and outdoor adventure play equipment (www.dobwallsadventurepark.co.uk).

Wadebridge

CORNWALL

The Tarka Trail – Instow to Barnstaple

Fremington Quay

There's little evidence at Fremington Quay today to suggest that in the mid 19th century this was said to be the busiest port between Land's End and Bristol. The deepwater quay was built in the 1840s (with a horse-drawn rail link to Barnstaple), when silting of the River Taw prevented large ships from going further upriver. Before that time a local port operated from Fremington Pill, which the trail crosses en route for Fremington Quay. The main exports were clay and minerals, the main imports coal and limestone from south Wales for burning in local limekilns.

The quay received another boost to its fortunes in 1854 when the main line railway reached Barnstaple, and lead to further development of the line to Bideford, which opened to passengers in late 1855. Exports of clay – from as far away as Peters Marland, 16 miles (25.7km) away – continued until the early 20th century.

The railway was closed in the 1960s, and the quay was taken out of use in 1969. Today the café and heritage centre, which opened in 2001, are housed in the reconstructed station building and signal box. There are picnic tables outside the café with lovely views across the Taw. The decline of shipping in the estuary, and the disappearance of local railways, has had a beneficial effect on local flora and fauna.

the ride

1 Turn left out of the car park and cycle along Marine Parade, passing **The Quay Inn** on the left. At the restored signal box (built in the early 1870s) turn left onto the **old railway line**.

2 The trail runs through a long cutting before emerging through an area of **wooden chalets**, with views left across dunes to the junction of the Torridge and Taw rivers, with the southern end of the sand dunes at Braunton Burrows beyond. Pass the **cricket ground** left, and then a picnic area and car park.

3 Continue over the access road to a **small industrial area** and then you're right out in the open. Pass East Yelland and Home Farm marshes and then the RSPB's **Isley Marsh reserve**, a saltmarsh habitat and high-tide roost. A short run through a wooded cutting leads to the viaduct over Fremington Pill – look left to see a lime kiln – and **Fremington Quay**.

4 The trail (now tarmac) passes in front of the café, then bears right past a parking and **picnic area** (left) and through a wooded cutting. A long embanked stretch leads all the way to Barnstaple. Penhill Marshes (jutting out into the estuary just east of Fremington Quay) have been reclaimed for grazing livestock. Along the trail you'll spot the 'creeps' – tunnels through the embankment enable cattle to access drier land at times of high tide. The large expanses of saltmarsh and mudflats along the estuary provide important habitats for a wide range of highly specialised plants and wildlife. Oystercatcher and redshank, among many other species, overwinter here. In late summer look out for the golden flowers of the sea aster, one of the few plants that can cope with being submerged by saltwater, and which helps to stabilise the marshes. In the cuttings either side of the Quay see if you can spot blue field

2h30 — **13 MILES** — **20.9 KM** — **LEVEL 123**

MAP: OS Explorer 139 Bideford, Ilfracombe & Barnstaple

START/FINISH: Instow car park (fee-paying), grid ref: SS 472303

TRAILS/TRACKS: level tarmac and gritty former railway track

LANDSCAPE: townscape, estuary

PUBLIC TOILETS: Instow; Fremington Quay

TOURIST INFORMATION: Barnstaple, tel 01271 375000

CYCLE HIRE: Biketrail, Fremington Quay, tel 01271 372586; Bideford Cycle Hire, East-the-Water, tel 01237 424123

THE PUB: The Quay Inn, Instow

🛑 Fremington Quay very busy with bikes and people at peak holiday times

Getting to the start

Instow lies on the Torridge Estuary signed off the B3233 Barnstaple to Bideford road. Approaching from Barnstaple, take the second sign right. From Bideford, take the first sign left. Pass The Quay Inn on the right and the car park in about 100yds (91m).

Why do this cycle ride?

This second chunk of the Tarka Trail can be linked with either the route from Torrington to Bideford, or that from Braunton to Barnstaple. It stands on its own, however, as an easy ride from the delightful village of Instow along the southern side of the Taw Estuary to Barnstaple, passing historic Fremington Quay.

Researched and written by: Sue Viccars

Instow

DEVON

scabious in summer, and spotted meadow brown butterflies feeding on its flowers.

The trail narrows as the edge of **Sticklepath** (opposite Barnstaple) is reached: cyclists are asked to give way to pedestrians.

5 Where the road bridge (A3125) can be seen ahead, bear left for 20yds (18m). At the next junction bear left for the **Long Bridge** if you want to go into Barnstaple; if not, retrace your route to the cricket ground (see Point 2).

6 Just after the entrance to the ground, turn right on a narrow path as signed for the Wayfarer Inn and **beach café**. Meet a track running through the dunes and turn left, passing the café on the right. Emerge onto the road and keep ahead along the seafront, to find the car park on the left. This alternative return gives lovely views over **the Torridge** towards the attractive fishing village of Appledore, an important port in Elizabethan times. During the 18th century Bideford and Appledore were the largest importers of tobacco in the country; today Appledore is famous for its shipbuilding tradition. Much of the village's network of narrow streets and cobbled courtyards is a conservation area; catch the ferry from Instow Quay for a closer look.

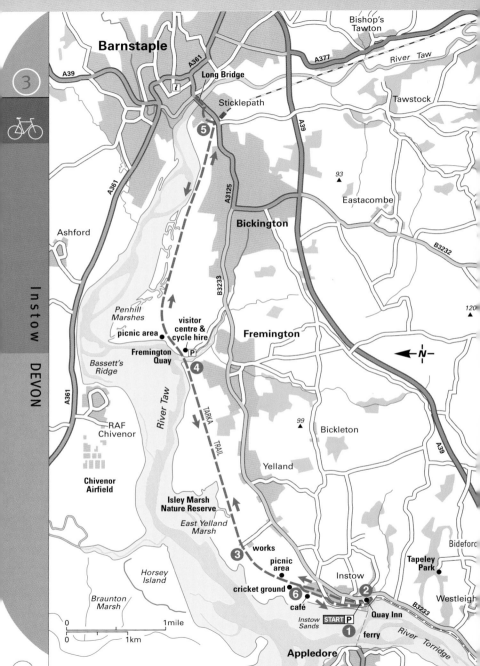

Barnstaple

A39

A361

A377

River Taw

Bishop's
Tawton

A361

Long Bridge

i

Sticklepath

Tawstock

5

A39

93 ▲

Ashford

A3125

Eastacombe

Bickington

B3232

A361

B3233

Penhill
Marshes

picnic area

visitor
centre &
cycle hire

P

Fremington

120 ▲

**Fremington
Quay**

4

←N—

*Bassett's
Ridge*

River Taw

TARKA TRAIL

99 ▲

Bickleton

**RAF
Chivenor**

A361

**Chivenor
Airfield**

Yelland

A39

**Isley Marsh
Nature Reserve**

*East Yelland
Marsh*

3

works

picnic
area

Instow

Bideford

**Tapeley
Park**

Westleigh

*Horsey
Island*

cricket ground

6

café

2

B3233

*Braunton
Marsh*

0 ———— 1mile
0 ———— 1km

*Instow
Sands*

START P

1

Quay Inn

ferry

River Torridge

Appledore

The Quay Inn

Lively and interesting little pub situated right on the quay with super views across the estuary from waterside tables outside the pub. The interior is rustic, open-plan and full of character, attracting a mixed clientele, from local fishermen and holidaymakers to walkers and cyclists on the Tarka Trail in search of refreshment. Locally brewed beers, perhaps Jollyboat ales from Bideford or Barum ales from Barnstaple, are particularly popular, as are the summer afternoon teas.

Food

The bar menu is huge, offering something for everyone, from crusty baguettes and crab salad to breaded plaice, fish pie, salmon and prawn fishcakes, and lamb shank with mash and rosemary gravy. Daily specials include fresh local fish like sea bass and plaice.

Family facilities

Although there is no specific family room children are welcome inside the pub. There are special meals for younger children and smaller portions are available.

Alternative refreshment stops

There are plenty of pubs, cafés and restaurant to choose from in Barnstaple. There's a café at the old station at Fremington Quay and the New Inn in Fremington.

☞ Where to go from here

Appeldore is home to the North Devon Maritime Museum where you can learn about the ship and boat building industry and the maritime activities of the area. Youngsters will love the Gnome Reserve and Wildflower Garden near Bradworthy (www.gnomereserve.co.uk), and the exhilarating rides and shows at the Milky Way Adventure Park near Clovelly (www.themilkyway.co.uk). Equally fascinating is the Quince Honey Farm at South Molton where you can follow the story of honey and beeswax from flower to table, as well as see the world of bees close up and in complete safety (www.quincehoney.co.uk).

about the pub

The Quay Inn
Marine Parade, Instow
Bideford, Devon EX39 4HY
Tel; 01271 860624

DIRECTIONS:	see Getting to the start
PARKING:	none
OPEN:	daily; all day
FOOD:	daily
BREWERY/COMPANY:	free house
REAL ALE:	changing local guest beers

The Tarka Trail – Braunton to Barnstaple

A gentle ride along the Taw estuary from historic Braunton to Barnstaple's old quayside.

Braunton Burrows

As you set off along the Tarka Trail from Braunton look right and in the distance you'll see a ridge of sand dunes (dating from the last Ice Age) – those nearest the sea are around 100ft (over 30m) high. This is Braunton Burrows, the second largest dune system in the UK, designated as an UNESCO International Biosphere Reserve in November 2002. The whole dune system is moving gradually inland, in some places as much as 10ft (3m) per year, and is well worth exploring. There are areas of managed meadowland, grassland, marsh and sandy habitats. Almost 500 different species of flowering plant have been identified, including 11 orchids. Sustainable tourism is the keyword here, and access for visitors is managed carefully so that fragile parts of the site are protected. The area is easily accessible by road or bike.

Braunton has a fascinating agricultural history, too. Between the village and the Burrows lies Braunton Great Field, a rare example of medieval strip farming. This area once lay beneath the sea and is extremely fertile. There's also an area of tidal saltmarsh, enclosed in the early 19th century for grazing cattle.

the ride

1 The car park marks the site of the old Braunton railway station, closed in 1965. The line – Barnstaple to Ilfracombe – was opened in 1874, and the last train ran in 1970. Cycle to the far end of the **car park** and turn right into the overflow area. Bear left and leave the car park by the police station (right). Bear right onto Station Road and cycle down it, passing the cycle hire on the left. Turn right into **Station Close** and then immediately left down a tarmac way. At the end cross the lane; keep ahead through black bollards to cross another lane, with a roundabout right.

On the Tarka Trail

2 Follow signs left to pick up the **old railway line**. Pass a wetland conservation area (left) and pass round a staggered barrier to cross a lane (the wire fences right mark the boundary of RAF Chivenor).

3 (Note: For The Williams Arms turn left here; at the end of the lane cross the A361 with care; the pub is on the other side.) Cycle on to reach a roundabout at the entrance to **RAF Chivenor**. The church ahead left is St Augustine's at Heanton Punchardon, built by Richard Punchardon (owner of Heanton estate) after his return from the Crusades in 1290. The village, formerly Heanton (Saxon Hantona – High Town) took on his name from that time. Cross the road by the roundabout and keep ahead through a wooded section.

4 Emerge suddenly from woodland onto the **Taw Estuary**, with far-reaching views. Listen for the oystercatcher's piping call, and watch out for curlew, easily identified by its curving bill. In winter thousands of migrant birds feed on the broad sandbanks here. Pass castellated **Heanton Court** on the left, a refuge for Royalists in the Civil War. The then owner of the Heanton estate, Colonel Albert Basset, fought for Barnstaple, which eventually fell to the Parliamentarians. Continue along the banks of the Taw to pass the **football club** (left).

5 Cross arched **Yeo Bridge**, a swing bridge over a tributary of the Taw, and pass the **Civic Centre** on the left (cyclists and pedestrians separate here). Bear left away from the river to meet the road. Turn right

MAP: OS Explorer 139 Bideford, Ilfracombe & Barnstaple

START/FINISH: Braunton car park (contributions), grid ref: SS 486365

TRAILS/TRACKS: level tarmac and gritty former railway track

LANDSCAPE: townscape, estuary

PUBLIC TOILETS: at start and in Barnstaple

TOURIST INFORMATION: Barnstaple, tel 01271 375000

CYCLE HIRE: Otter Cycle Hire, tel 01271 813339; Tarka Trail Cycle Hire, Barnstaple, tel 01271 324202

THE PUB: The Williams Arms, Wrafton

🅛 Busy crossing of A361 on route to the Williams Arms

Getting to the start

Braunton lies on the A361 Barnstaple to Ilfracombe road in north Devon. The car park is signed from the traffic lights in the centre of the village. If approaching from Barnstaple, turn left, and 100yds (91m) later turn left into the car park.

Why do this cycle ride?

Visiting Barnstaple by car at the height of the tourist season can be something of a trial as this north Devon market town, the oldest borough in the country, can get pretty choked by traffic. So what better way to get into the heart of Barnstaple than by cycling from Braunton via the Tarka Trail along the edge of the Taw estuary?

Researched and written by: Sue Viccars

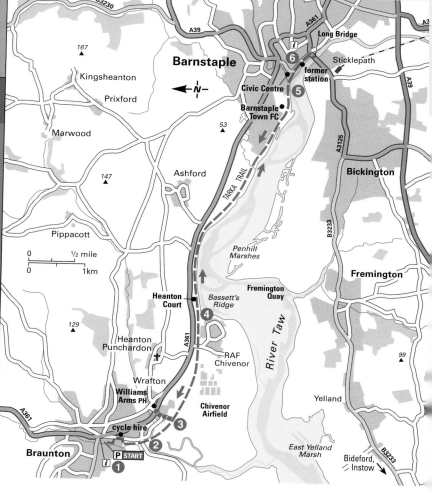

along the cycle path past **old Barnstaple Town Station** on the right (the railway reached the south side of the river in 1854, and this side in the early 1870s). Bear right as signed, then left along the **quay** (note: there is no wall along the edge).

6 Continue on to pass **Barnstaple Heritage Centre** (left), with its elaborate statue of Queen Anne. The Riverside Café (with cycle racks) lies a few yards along on the left, just before Barnstaple's Long Bridge over the Taw (there has been a bridge here since the 13th century). There is evidence of a settlement at Barnstaple from early Saxon times; trade via the Taw was vital to the town's prosperity for centuries. Queen Anne's Walk marks the site of the Great and Little Quays, once bustling with ocean-going ships, including five bound for Sir Francis Drake's Armada fleet in 1588.

The Williams Arms

A modernised thatched village pub that is well worth the short diversion off the trail as it is really geared up to family dining and has the added attractions of a play area and aviary in its spacious garden. Popular with both holidaymakers and locals, the two huge bars have been smartly refurbished with plush red carpets, a mix of modern furnishings and a self-service carvery, yet they retain some character in the form of low-beamed ceilings and open fires. Separate games area with pool table, darts and TV.

Food
The lounge bar menu offers a good choice of filled rolls and paninis, ploughman's lunches with home-cooked ham or local cheddar, steaks from the grill, and specialities like steak and venison pie, Exmoor venison braised in red wine and brandy, roast duck with orange sauce, and roast meats from the daily carvery.

Family facilities
Children are welcome thoughout the pub. It is really geared to family dining and you'll find a games/TV room, a basic kid's menu, smaller portions for older children, high chairs, and a play fort and aviary in the large garden.

about the pub

The Williams Arms
Wrafton, Braunton
Devon EX33 2DE
Tel 01271 812360
www.williams-arms.co.uk

DIRECTIONS: the pub is beside the A361 Braunton to Barnstaple road, 1 mile (1.6km) south east of Braunton. See Point 3
PARKING: 100
OPEN: daily; all day
FOOD: daily
BREWERY/COMPANY: free house
REAL ALE: Bass

Braunton
DEVON

Alternative refreshment stops
There are plenty of pubs and cafés in Braunton and Barnstaple, and en route you'll find Heanton Court, another family-friendly pub.

☛ Where to go from here
On the edge of Exmoor at Blackmoor Gate is the Exmoor Zoological Park, which specializes in smaller animals, many endangered, such as the golden headed lion tamarins. There are contact pens and children are encouraged to participate (www.exmoorzoo.co.uk). Combe Martin Wildlife Park and Dinosaur Park is a subtropical paradise with hundreds of birds and animals and animatronic dinosaurs, plus there are sea lion shows, falconry displays and animal handling sessions (www.dinosaur-park.com).

The Granite Way

A glorious, easy ride along an old railway line around the northwestern edge of Dartmoor, with an optional hilly extension to Bridestowe and historic Lydford.

Okehampton Castle and Lydford Gorge

The atmospheric ruins of Okehampton's Norman castle – once the largest in Devon – peep through the trees north of the line near the start of this ride. Built soon after the Norman Conquest, most of what can be seen today dates from the 13th and 15th centuries. The castle – seat of the Earls of Devon in medieval times – is beautifully situated on the banks of the West Okement River, with walks and picnic areas near by. It lies at one end of the Two Castles Trail, a 24-mile (39km) walking route linking it with the Norman castle at Launceston in east Cornwall.

At the other end of the ride lies Lydford, once an administrative centre for the Forest of Dartmoor. Lydford Castle, a tower built in the late 12th century as a prison and courtroom, was used by the Royalists in the Civil War. There's also the National Trust's Lydford Gorge. During the Ice Age the River Lyd carved a new and tortuous route through solid rock as it coursed west towards the River Tavy. The waters now hurtle through the 1.5 mile- (2.4km) long gorge via a succession of waterfalls and pools, including the beautiful 98ft (30m) White Lady waterfall. Various paths, some narrow and slippery, wend their way through the surrounding oak woodlands.

the ride

1 From Okehampton Station cross **Station Road** and keep ahead, as signed, parallel to the railway. After 50yds (46m) turn left onto a tarmac way that then bears right to run parallel to the railway. Follow this as it bears left under a bridge. Continue on to pass through a gate, left under the A30, through another gate, and right on the other side. The route bears away from the railway to reach **Meldon Quarry**, which started 200 years ago to produce a variety of materials, including 'Hornfells' used in construction work, and which was exposed when the railway cuttings were dug.

2 The next stop is **old Meldon Station** with its visitor centre. There's a buffet in a couple of old railway carriages, and a picnic area, with glorious views over Meldon's steel viaduct and towards Dartmoor's highest ground. The Devon and Cornwall Railway reached Okehampton in 1871 and was absorbed into the London and South Western Railway the following year. The line was extended to Lydford via the viaduct (which soars 150ft/46m over the West Okement Valley) in 1874, and

| 4h00 | 18 MILES | 29 KM | LEVEL 123 |

SHORTER ALTERNATIVE ROUTE

| 2h15 | 11 MILES | 17.7 KM | 17.7 KM |

MAP: OS Explorer OL28 Dartmoor
START/FINISH: Okehampton Station, grid ref: SX 591944
TRAILS/TRACKS: level tarmac track, rough bridlepath to Bearslake Inn, narrow lanes/level track to Lydford
LANDSCAPE: moorland edge, farmland, woodland
PUBLIC TOILETS: at start and in Lydford
TOURIST INFORMATION: Okehampton, tel 01837 53020
CYCLE HIRE: YHA, Okehampton Station, tel 01837 53916
THE PUB: The Bearslake Inn, Lake
⬤ Crossing of A386 on Lydford extension, steep descent/ascent into/out of Bridestowe

Getting to the start

Okehampton lies off the A30 on the northern edge of Dartmoor. Make your way to the town centre and follow signs for the railway station.

Why do this cycle ride?

There are so many options on this ride that it's hard to know which to recommend! It really is a route to suit all tastes and abilities. Quite apart from traversing stunningly beautiful landscapes, here are several possible picnic and refreshment stops along the way. Keen cyclists can extend the route via quiet country lanes to rejoin the old railway line and continue on to Lydford.

Researched and written by: Sue Viccars

closed to commercial passenger traffic in 1968. Today the 'Dartmoor Pony' runs out here from Okehampton on weekends and during the summer holidays.

3 Continue on over the **viaduct** – a fantastic ride, but take care in high winds (for Meldon Reservoir leave the route left just after the viaduct; on reaching the lane go straight over). Pass through a long cutting on the edge of **Prewley Moor**, after which views open up towards Sourton Tor (unusually formed of basalt, not granite). Cross the access lane to **Prewley Works**, and pass the pretty church of St Thomas à Becket at Sourton. The Highwayman pub can be accessed over the A386 here. Continue on through a short gated section at **Albrae**, and on past ponds to reach **Lake Viaduct**, built of local stone in 1874, and more lovely views.

4 Here you have a choice. The line ends 0.75 mile (1.2km) further on at **Southerly Halt picnic site**, so you can cycle on and turn round there. If you want to either go to **The Bearslake Inn**, or onto Lydford, turn left off the track just after the viaduct and descend steeply to a gate. Turn

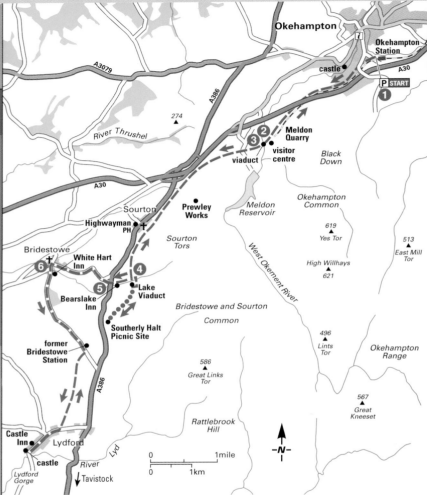

left under the **viaduct** and follow this rough track downhill to meet the A396. Turn left into the grounds of the pub, originally a 13th-century longhouse.

5 To continue to the ancient Saxon burgh of Lydford, cross the A386 – take great care – and cycle up the quiet lane opposite. At the T-junction turn left and follow the lane downhill into **Bridestowe**.

6 Turn left opposite the church, passing the White Hart Inn on the left. Cycle up Station Road (steep) and follow this for 1.5 miles (2.4km) to **old Bridestowe Station**. Cross the bridge and turn right onto the old railway track again. Follow this to Lydford. Leave the track and turn right down the road for the Castle Inn, castle and **Lydford Gorge**. Retrace your route back to Okehampton.

The Bearslake Inn

Standing on the edge of the National Park and built as a farm in the 13th century, this thatched and stone-built Devon longhouse is conveniently located beside the Granite Way cycle trail. Oozing old-world charm and character, expect to find flagstone floors, exposed beams and timbers, head-crackingly low ceilings, old pews, and a fine inglenook fireplace with crackling log fire in the rambling interior. Food is freshly prepared on the premises using local produce, including fish landed at Plymouth Quay and Taw Valley cheeses. Cyclists are very welcome and there's plenty of space in both the front and rear gardens to rest and relax on fine summer days.

Food

Lunchtime snacks take in sandwiches and filled baguettes (hot sausage and onion), traditional ploughman's with Taw Valley Brie, home-made soups, salads and the Bearslake burger with chips. Imaginative evening meals range from salmon and broccoli tart and beef casserole to chargrilled mackerel and whole baked sea bass.

Family facilities

Although children are not allowed in the bar there are two family dining areas. Smaller portions are available and children are welcome overnight.

Alternative refreshment stops

Plenty of pubs and cafés in Okehampton and the eccentric Highwayman Inn at Sourton. If continuing to Lydford, you'll pass the White Hart in Bridestow and the Castle Inn in Lydford.

about the pub

The Bearslake Inn
Lake, Sourton, Okehampton
Devon EX20 4HQ
Tel: 01837 861334
www.bearslakeinn.com

DIRECTIONS: pub is situated north of Lydford on the A386 Okehampton to Tavistock road

PARKING: 18

OPEN: daily; all day Sunday; all day all week June to September

FOOD: daily

BREWERY/COMPANY: free house

REAL ALE: Teignworthy Golden Sands and Reel Ale, Otter Nitter, Summerskills Best, guest beers

ROOMS: 5 en suite

☛ Where to go from here

Discover how people lived, worked and played on and around Dartmoor at the Museum of Dartmoor Life in Okehampton, housed on three floors in a 19th-century mill (www.museumofdartmoorlife.co.uk). Visit Okehampton Castle and enjoy the free audio tour which brings this romantic ruin to life (www.english-heritage.org.uk). Daily demonstrations at the Finch Foundry Working Museum in Sticklepath show how water-powered hammers made sickles, scythes and other hand tools. In Lydford, explore the spectacular gorge formed by the River Lyd (www.nationaltrust.org.uk), and look round Lydford Castle, a 12th-century tower that was once a notorious prison.

Okehampton DEVON

Bristol and Bath railway path

Park and ride with a
difference, an easy ride
to explore Bath's fine
18th-century architecture.

Avon Valley Railway

The first section of the Avon Valley Railway opened in 1835, between Mangotsfield, just north of Warmley and Bristol. Originally a horse-drawn tramway, it transported local coal to Bristol. With growing industrialisation, the track was upgraded for steam and by 1869 had been extended all the way to Bath, following the course of the River Avon as it neared the city. After publication of the Beeching Report, passenger trains were withdrawn in March 1966, although goods traffic continued for a further five years, supplying coal to the gasworks in Bath. In 1972 the track was finally dismantled, but even as British Rail was removing the rails, the Bristol Suburban Railway Society was planning to reopen the line. A 2.5 mile (4km) section is now operational with extensions planned.

Known the world over for its Roman baths and elegant Cotswold-stone Georgian architecture, Bath simply demands exploration. Dedicated to the goddess Sulis, the baths were begun in the 1st century, the focus of a sophisticated city that thrived for

nearly 400 years. After the Romans left, the baths were gradually forgotten and when Nash created his fashionable spa town, nobody even dreamed of their existence. The former complex was only rediscovered in 1880 when sewer works broke into the subterranean ruin, and subsequent excavation revealed the finest Roman remains in the country.

the ride

1 Leaving the car park adjacent to the former Warmley Station, go left to cross the main road at a traffic light controlled crossing and follow the path away beside the old signal box. Hidden behind the trees lining the path are small units, occupying the sites of the former industries that once supported the town. After passing beneath **St Ivel Way**, look for a sculpture that represents a Roman centurion quaffing wine from a flask: it recalls that a Roman road passed nearby. A little further along is a controlled crossing at **Victoria Road**.

2 Pedalling on brings you to **Oldland Common**, the northern terminus of the restored section of the Avon Valley Railway. The path continues beside the track, passing beneath North Street to enter a shallow cutting. The stone here, known as Pennant sandstone, is particularly hard and proved an excellent construction material. The excavated stone was used for several buildings in the vicinity. There are also coal deposits in the area, laid down during the same carboniferous period and these

The former Warmley Station

Pulteney Bridge over the River Avon in Bath

3h30 — **18.25 MILES** — **29.4 KM** — **LEVEL 123**

fuelled local brass foundries and other industries. Later on, at **Cherry Gardens**, the way enters a second cutting, exposing much younger rocks containing fossils of graptolites, belemnites and ammonites, creatures that lived in the Jurassic seas covering the region 200 million years ago. Before long, the **railway yard** at Bitton appears ahead, the cycle track swinging across the line through a gate (look out for passing trains) to reach the station.

3 Even if the trains are not running, there is always something of interest to see in the goods yard, with an assortment of engines and rolling stock either awaiting refurbishment or dismantling for spares. The buffet is generally open and for a small donation you are welcome to wander onto the platform. Go through the car park, over a small level crossing and continue beside the railway. Carry on along an embankment overlooking the Avon's flood meadows, crossing the river to reach **Avon Riverside Station**, where a path on the right drops to a picnic area by the water's edge.

4 At **Saltford**, the Bird in Hand below the embankment invites a break for refreshment. You can also wander into the village and have a look at the restored **Saltford Brass Mill**, which is open on some Saturdays during the summer months. Re-crossing the river the way continues towards Bath, the Avon winding below you twice more before you reach the outskirts of the city.

5 Eventually you emerge on **Brassmill Lane**. Follow the road to the right, keeping ahead on a short cycle lane further

MAP: OS Explorer 155 Bristol & Bath
START/FINISH: car park beside the A420 at Warmley, Kingswood; grid ref: ST 670735
TRAILS/TRACKS: former railway line
LANDSCAPE: wooded cuttings and embankments with occasional views across riverside path into Bath
PUBLIC TOILETS: at car park at start
TOURIST INFORMATION: Bath, tel 01225 477101
CYCLE HIRE: Webbs of Warmley, High Street, Warmley, Bristol, tel 01179 673676
THE PUB: Bird in Hand, Saltford
🚦 Traffic lights control major road crossings; dismount when crossing the railway line; care when riding alongside the River Avon; route shared with pedestrians

Getting to the start

Warmley is on the A420 to the east of Bristol. The car park lies 0.25 mile (400m) east of the roundabout junction with the A4174.

Why do this cycle ride?

Bath is notorious for its traffic problems. For the cyclist, however, there is a splendid route along the track bed of the former Avon Valley Railway. It penetrates the heart of the city and has attractions of its own along the way: you can visit a brass mill, or ride along a section of the line, pulled by a vintage steam or diesel engine. The cycling is not strenuous, but for a shorter ride, turn around at Saltford.

Researched and written by: Dennis Kelsall

Bath

BATH & NE SOMERSET

on past a 'no entry' sign for motorised traffic. Where the cycle lane ends, turn right (watch for oncoming traffic) to gain a riverside path behind a tool hire shop. Signed towards **Bath city centre**, keep going past the 19th-century industrial quarter of Bath, where more brass and other mills took advantage of the water for both power and transport. The factories have now gone, replaced by modern light industry, but some of the old riverside

warehouses remain. The path finally ends near **Churchill Bridge** in the centre of Bath.

6 Although cyclists are common on Bath's streets, the traffic is busy and it is perhaps a good idea to find a convenient spot to secure your bikes whilst you explore on foot. When you are ready to head back, retrace your outward route to **Warmley** along the riverside path and cycleway.

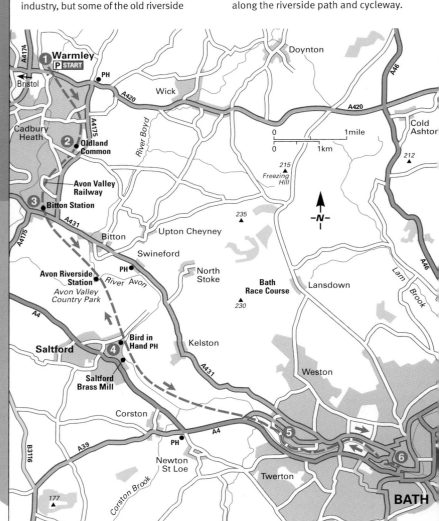

Bird in Hand

Converted in 1869 from two cottages in the original village close to the River Avon, the Bird in Hand first served the workers building the railway through the valley between Bath and Bristol. Now that the railway has gone, this homely village local, which is smack beside the old route, is a favoured resting and refuelling stop for cyclists pedalling the peaceful cycle path between the two cities. There's a comfortable bar area adorned with old pictures of the pub and village, a light and airy conservatory and plenty of outdoor seating for fine-weather eating and drinking.

Food

Lunchtime food ranges from Stilton ploughman's and salad platters to steak and ale pies, omelettes and ham, egg and chips. Evening additions include a mixed grill and daily specials such as salmon fishcakes, sea bass with prawn and lemon butter sauce, dressed crab and rack of lamb with redcurrant and port sauce.

Family facilities

Children are very welcome inside. There's a family area with a box of toys to keep youngsters amused, and a basic children's menu.

Alternative refreshment stops

Range of pubs and cafés in Bath; café at Bitton Station.

☛ Where to go from here

In Bath visit the Abbey, the Roman Baths and Pump Rooms (www.romanbaths.co.uk) or the museums (www.bath-preservation-trust.org.uk). In Bristol head for the superb zoo (www.bristolzoo.org.uk) or savour the unique sights and sounds of steam trains along the Avon Valley Railway at Bitton (www.avonvalleyrailway.co.uk).

about the pub

Bird in Hand
58 High Street
Saltford, Bristol
BS31 3EN
Tel: 01225 873335

DIRECTIONS: 3 miles (4.8km) along the cycle track from Bitton railway station	
PARKING: 36	
OPEN: daily	
FOOD: daily	
BREWERY/COMPANY: free house	
REAL ALE: Abbey Bellringer, Butcombe, Courage Best, guest beers	

From Bradford-on-Avon along the Kennet & Avon Canal

Discover one of Brindley's great canal masterpieces.

Kennet & Avon Canal

John Rennie began the construction of the Kennet and Avon Canal in 1794 to link the Avon and Kennet Navigations between Bath and Bristol and thus create a continuous waterway between Bristol and London. The 57 mile (92km) canal took 16 years to complete and was quite an achievement, requiring two great aqueducts and a spectacular flight of 29 locks at Caen Hill outside Devizes to lift the waterway over 240ft (73m) onto the summit level. It proved a highly profitable venture and was soon carrying over 350,000 tons a year

between the two great cities. By the middle of the 19th century, competition from railways foreshadowed its decline, and in 1846 was taken over by the Great Western Railway Company. GWR signs remain on some of its bridges, ominously mounted on the instrument of its ruin, an upended length of railway track. Re-opened in 1990, many of the canal's original features still excite the imagination, none more so than the two splendid stone aqueducts carrying the canal across the Avon Valley, one of them named after the canal company's founding chairman, Charles Dundas. They presented major technical difficulties for Rennie as they had not only to carry a great weight but remain watertight, yet his

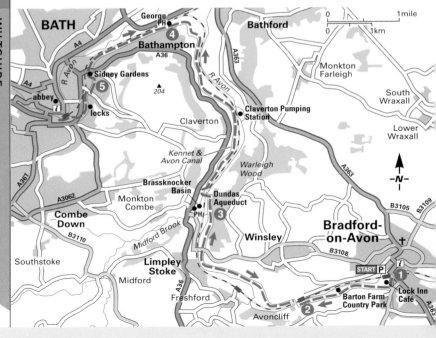

7

| 4h00 | 20 MILES | 32 KM | LEVEL 123 |

SHORTER ALTERNATIVE ROUTE

| 3h00 | 15 MILES | 24 KM | LEVEL 123 |

MAP: OS Explorer 155 Bristol & Bath & 156 Chippenham & Bradford-on-Avon

START/FINISH: Bradford-on-Avon railway station (pay car park); grid ref: ST 825606

TRAILS/TRACKS: gravel tow path, short section on road

LANDSCAPE: canal tow path through the wooded and pastoral Avon Valley

PUBLIC TOILETS: at start

TOURIST INFORMATION: Bradford-on-Avon, tel 01225 865797

CYCLE HIRE: The Lock Inn Café, 48 Frome Road, Bradford-on-Avon tel: 01225 868068

THE PUB: The George, Bathampton

🅛 Care through town; unguarded canal tow paths shared with pedestrians; blind approaches to bridges; dismount in tunnels; flight of steps on approaching Bath

Getting to the start

Bradford-on-Avon is only 5 miles (8km) south east of Bath and lies on the A363 to Trowbridge. Park at the railway station, from where the ride begins.

Why do this cycle ride?

The Kennet and Avon Canal passes through picturesque countryside. An attractive riverside pub at Bathampton offers a turning point although the locks passed into Bath on the longer ride are worth seeing.

Researched and written by: Dennis Kelsall

Bradford-on-Avon WILTSHIRE

creations combined both aesthetic quality and practicality in the best tradition of the great architects.

the ride

1 Leaving the station car park, turn right along the main road in the direction of Frome. Continue past a mini-roundabout to the Canal Tavern and Lock Inn Café. Go between them to join the towpath and follow it past **Grange Farm** with its massive 600-year-old tithe barn. The River Avon runs below to the right, containing Barton Farm Country Park's picnic and wildlife areas within the intervening spit of land. Beyond a gate, continue beside the canal to **Avoncliff**.

2 The canal now makes an abrupt turn across the Avon Valley, carried above both the river and railway on an imposing aqueduct. Do not cross, but at a sign to Dundas just before, drop steeply right towards the **Cross Guns** pub, then double back left underneath the bridge, climbing left to gain the opposite towpath. Tacked along the wooded valley, the waterway runs pleasantly on, harbouring an assortment of ducks, coots and moorhens. Turning a corner opposite **Limpley Stoke**, pass beneath a road bridge, then look out on the left for a glimpse of a viaduct taking the A36 across the Midford Brook valley.

Taking life at a leisurely pace along the canal

3 Another sharp turn heralds the **Dundas Aqueduct**, immediately beyond which is the last remnant of the Somerset Coal Canal, completed in 1805 to transport coal from Radstock and Paulton to Bristol. The track just before it leads to **Brassknocker Basin**, where a small exhibition (open daily in summer) describes its history. The route, however, continues ahead, signed 'Bath and Claverton', winding behind a **derrick** and maintenance building and onto the opposite bank. A mile (1.2km) further on, immediately beyond a bridge, a track drops across the railway to the river where there is a restored pump house (**Claverton Pumping Station**), built in 1813 to replenish the water drained by the locks descending to Bath. There are views to Bathford and Batheaston as you pedal the last 1.75 miles (2.8km) to **Bathampton** and The George.

4 To extend the ride, continue beside the canal, the eastern suburbs of Bath rising on the opposite side of the valley. Eventually the city itself comes into view with a glimpse of the abbey at its heart. There are a couple of short tunnels to pass through at **Sidney Gardens**, where you should dismount. Between them, two **ornate cast-iron bridges** span the canal, which, together with the elaborate façade of the second tunnel beneath Cleveland House, were added to placate the owners of Sidney Park, who rather disapproved of common cargo barges passing through their land.

5 Emerging below **Cleveland House**, the towpath doubles back onto the opposite bank, passes former warehouses, now a **marina**, and rises to a road. Taking care, diagonally cross and drop back to the tow path, here having to negotiate a flight of steps. Beyond, the canal falls impressively through a succession of locks, the path periodically rising to cross a couple of roads and a track before meeting the River Avon. To explore Bath, carry on a little further by the river to emerge on the road beside **Churchill Bridge** in the city centre. As the city is busy, it is perhaps preferable to secure your bikes whilst you wander around. The return is back the way you came, but remember you have to climb steps to the road at Bathwick Hill and dismount through the tunnels at Sidney Gardens, or you could return by train.

The George

The pub's enviable position by the parish church and a bridge over the Kennet and Avon Canal is one of its attractions. The creeper-clad building is so close to the water that the entrance to the upper dining room is from the tow path. When the weather is fine, the tables on the canalside terrace fill quickly with walkers, cyclists and barge visitors, and you can watch the many activities on the canal. Inside, there's a warren of wood-beamed rooms radiating out from the flagstoned central bar, with plenty of space away from the bar for families. The George oozes history, dating back to the 13th century when it was originally a monastery. The last official duel in

England was fought on nearby Claverton Down in 1778 following a quarrel over a game of cards at The George. The fatally wounded Viscount du Barré was buried in the churchyard opposite.

Food
Expect traditional pub food – sandwiches and filled rolls (roast beef and horseradish), salads, ploughman's lunches, and changing blackboard specials, perhaps roast monkfish, steak and kidney pudding or Tuscan-style swordfish.

Family facilities
Children are welcome away from the bar and a children's menu is available. Keep an eye on children on the canalside terrace.

Alternative refreshment stops
Plenty of eating places in Bradford-on-Avon and Bath. The Lock Inn Café near the start, the Cross Guns at Avoncliff, the Hop Pole and a canalside tea room at Limpley Stoke.

☛ Where to go from here
Take a closer look at the tithe barn and seek out the unspoiled Saxon church in Bradford-on-Avon. Visit the Claverton Pumping Station (www.claverton.org) or explore Bath's famous buildings and museums (www.bath-preservation-trust.org.uk). Peto Gardens at Iford Manor (www.ifordarts.co.uk) are worth seeing.

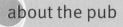

about the pub

The George
Mill Lane
Bathampton, Bath
Bath & NE Somerset BA2 6TR
Tel: 01225 425079

DIRECTIONS: at Bathampton on the A36 east of Bath, take minor road left downhill to village centre, crossing the canal to the church. The George is beside the canal near the church

PARKING: 50

OPEN: daily; all day

FOOD: daily; all day

BREWERY/COMPANY: Chef & Brewer

REAL ALE: Wadworth 6X, Courage Best & Directors, Greene King Old Speckled Hen

Malmesbury and the Fosse Way

Visit the splendid remnants of an ancient abbey church and follow in the footsteps of Roman soldiers.

in fine arches, vaulting and tracery, while the early Norman carving in the porch is particularly striking.

An unusual and rare feature is the curious watching loft that projects from the

Malmesbury Abbey

All that is left of Malmesbury's great monastery, founded in 676 by St Aldhelm, is part of the abbey church, which survived Henry VIII's Dissolution only because it was granted to the town for use as its parish church. The building dates from the 12th century and was constructed on a vast cruciform plan. Beside it stood a secluded cloister surrounded by the domestic buildings in which the monks lived.

If what remains is anything to go by, then the medieval building must have been a truly magnificent sight, a long avenue of soaring columns lifting the roof high above the church. Exquisite stonework is revealed

upper wall high above the southern side of the nave; nobody is really sure what purpose it served. Also of interest is the tomb of Alfred the Great's grandson, King Athelstan. He commissioned the first translation of the Bible into English, and his tomb stands near the north west corner of the church, while outside is the grave of Hannah Twynnoy, a servant at the town's White Lion Inn, who died after being mauled by a tiger in 1703.

the ride

1 Out of The Vine Tree car park, pedal easily away along the lane to the left, reaching a junction after 0.75 mile (1.2km).

Keep left with the main lane, before long arriving at **Foxley**. Go right, passing the community's tiny church.

2 Continue along the lane for 2 miles (3.2km) to the outskirts of Malmesbury, where **Common Road** joins from the right. Keep going as the road shortly winds down to cross the Sherston branch of the River Avon, where there is a view right to the **abbey church**. Climb away, remaining with the main road as it bends right to a T-junction. Go right, and then at the next junction, in front of The Triangle and **war memorial,** go right again to the abbey. It is perhaps a good idea to park your bike there while you explore the town centre, just a short walk away.

3 Ride back to the junction by the war memorial and now turn right along Gloucester Road, passing through the town to a mini-roundabout. There, bear left into Park Road, signed to **Park Road Industrial Estate**. Fork off right after 300yds (274m) to remain with Park Road. After passing a few more houses, the route abruptly leaves the town, and continues beside the Avon's **Tetbury Branch** along a narrow hedged lane.

4 Reaching a T-junction, go right, crossing the river towards **Brokenborough**. The lane climbs easily to the village, passing the **Rose and Crown** and then falling to the church and Church Lane. After 100yds (91m), turn off left into a lane marked as a cul-de-sac. After dropping to re-cross the river, the narrow lane climbs past **Brook Farm**, initially steeply, but soon levelling to continue between the fields.

MAP: OS Explorer 168 Stroud, Tetbury & Malmesbury

START/FINISH: The Vine Tree, Norton (ask permission first); grid ref: ST 887846

TRAILS/TRACKS: country lanes and gravel tracks, a short town section at Malmesbury

LANDSCAPE: undulating hill farmland

PUBLIC TOILETS: in Malmesbury behind the town square

TOURIST INFORMATION: Malmesbury; tel: 01666 823748

CYCLE HIRE: C H White & Son, 51 High Street, Malmesbury, tel 01666 822330 (prior bookings only) – alternative start

THE PUB: The Vine Tree, Norton

🚳 Great care to be taken through Malmesbury; steep descent and climb at Roman Bridge on the Fosse Way

Getting to the start

Malmesbury stands midway between Chippenham and Cirencester just off the A429 on the B4040. Norton is 3 miles (4.8km) to the south west. On entering the village, turn right, signposted Foxley, follow the road round to the right for the pub.

Why do this cycle ride?

This undemanding ride combines historic Malmesbury with quiet lanes and good off-road cycling. The route roughly follows part of two shallow valleys which converge on Malmesbury. The 'circle' is completed along a straight stretch of the Fosse Way.

Researched and written by: Dennis Kelsall

Malmesbury WILTSHIRE

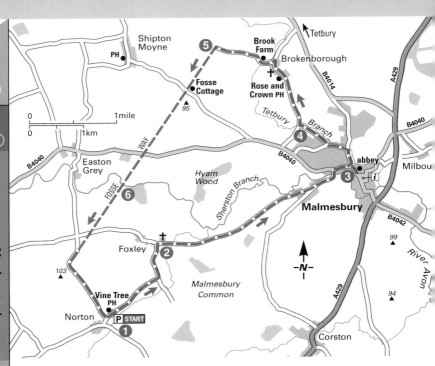

5 The track ends at a T-junction with a broad, straight track, the **Fosse Way**. Go left. Very soon, the tarmac gives way to coarse gravel and stone, and although the way is firm, the surface is loose in places and there is a risk of skidding if you travel at speed. After 0.5 mile (800m), cross a lane by **Fosse Cottage** and carry on past a water-pumping station for another mile (1.6km) to the B4040. Keep an eye open for fast-moving traffic as you cross and

continue, the track, before long, starting a steepening descent. It bends at the bottom to a bridge over the **Sherston Branch**.

6 Although widened in modern times the upstream portion of the bridge is original and dates back to a Roman settlement beside the river. The climb away on the far bank is very steep, and you may have to get off and push. Beyond, the way runs easily again for 0.5 mile (800m) to another road crossing. Keep ahead with the byway, the surface now of earth and a little rutted, shortly emerging onto another lane. Go ahead, staying with it as it soon bends left away from the line of the Roman road. Eventually dropping to a T-junction at the edge of **Norton**, go left to The Vine Tree.

The south view of the remnants of Malmesbury Abbey

The Vine Tree

The Vine Tree is a converted 16th-century mill house close to Westonbirt Arboretum, and is well worth seeking out for its interesting modern pub food and memorable outdoor summer dining. The tranquil sun-trap terrace includes a fountain, lavender hedge, pagodas, trailing vines and a barbecue. There's also a 2 acre (0.8ha) garden with a play area, and two boules pitches. If the weather is wet, be consoled with a pint of Fiddlers Elbow by the log fire in the main bar, with its old oak beams and flagstone floors. As well as a changing selection of real ales, there's a carefully selected list of wines (up to 30 by the glass), and decent coffee. Cooking is modern British, everything is made on the premises, and meals are served in the pine-furnished dining areas.

Food

The menu changes daily and closely follows the seasons, using local produce wherever possible. Choose from light bites (smoked haddock kedgeree, roast Cotswold pork baguette) and vegetarian options (wild mushroom and feta risotto) or trio of local award-winning sausages with bubble and squeak and a grain mustard sauce, or gilthead bream with lemongrass and sweet basil broth. Imaginative puddings.

Family facilities

Well-behaved children are welcome in the pub. High chairs are at hand, a children's menu, including home-made chicken nuggets, is available as are smaller portions, plus colouring equipment to keep youngsters amused. Sun-trap terrace and a huge garden/field with play area and space for impromptu football and cricket.

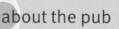

about the pub

The Vine Tree
Foxley Road, Norton
Malmesbury, Wiltshire SN16 0JP
Tel: 01666 837654
www.thevinetree.co.uk

DIRECTIONS: see Getting to the Start
PARKING: 100
OPEN: daily; all day Sunday
FOOD: daily; all day Sunday (& Saturday if fine) in summer
BREWERY/COMPANY: free house
REAL ALE: Butcombe Bitter, Wychwood Fiddlers Elbow, Hook Norton Bitter, guest beers
ROOMS: 4 en suite

Alternative refreshment stops

Various pubs and cafés in Malmesbury; the Rose & Crown at Brokenborough.

☛ Where to go from here

Visit the impressive remains of Malmesbury's Benedictine abbey, and in the spring and summer visit the Abbey House Gardens (www.abbeyhousegardens. co.uk). In nearby Tetbury the Police Museum (www.tetbury.org) explains how policing was carried out in the early 1900s.

8

Malmesbury WILTSHIRE

Around the Moors Valley Country Park

Exploring woodland and lakes, with extra loops to create your own route.

A miniature railway

The tracks may only be 7.25 inches (18.5cm) wide, but there's a real railway atmosphere to the miniature line at the Moors Valley Country Park. Its steam locomotives, carriages and goods vans thread their way around a landscaped loop beside the Moors Lake, and the 1-mile (1.6km) circuit is complete with a station, signal box and four tunnels.

The Moors Lake itself was built as a 'safety valve' to contain flooding in the area, which is liable after heavy rainfall. Some of the spoil from the lake was used to landscape the golf course and these developments provided the inspiration for the 1,500-acre (608ha) country park.

Work on the miniature railway began in 1985 as tracks were laid out and Kingsmere station was created from former farm buildings on the site. Many of the locomotives, rolling stock and carriages were brought from the Tucktonia Leisure Centre at Christchurch, and the new line opened to the public in July 1986. The railway is popular with both adults and children, and the ten-minute ride takes you past the main signal box and along the banks of the lake before looping around the play area on the way back to Kingsmere station. The railway is open daily from late May to early September, as well as during Easter and the Christmas holidays.

the ride

1 Leave the car park by the road entrance, zig-zag across **Hurn Lane** and join the combined cycleway/pavement under the A31. Bear left past the **phone-box**, then stop at the A31 slip road. Cross with care, then bear left on to the **Castleman Trail** towards Ashley Heath. The narrow gravel track bears to the right and pulls clear of the A31 through a tunnel of **young oak trees**. Soon the old line widens out into a 'dual carriageway' of narrow tracks separated by gorse and brambles. Watch out for cars as you cross the lane at **Holly Grove Farm**. You'll speed along the next

A packed model railway ride through Moors Valley Country Park

section to the road crossing at **Ashley Heath**. Stop here, and cross **Horton Road** with care. There's a convenience shop on your right as you rejoin the Castleman Trail and continue along the tree-shaded **cycleway**. Very soon, pass a section of the **former platform** at Ashley Heath, complete with its railway name-board. Continue for 600yds (549m), then look out for the narrow exit into **Forest Edge Drive** on the right.

2 Go through here and follow this residential road to the T-junction with Horton Road. Take care as you zig-zag left and right into the **Moors Valley Country Park** – it's only 50yds (46m), but you may prefer to wheel your bike along the pavement beside this busy road. Follow the tarred entrance road for the last 0.5 mile (800m) to reach the **visitor centre**, with a restaurant, toilets and other facilities. For the shortest ride, turn here and retrace the outward route back to the start. But it's well worth extending your visit by picking up a park map and following one of the four waymarked cycle routes around the forest.

3 The **Corsican Circuit** (2 miles/3.2km) is the basic ring at the heart of the park, which you can extend by adding one or more of the loops. It leads east from the visitor centre and loops anti-clockwise. The level route passes the **Play Trail entrance**, then circles back on good, gravelled forest rides.

4 Take the **Watchmoor Loop** (1.5 miles/2.3km) off the Corsican Circuit. It follows sandy tracks and penetrates some of the quieter areas of the forest. You'll see areas of open heathland, as well as plenty of light conifer woodland where the smell of the

---

2h00 — **12 MILES** — **19.3 KM** — **LEVEL 1 2 3**

SHORTER ALTERNATIVE ROUTE

1h00 — **5.5 MILES** — **8.8 KM** — **LEVEL 1 2 3**

MAP: OS Explorer OL22 New Forest
START/FINISH: Ashley Twinning (free) car park; grid ref: SU 139048
TRAILS/TRACKS: old railway cycleway, roads and forest tracks
LANDSCAPE: the tree-lined old railway leads into mixed woodland, heath and lakes
PUBLIC TOILETS: Moors Valley Country Park
TOURIST INFORMATION: Ringwood, tel: 01425 470896
CYCLE HIRE: Moors Valley Country Park visitor centre, tel: 01425 470721
THE PUB: The Old Beams, Ibsley
🛈 Two main road crossings and slow-moving traffic on country park access road. Suitability: inexperienced riders and children over 7 depending on trail option selected

Getting to the start

The car park is 0.5 miles (800m) south west of Ringwood off the A31. Leave the A31 at the B3081 junction, then take the Hurn Lane exit from the junction roundabout for the car park.

Why do this cycle ride?

A versatile route: at its simplest, you'll follow a level, traffic-free cycleway to the Moors Valley Country Park, with its superb range of family-friendly facilities and attractions. You can extend or vary this basic route by following one or more of the traffic-free cycle trails within the park.

Researched and written by: David Foster

pines mixes with the sweet scent of bracken, before rejoining the Corsican Circuit.

5 At this point you can also detour off on the **Somerley Loop** (1 mile/1.6km). This weaves its way over gravel and dirt tracks through some of the denser parts of the forest, though there are still some wide heather verges in places. It is the most undulating of the park trails, with a steep downhill section near the end.

6 The Somerley Loop joins on to the **Crane Loop** (2 miles/3.2km), which on its own is great for young families. This pretty route heads out beside the **golf course** and **Crane Lake**, before returning beside the miniature railway. You'll mainly follow tarred trails, though there are some gravel and dirt sections, too. Watch out for cars on the final section, which shares one of the park roads.

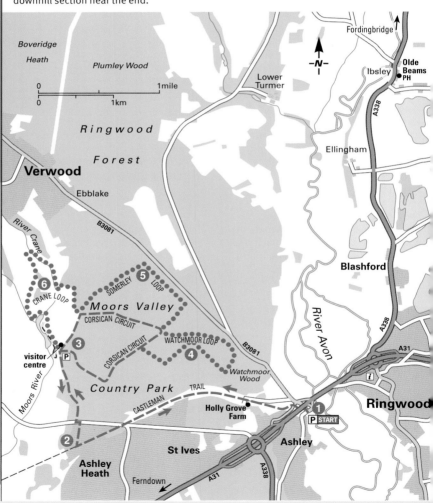

The Old Beams

The exterior of this 600-year-old cruck-beamed cottage is everything you would expect of an untouched country pub. The roof is neatly thatched, the walls are half-timbered and the building is flanked by an orchard garden. But all is not what it seems. Venturing inside is like entering Dr Who's Tardis, and beyond the pretty façade you will find a vast open-plan area, with a conservatory-style extension dominated by a central hooded fireplace. Furnishings range from dark wood tables and chairs to pine farmhouse tables. Along one side is the grand buffet table, laden with cold meats, seafood and fresh salads, drawing diners all day long.

Food

In addition to the usual sandwiches and ploughman's, there's a buffet counter displaying a wide range of cold meats and

about the pub

The Old Beams
Salisbury Road, Ibsley
Ringwood, Hampshire BH24 3PP
Tel: 01425 473387

DIRECTIONS: beside the A338 Ringwood-to-Salisbury road, 3 miles (4.8km) north of Ringwood

PARKING: 100

OPEN: daily, all day

FOOD: daily, all day

BREWERY/COMPANY: Greene King Brewery

REAL ALE: Greene King IPA & Abbot Ale, Ringwood Best

salads. Hot dishes include steak and ale pie, fish and chips, lamb slow cooked with rosemary and red wine on thyme mash, mixed grill and chargrilled tuna with white wine and coriander sauce. Sunday roast carvery lunches are served all afternoon.

Family facilities

Expect a genuine welcome, with smaller portions and standard children's menu available. There are also high chairs and baby-changing facilities.

Alternative refreshment stops

Seasons Restaurant at Moors Valley Country Park serves breakfast, lunches and afternoon teas.

☞ Where to go from here

At the Dorset Heavy Horse Centre near Verwood you'll see magnificent Shire horses, meet and groom donkeys and miniature Shetland ponies, and help feed the many animals at the centre, including Lulu the llama. Café, picnic and play areas (www.dorset-heavy-horse-centre.co.uk).

A New Forest loop from Burley

10

A varied ride from a popular village via 'Castleman's Corkscrew'.

The Castleman Trail
Railway interest is all around you on the mid-section of this ride, which reaches its climax at Holmsley's old station. The Castleman Trail follows the broad, level trackbed of the original main line to Dorchester. The railway was promoted by Charles Castleman, a Wimborne solicitor, who planned the line through his home town. This wasn't exactly the most direct route, and critics quickly dubbed it 'Castleman's Corkscrew'.

The railway opened in 1847, but was swallowed up by the larger and more powerful London & South Western Railway in the following year. At this time Bournemouth was little more than a sleepy village, but passengers for Christchurch could catch a linking coach service from Holmsley station, which was originally known as 'Christchurch Road'. After Bournemouth and Christchurch were linked to the national rail network, Holmsley's traffic evaporated. The station continued to serve its small local community, and handled timber from the nearby inclosures. Its rural seclusion was interrupted for a few years during the Second World War, when the little station became the gateway for a

Burley

HAMPSHIRE

Above: The war memorial in Burley
Below: An open path though woodland

new RAF airfield at Plain Heath. After the war, the railway fell victim to the growing popularity of road transport. Passenger traffic dwindled again and, in 1964, 'Castleman's Corkscrew' was finally axed in the notorious cuts made by Dr Beecham.

the ride

1 Turn right out of the car park, stop at the road junction, and continue straight ahead. Fork left at the **war memorial** into Pound Lane, signed to Bransgore. Pass the Forest Teahouse and cider shop, then follow the lane out over the heath to **Burbush Hill**.

2 Fork left just before the old railway bridge, following the waymarked off-road cycle track through the Forestry Commission's car park and down on to the **old railway line**. The Castleman Trail begins in a lovely sandy cutting, which is smothered with brilliant purple heather in late summer. Soon the old line emerges from the cutting onto a low embankment, with good views out over the boggy heath. You'll often see horse riders in the area and birdwatchers should look out for green woodpeckers, as well as for lapwings, curlews and redshanks, which nest on the heath in early summer. The trail rises briefly to the broken brickwork of **Greenberry Bridge**, which survived the closure of the

1h00	**6** MILES	**9.7** KM	**LEVEL** 123

MAP: OS Explorer OL22 New Forest
START/FINISH: public fee-paying car park, Burley; grid ref: SU 211030
TRAILS/TRACKS: busy village centre, quiet lanes and an old railway route
LANDSCAPE: bare open heathland contrasts with pretty cottages and wooded village lanes
PUBLIC TOILETS: opposite car park, Burley
TOURIST INFORMATION: Lyndhurst, tel: 023 8028 2269
CYCLE HIRE: Forest Leisure Cycling, The Cross, Burley, tel: 01425 403584
THE PUB: The Queens Head, Burley
🅫 Burley's streets get busy at weekends and during holiday periods. Good traffic sense required

Getting to the start

Burley village is on a minor road south east of Ringwood, between the A31 and the A35. Leave the A31 at Picket Post, 1 mile (1.6km) east of Ringwood, and follow the signposted route through Burley Street to Burley. Keep left at the war memorial in the centre of the village, and you'll find The Queens Head immediately on your left, with the public car park entrance just beyond the pub's own car park.

Why do this cycle ride?

This route takes you through the heart of the bustling New Forest village of Burley, with its antique shops, tea rooms and horse-drawn wagon rides. In complete contrast, the Castleman cycle trail is the perfect way to experience the surrounding heathland from a level stretch of old railway line. There are good opportunities for birdwatching, and you can visit the Old Station tea rooms at Holmsley.

Researched and written by: David Foster

Burley

HAMPSHIRE

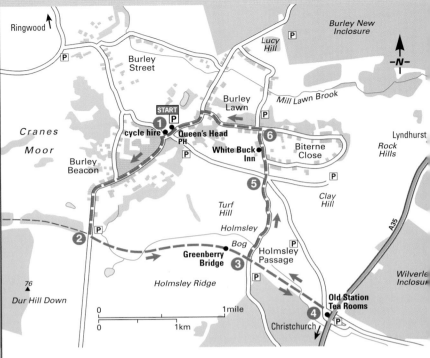

railway, only to be demolished in 1995 when it became unsafe. Continue to the low **wooden barriers** that guard the minor road crossing at **Holmsley Passage**, where you can still see short sections of the original railway lines embedded in the road surface.

3 If you wish, you can shorten the ride by turning left here. To complete the full route, cross the road and continue along the **old railway line**. The trail becomes more shaded as it runs perfectly straight through an avenue of young oak trees. The track crosses **two small bridges** that herald the approach to Holmsley Station. Look out for the **old brick platform** on your right before dismounting at the wooden gate that marks the end of the cycle track.

4 Beyond the gate and across the road, the **Old Station tea rooms** are well worth a visit for morning coffee, home-cooked lunches and cream teas. There's a pleasant garden, as well as a gift shop where you can buy a souvenir of your visit to this unusual refreshment stop. Turn here and retrace your outward route to **Holmsley Passage** (Point 3). Turn right on to the quiet lane, follow it up the hill and stop at the 5-way junction.

5 Cross straight over towards **Burley Lawn** and zig-zag left, then right, past the **White Buck Inn** into Bennetts Lane.

6 Bear left at the next junction into Beechwood Lane and keep straight on through **Lester Square** until you reach a T-junction. Turn left here towards Burley, and continue past the little brick-built **church** of St John the Baptist for the final 400yds (366m) back to the car park.

The Queens Head

Family facilities
Children are very welcome in the pub and there's a separate family area and children's menu. Youngsters will love to see the New Forest ponies that often congregate outside the pub.

Alternative refreshment stops
Tea rooms and the Burley Inn in Burley, the White Buck Inn at Burley Lawn, and the Old Station tea rooms at Holmsley are all good alternatives.

☛ Where to go from here
For more information about the New Forest area and its varied wildlife, visit the New Forest Museum and Visitor Centre in nearby Lyndhurst, with exhibitions and an audio-visual show (www.newforestmuseum.org.uk).

The Queen's Head was built in 1633, which makes it one of the oldest buildings in the New Forest. It became a smugglers' haunt in the 17th century, when contraband rum, brandy and tobacco was stored in the spacious cellars, well away from the coast. The main bar is named after Jack Warnes, an infamous local smuggler. The pub has been well modernised over the years and retains plenty of old timbers and panelling, wooden, flagstone and carpeted floors, and a fine Jacobean fireplace where a log fires blazes in winter. You'll find local beers from Ringwood Brewery on handpump and, for sunny summer days, a shaded courtyard garden with picnic tables.

Food
Food is traditional and the lunch and dinner menus are extensive. At lunch expect 'light bites' – seasonal soups, ploughman's and risotto, pasta, salads and sandwiches, alongside beer battered cod, steak and ale pie and specials such as lasagne and cottage pie. Dinner adds potted crab, rack of lamb, venison pie and roast duck with orange and shallot sauce. Sunday roast lunches.

about the pub

The Queens Head
The Cross, Burley
Ringwood, Hampshire BN24 4AB
Tel: 01425 403423

DIRECTIONS: in the centre of the village
PARKING: 30
OPEN: daily, all day
FOOD: daily, all day
BREWERY/COMPANY: Greene King
REAL ALE: Ringwood Best and Fortyniner, Greene King IPA

A circuit of Queen Elizabeth Country Park

A wooded ride through the heart of Hampshire's largest country park.

Butser Ancient Farm

Butser Ancient Farm was founded by Dr Peter Reynolds in 1972 to improve the understanding of prehistoric farming methods. The original farm was established west of the A3 at Rakefield Hanger, some 3 miles (4.8km) north of the present site. Although research continued at this remote location until 1989, Rakefield Hanger wasn't the ideal place to develop the farm's educational role. So, in 1976, a new site was developed at Hillhampton Down, just

across the A3 from the country park visitor centre. This site boasted a large, thatched roundhouse, with fields of crops and an industrial research area for producing charcoal and early metals like iron, copper, tin and bronze. In 1991 the farm moved to its present site at Bascomb Copse, where the buildings, animals and crops recreate the living conditions on a British Iron Age farm about 2,300 years ago. The farm has a reception area with a video introduction, souvenir shop and toilets. There's also an activity centre where visitors can try their hand at grinding corn, spinning, weaving or making clay pots. The ancient farm is open to the public between March and September for weekend events, including

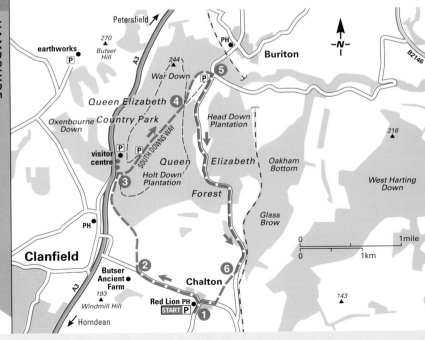

1h00	**6** MILES	**9.7** KM	**LEVEL** 1**2**3

MAP: OS Explorer 120 Chichester

START/FINISH: public car park next to the Red Lion, Chalton; grid ref: SU 731160

TRAILS/TRACKS: rough off-road trails, quiet rural lanes

LANDSCAPE: thickly wooded rolling chalk hills, with open fields grazed by sheep

PUBLIC TOILETS: Queen Elizabeth Country Park visitor centre

TOURIST INFORMATION: Petersfield, tel: 01730 268829

CYCLE HIRE: Owens Cycles, Petersfield, tel: 01730 260446

THE PUB: The Red Lion, Chalton

🛈 There are two short, steep sections in the Country Park where you may prefer to push your bike; bumpy off-road tracks. Suitable for older children, some off-road experience useful

Chalton **HAMPSHIRE**

demonstrations of prehistoric cookery, textiles and clothing.

the ride

1 Leave the car park and turn left past **The Red Lion,** then left again at the junction towards **Clanfield and Petersfield**. Pass under the power lines and continue for 700yds (640m) to the bottom of the hill opposite **Butser Ancient Farm**.

2 Fork right here on to the bridleway and **off-road cycle trail**, a bumpy track with lovely views across the fields to **Windmill Hill** and the ancient farm behind you on your left. The bridleway climbs steeply as it approaches the woods at the corner of the country park, and it's probably safer to dismount and push your bike at this point. Follow the bridleway as it skirts the western edge of the forest and drops gently down to the tarred **Forest Drive** and **picnic areas**.

3 Here you can turn left for the 300yds (274m) diversion to the park's **visitor centre,** with café and toilets. Alternatively, turn right to continue your ride. This

Above: Cycling through the Country Park

Getting to the start

Chalton lies east of the A3 between Petersfield and Horndean. Leave the A3 at the Clanfield exit, and follow signs to Chalton and the Red Lion pub (about 1 mile/1.6km). Bear right in the village and you'll find the public car park tucked away on the right hand side, just past the Red Lion.

Why do this cycle ride?

This route links Hampshire's oldest pub with its largest country park. Twenty miles of trails thread their way through the park's 1,400 acres (567ha). There's an excellent visitor centre with a shop, information desk and café. The route takes in a section of the South Downs Way before returning to Chalton on a quiet country lane.

Researched and written by: David Foster

section, which follows part of the **South Downs Way** national trail, takes you past the **Benhams Bushes barbecue site** (advance booking required). Follow the Forest Drive for 600yds (549m). When you reach the hairpin bend, fork right through **Benhams Bushes car park** on to the waymarked off-road cycle trail. Follow the bumpy gravel road for just over 0.5 mile (800m) to a junction near the top of the hill.

4 Bear left here, then fork right a few yards further on, sticking with the gravel road as it drops to a **wooden gate** at the Forestry Commission's **Hall's Hill car park**. Continue through the car park and stop at the road exit.

5 Leave the South Downs Way here, and turn right on to the **narrow lane** that drops down towards Chalton and Finchdean. This easy ride takes you through a deeply rural, **wooded landscape**; sheep graze in small open fields between the beechwoods and hazel coppices, and you may spot the occasional deer. Eventually you'll pass under a line of **electricity wires**, before the road climbs around a right-hand bend and runs beside the railway for a short distance. Two hundred yards (183m) further on, look out for a **signposted byway** on your right-hand side.

6 Fork right here for the short, sharp climb up on to **Chalton Peak**. There are fine views on your right towards Windmill Hill, with dog rose, bramble and knapweed colouring the hedges beside this pleasant, level section. At the end of the byway turn right for the final 200 yds (183m) back to the junction where you fork left to return to The Red Lion and the car park.

Negotiating a bend in the Queen Elizabeth Country Park

The Red Lion

mash with rich gravy, and puddings such as cherry pie and bread pudding.

Family facilities
Children are welcome in the dining room (where there's a small standard children's menu) and the spacious rear garden. The latter offers lovely views to Windmill Hill and Butser Ancient Farm.

This beautiful timbered and thatched pub – a typical Hampshire cottage, reputedly built in the 12th century as dwellings for the craftsmen building the parish church – stands at the heart of the quaint village, opposite the lych-gate. Tourists, walkers and weary A3 travellers are attracted into its cosy and rustic main bar and modern dining bar extension – not least for the tip-top ale and the impressive range of whiskies and country wines. Both the old-fashioned public bar and the lounge bar are contained in the original building, the high-backed old settles of the former providing the perfect foil to the black beams and huge inglenook. This is reputedly Hampshire's oldest pub, and it is immaculately maintained by the very local Gales Brewery.

Food
In addition to sandwiches and filled baguettes (hot roasted vegetables), ploughman's lunches and filled jacket potatoes, daily specials may include braised mixed game with mushrooms and red wine, local pork and watercress sausages on chive

Alternative refreshment stops
The Coach House Café in Queen Elizabeth Country Park or the Five Bells in Buriton.

☛ Where to go from here
Gale's Brewery at Horndean has tours and a shop (www.galesales.co.uk).

Chalton HAMPSHIRE

about the pub

The Red Lion
Chalton, Waterlooville
Hampshire PO8 0BG
023 9259 2246
www.gales.co.uk

DIRECTIONS: in the centre of the village
PARKING: use adjacent village car park
OPEN: daily
FOOD: daily
BREWERY/COMPANY: Gales Brewery
REAL ALE: Gales Best, Butser and HSB, guest beer

The Centurion Way from Chichester

Centurion Way

WEST SUSSEX

Encounter the sculptures along the Centurion Way cycle route, and scale the Iron Age banks of The Trundle.

The Centurion Way and The Trundle

This traffic-free bike and pedestrian trail opened in full in 2002, and was named the Centurion Way because it crosses a Roman road at one point. For most of its length it follows the trackbed of a defunct railway that ran between Chichester and Midhurst. This existed from 1881 until 1957; the stretch southwards from Lavant was kept in operation for transporting sugar beet and gravel up to 1991. Along the route you will see some highly quirky modern sculptures: two of these, Roman Archway and Primary Hangers, were made with the help of local schoolchildren.

Huge grassy banks on The Trundle mark the extent of an Iron Age hillfort, which has two modern masts on it. The view is quite spectacular, including almost the entire east coast of the Isle of Wight, the watery expanses of Chichester Harbour and the stands of Goodwood racecourse. If you look carefully on a clear day, you can see the chalk cliffs of the Seven Sisters way over to the east, and the white tent-like structure of

Butlin's in Bognor Regis. There is no access for cyclists to the top, so lock up your bike by the car park and walk up.

the ride

1 Take the **Centurion Way** (signposted as cycle path to Lavant) to the right of the house at the end of the road, and to the left of the **school gates**. This joins the old railway track by a sculpture called **Roman Archway**, which spans the track. After going under a bridge, you will see the entrance to **Brandy Hole Copse**, a local nature reserve to the left. Among the oak coppice and chestnut trees are high, overgrown banks that were erected 2,000 years ago by a late Iron Age tribe as boundaries or fortifications, some years before the Roman Conquest in AD 43. Dragonflies and bats are attracted to this reserve, which also has three ponds to explore.

2 Before going under the next bridge (signposted Lavant), you will see sculptures called **The Chichester Road Gang**, resembling road workers carrying tools, but made out of metal canisters. Away to the left is another artwork called the **Roman Amphitheatre**. It is here that the now invisible Roman road once passed.

3 After the next bridge, with its **dangling metal sculptures** – Primary Hangers – the route leaves the old railway track and joins a residential road in Mid Lavant. Just down to the right is an excellent **adventure playground**. Carry along the road, following

Roman Amphitheatre is one of several unusual works of art on the route

Cycling along a quiet lane on the route

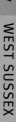

MAP: OS Explorer 120 Chichester

START/FINISH: Westgate, Chichester, at the end of the road by the railway line and Bishop Luffa School; grid ref SU 847047

TRAILS/TRACKS: surfaced cycle path, compacted earth cycle path; full ride returns via chalk field track, stony track and roads

LANDSCAPE: old railway track, woodland, farmland; chalk downland on the full ride

PUBLIC TOILETS: none on route

TOURIST INFORMATION: Chichester, tel: 01243 775888

CYCLE HIRE: Shed End Bikes, Preston Farm, near West Dean (on this route) tel: 01243 811766, 07946 341685

THE PUB: The Selsey Arms, West Dean

🚴 The full ride has long, stony descent: ride with care and wheel your bike if necessary. There's a short section along the main road

Getting to the start

Turn off the A27 on the western side of Chichester, along the A259 into Chichester. Turn left at the roundabout, then left at the next mini-roundabout, along Westgate. Roadside parking at the end of the road.

Why do this cycle ride?

There's an adventure playground and sculptures on the Centurion Way, a level path shared with walkers. From Chichester, head out into the country, reaching West Dean. Either return the same way or take a more demanding off-road route up to The Trundle.

Researched and written by: Tim Locke

signs for West Dean. After concrete bollards, and soon after a **postbox** on the left, then St Mary's Close on the right, turn right at a **square green** to rejoin the old railway track (not signposted at time of writing). Later the Centurion Way turns left to leave the old railway track, then turns right along a cycle path parallel to the **A286**.

4 This path ends at the village of **West Dean**. Turn right along the small road, round the back of the village (take the next turning on the left for **The Selsey Arms**, or to see the churchyard, with its fine old tombstones, carry straight on). For the short route, return the same way to the start. For the full route bear to the right where the road first bends left, towards ornate **iron gates** in a flint wall. Follow the bridleway uphill, alongside the wall and along the field edge, and later through a forest. Finally emerge at the top as the view opens out by a **house**. Keep forward on a track to a car park.

5 Before turning right (towards the sea) to continue, walk up ahead to the summit of **The Trundle**, marked by two prominent **masts**, to enjoy the view. Now carefully ride the stony route down a long hill to **East Lavant**. Turn right along the main village street, avoiding a left fork, and past the Royal Oak. Ignore side turns and go past a **triangular recreation ground** on your right.

6 Turn left along the **A286** for 350 yards (320m). Take the first turning on the right (with the cycle route sign for Chichester) by stopping at a small lay-by (just before this turning) on the left and then crossing the road when it is safe to do so. After crossing the bridge, turn left to rejoin the **Centurion Way**, and turn right to return to the start.

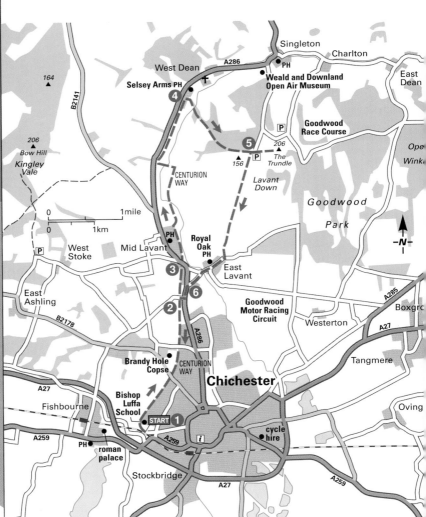

The Selsey Arms

The Selsey Arms is a traditional late 18th-century village pub, well placed for Goodwood, the Weald and Downland Museum and visitors heading to West Dean Gardens. The front bar rooms feature bare boards, horse brasses on beams, dark wood pub tables and chairs, and a friendly, welcoming atmosphere. Daily papers are strewn on a table for customers to read. There's a separate, carpeted restaurant with open fires, beamed ceilings and plain wooden furnishings.

Food

Good-value bar food ranges from sandwiches and ham ploughman's to haddock and chips and home-made steak and kidney pie. A blackboard highlights the bargain two-course lunch and evening extras such as lamb's liver and bacon, red bream, and smoked haddock topped with Welsh rarebit.

Family facilities

Children are welcome inside the pub. The sheltered patio with picnic benches is ideal in fine weather.

Alternative refreshment stops

Try the Royal Oak, East Lavant (on full ride only) or the café at the Weald and Downland Open Air Museum (if visiting).

☛ Where to go from here

The Weald and Downland Open Air Museum (www.wealddown.co.uk) at Singleton, 1 mile (1.6km) east of West Dean, can be reached by driving or cycling along the A286. More than 45 historic buildings, from medieval to Victorian, rescued from south east England, have been rebuilt here. About 0.75 mile (1.2km) along a signposted route from the beginning of this ride or by car via the A259, is Fishbourne Roman Palace (www.sussexpast.co.uk). The largest Roman building north of the Alps, it has outstanding mosaics.

Centurion Way

WEST SUSSEX

about the pub

The Selsey Arms

West Dean, Chichester
West Sussex PO18 0QX
Tel: 01243 811465

DIRECTIONS: on the A286 at West Dean, between Singleton and Mid Lavant
PARKING: 20
OPEN: daily; all day Saturday and Sunday April to October
FOOD: daily; all day Saturday and Sunday April to October
BREWERY/COMPANY: free house
REAL ALE: Greene King Abbot Ale, Fuller's London Pride, Young's Bitter

Hamsey and Barcombe Mills

Peaceful hamlets, mill pools, Roman sites, a pub that offers boat hire and a fair-weather extension to see a steam railway.

The Lavender Line

Old advertising signs and railway paraphernalia adorn the beautifully painted and restored station at Isfield. If you visit Cinders Buffet, on the platform, you can see 'before and after' photos that show how much volunteers and lovers of this little country railway have put into running a short section of the line that once ran from Lewes to Uckfield. Steam and diesel trains run during most weekends throughout the year, and on some other days during summer; one ticket allows you to ride all day. You can also go into the signal box at Isfield, try pulling the levers and operating a signal, while the former coal office houses a model railway layout. This ride crosses a bridge at Hamsey over the old railway (where the track has been removed), and from The Anchor Inn it follows a section along the trackbed itself (a licensed bridleway, which the landowner allows the public to use) to reach Barcombe Mills station, now a private house. You also cross twice over another line that ran from Lewes to East Grinstead.

Barcombe Mills

Two Roman roads – one from the west and the other from London – once met here. There was a mill here for 900 years until 1939; all that remains are the huge mill pool and gushing weirs. A plaque tells you this was, in 1066, the first place in Sussex

to have a tollgate: look out for the list of tolls by the bridge, showing charges in old money – 's' for a shilling (5p) and 'd' for a penny (12 pennies to the shilling).

the ride

1 With the Royal Oak pub on your right go along the main street in Barcombe and turn left in front of the village sign for **The Anchor Inn and Newick**. At the bottom of the hill turn right on Boast Lane, signposted Anchor Inn. After passing **Delves Farm**, and just before a house on the right, look for a track signposted '**bridleway**' on the left, into a triangular field. At the next triangular area, look to your left for a gate with a yellow arrow on it: at the far end of the field a line of hedgerow trees rising up to the top right skyline marks the line of a Roman road that ran from London to Lewes. Continue along the track, which later follows the left side of a field and passes a wartime **brick pillbox**. The route drops to a **footbridge**. Continue across a meadow to the gate ahead, up over another footbridge and along a track; ignore driveways to the right.

| 3h00 | 12 MILES | 19.3 KM | LEVEL 1 2 |

SHORTER ALTERNATIVE ROUTE

| 1h00 | 4 MILES | 6.4 KM | LEVEL 1 2 |

MAP: OS Explorer 122 South Downs Way: Steyning to Newhaven

START/FINISH: Barcombe village centre; roadside parking; grid ref: TQ 418157

TRAILS/TRACKS: back lanes, hard stony track; optional extension along a track and through fields that get muddy after rain

LANDSCAPE: farmland and river, with distant views of the South Downs

PUBLIC TOILETS: none; when open, Barcombe Mills station has toilets

TOURIST INFORMATION: Lewes tel: 01273 483448

CYCLE HIRE: Lifecycle, The Tile House, Preston Park, Preston Road, Brighton tel: 01273 542425 (www.lifecyclebrighton.com)

THE PUB: The Anchor Inn, Barcombe

🚩 One short climb after Barcombe Mills, otherwise more gentle ups and downs. Take care on blind bends

Getting to the start

Barcombe is signposted from the A26 and A275, 4.3 miles (7km) north of Lewes.

Why do this cycle ride?

Along this route of quiet lanes you'll find everything from Roman sites to wartime defences. Off-road sections follow a disused track, with distant views of the South Downs, and an ancient 'green lane' that crosses fields and leads to the Lavender Line preserved railway.

Researched and written by: Tim Locke

At the road T-junction turn right into **Isfield**. Pass the Laughing Fish pub on your left to visit the Lavender Line.

2 From Isfield retrace your route across the meadows and back past the pillbox. Turn left on the road to continue to **The Anchor Inn**.

3 Retrace your route a short distance from The Anchor Inn and, just before **Keeper's Cottage** on the left, turn left on the **old railway track**, signposted 'licensed bridleway to Barcombe Mills'.

4 On reaching a road opposite the old **Barcombe Mills station**, detour left and take the first road on the left. Turn right at the junction in front of the driveway to **Barcombe House** to reach the millpond and weirs of **Barcombe Mills**. Return the same way to the road, past **Barcombe Mills station**. At the next junction go straight ahead for a short-cut back into Barcombe. For the main route, turn left here, and pass

Isfield Station on the Lavender Line

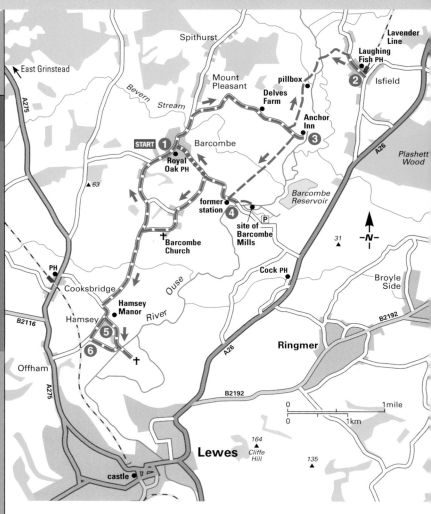

Barcombe church. Carry on along the road, keeping left at the next two junctions towards Hamsey.

5 Just after **Hamsey Manor** turn left down Whitfeld Lane to Hamsey. There is a lovely half-timbered house called **Yeoman's** dated 1584; just after, turn left at a T-junction. The road crosses a former canal via a bridge. After the bridge, you can pick up the keys to **Hamsey church** from **Pine**

Barn, the first house on the left. The road rises over the old railway to reach Hamsey church, a wonderful example of what medieval country churches used to look like. Return to **Hamsey,** keep left at the road junction by the **canal bridge,** past a pillbox.

6 Turn right at the T-junction, and after **Whitfeld Lane** joins from the right follow signs for Barcombe to return to the start.

The Anchor Inn

The white-painted Anchor, built in 1790 mainly to cater for the bargees, has an idyllic location in an isolated spot on the west bank of the River Ouse. It lost its liquor licence in 1895, after the landlord was convicted of smuggling, and didn't regain it until 1963. Refurbished after serious flooding in 2000, the interior features wood and flagstone floors, a warm décor, open fires and a welcoming atmosphere. The big attraction here is the large riverside decking area with views directly to the river and the open countryside beyond, The pub also has 27 boats available for hire by the hour.

Food
Expect classic pub food such as baked trout, cottage pie, chilli, lasagne and various steaks. There are also good snacks and daily specials.

Family facilities
The Anchor Inn has a children's licence so youngsters are welcome anywhere in the pub. There is a basic children's menu and smaller portions of adult dishes are offered. The large front garden is ideal for children; take care by the river.

about the pub

The Anchor Inn
Anchor Lane, Barcombe
Lewes, East Sussex BN8 5BS
Tel: 01273 400414
www.anchorinnandboating.co.uk

DIRECTIONS:	The Anchor Inn is at the end of Boast Lane (which becomes Anchor Lane), all by itself, and signposted from the centre of Barcombe village
PARKING:	100
OPEN:	daily; all day Easter to September; all day Saturday and Sunday only October to Easter. Phone for winter weekday opening times
FOOD:	no food Sunday evening
BREWERY/COMPANY:	free house
REAL ALE:	Harveys Best, Badger Tanglefoot
ROOMS:	3 rooms (1 en suite)

Hamsey

EAST SUSSEX

Alternative refreshment stops
The Royal Oak in Barcombe and the Laughing Fish in Isfield both serve pub food and have gardens. Cinders Buffet at Isfield Station has good-value snacks and light lunches.

☛ Where to go from here
About 4.3 miles (7km) south of Barcombe, Lewes Castle (www.sussexpast.co.uk) stands at the high point of the hilly, ancient town of Lewes. Your entrance ticket includes Barbican House Museum, with its scale model of 19th-century Lewes. The town of Lewes itself is fun to explore, with its many tiny lanes and paths.

The Cuckoo Trail around Hailsham

Well-signposted tracks and lanes link together to create a cycle-friendly ride along a railway track and through peaceful countryside to Michelham Priory.

The Cuckoo Trail

Part of the National Cycle Network, this well-signposted and popular route follows a former railway for most of its 11 miles (17.7km) between Heathfield and Polegate, with an extension to Eastbourne. The railway opened in 1880, linking Polegate with Eridge, and got its name because of a Sussex tradition that says the first cuckoo of spring was always heard at Heathfield Fair. The line closed in 1968, but was revived imaginatively in 1990 as a cycle path, shared with walkers. Quirky iron sculptures and carved wooden benches punctuate the route. Signposted by a former station, the Old Loom Mill complex has a café, crafts, playground, bike hire and the MasterPiece Studio where you can paint your own pottery and collect the results after firing a day or so later.

Michelham Priory

Despite its name, this is a Tudor mansion, set in England's longest medieval, water-filled moat and approached through a 14th-century gatehouse. Wander around the grounds and you will find a physic herb garden with plants that were used for medicine and cooking, re-created Iron Age huts, and the remains of the original priory, where Augustinian canons once lived and worshipped. Inside the house are tapestries, kitchen equipment and an 18th-century child's bedroom; by the entrance is a working watermill which grinds flour for sale.

the ride

1 From the car park, return along the main **driveway** to the road. Turn left and keep left at the first junction. Just after the next junction, turn left on to **Robin Post Lane**, and follow the '**cycle route 2**' signs. The surfacing ends after **New House Farm** on the right. Continue on a track, turning right at the next junction signposted **Cuckoo Trail/route 2**; you can see the South Downs away to the right in the distance.

The Cuckoo Trail has several unique sculptures along its route

Michelham Priory is actually a Tudor mansion with the remains of the original priory

2 At the end of the forest, where there is a house away to the right, ignore a track to the left but keep forward on **cycle route 2**. Beneath the embankment of the A22 turn right on a cycle path, following **Cuckoo Trail signs** which lead you under the main road and along the right side of a road. Avoid crossing a footbridge over the **A27** Polegate bypass and continue on the cycle path. At the next bridge turn left on the **Cuckoo Trail** and follow for 3 miles (4.8km) to Hailsham. The Cuckoo Trail itself is very well signposted and easy to follow. It follows the old railway track for much of the way, but occasionally diverts along small and quiet residential roads. Cross over via **traffic lights**. Later the Trail leaves the old railway track briefly and you enter **Freshfield Close**; follow the Cuckoo Trail signs to right and then to the left.

3 The Trail follows a road close to a **duck pond** and the small park surrounding it, then just after the Railway Tavern on the right, it turns left to leave the road, passing close to a **skateboard ramp**. Going under a bridge, it continues along the old railway track. After some playing fields appear on the right, the Cuckoo Trail bends left into a **housing estate**, then right and left on a **path**.

4 Go under **Hawk's Road bridge** and turn left up the ramp, signposted **Michelham Priory**. Turn right on the road, then forward at the mini-roundabout to follow **Hempstead Lane**.

3h15	11 MILES	17.7 KM	LEVEL 1 **2** 3

SHORTER ALTERNATIVE ROUTE

3h00	9.5 MILES	15.3 KM	LEVEL 1 **2** 3

MAP: OS Explorer 122, South Downs Way: Newhaven to Eastbourne

START/FINISH: Abbot's Wood car park; grid ref: TQ 558072

TRAILS/TRACKS: largely compacted gravel and earth tracks, muddy in places; some quiet back lanes and residential roads

LANDSCAPE: woodland, farmland, railway track, suburban roads

PUBLIC TOILETS: at the start

TOURIST INFORMATION: Eastbourne, tel: 01323 411400

CYCLE HIRE: MP Cycle Hire (passed on the Cuckoo Trail), the MasterPiece Studio, Old Loom Mill, Ersham Road, Hailsham BN27 4RG, tel: 01323 449245 or 07974 443119

THE PUB: The Old Oak Inn, Arlington

🚫 Often muddy for a short section after Point 5. Use the bike crossing point on the A22 at the edge of Hailsham, and take special care as this road is usually busy

Getting to the start

Abbot's Wood car park is signposted from the A27 between Lewes and Polegate. Take the north turn (Thornwell Road), signposted Arlington and Abbot's Wood. Keep left at the first road junction and right at the next junction, then soon turn right at the signpost to Abbot's Wood car park.

Why do this cycle ride?

This level ride uses the Cuckoo Trail and most of it is on a disused railway track.

Researched and written by: Tim Locke

Hailsham

EAST SUSSEX

5 At the **A22** dual carriageway, cross very carefully by the traffic islands indicated with blue bicycle/pedestrian symbols, and take the lane signposted to **Michelham Priory** opposite. The road surfacing ends by the last cottage on the left, and the lane continues as an often muddy track. Just after the track bears left, ignore a bridleway forking right, and continue along to a road. Before turning right along the road, you can detour left for a short distance to see the entrance to **Arlington Stadium**, a venue for stock-car racing and speedway.

6 At the next junction detour right to **Michelham Priory,** then right again at the access road to the Priory itself. Return to the previous road junction and turn right towards Arlington and Wilmington, past **The Old Oak Inn**. Take the next left to return to Abbot's Wood car park.

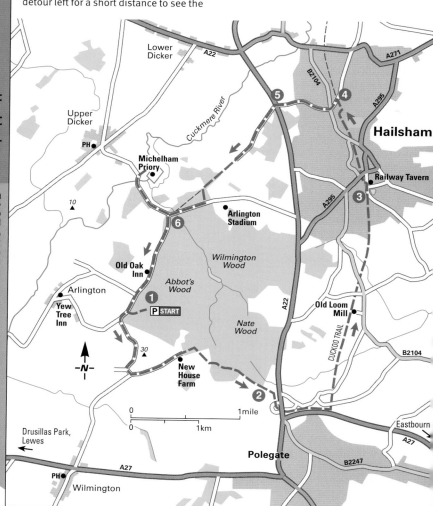

The Old Oak Inn

Built in 1733 as the village almshouse, the Old Oak became a pub in the early 1900s and supplied ale and cider to the workers in the local brick-making and charcoal-burning industries. The friendly, open-plan bar has big beams, blazing winter log fires, comfortable seating and a relaxed atmosphere. Ales are tapped from the cask and you will find a good choice of time-honoured pub games to while away an hour or two on inclement days. In sunny weather head out into the secluded rear garden and savour the South Downs views.

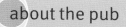

about the pub

The Old Oak Inn
Arlington, Polegate
East Sussex BN26 6SJ
Tel: 01323 482072

DIRECTIONS: follow directions to Abbots Wood car park (above), go past Abbots Wood for 0.5 mile (0.8km) and it's on the left side of the road
PARKING: 40
OPEN: daily; all day
FOOD: daily; all day Saturday and Sunday
BREWERY/COMPANY: free house
REAL ALE: Harveys Best, Badger Best, guest beers

Food
The menu offers light meals such as ploughman's salads and filled baguettes. More substantial dishes include 'Oak Favourites' like ham, egg and chips, home-made fishcakes and a large Yorkshire pudding filled with Cumberland sausage and rich gravy. Alternatives range from the daily curry and mixed grill to blackboard specials like seafood gratin and lamb shank in minted gravy.

Family facilities
Children of all ages are welcome inside. There are high chairs, children's portions of main menu dishes, a menu for young children and a wooden adventure frame and slide in the garden.

Alternative refreshment stops
The Railway Arms in Hailsham has a children's area in the garden, and there's a café with a playground at Old Loom Mill on the Cuckoo Trail and a café for visitors at Michelham Priory.

☛ Where to go from here
Four miles (6.4km) south west of Abbot's Wood, Drusillas Park (www.drusillas.co.uk), on the road to Alfriston, has a wonderful animal collection. Animals are kept in conditions similar to those they would experience in the wild. There are monkeys, meerkats, a farmyard area, and 'Penguin Bay' with underwater viewing points, plus play areas, a miniature railway and a paddling pool.

Hailsham   EAST SUSSEX

Chedworth Roman Villa

Discover a Roman villa set in a picturesque fold of the Cotswold Hills.

Roman Villa

Set amid idyllic Cotswold countryside, the Roman villa at Chedworth is perhaps the finest discovered in Britain. The area was well populated during the occupation, and Corinium (Cirencester) was the second largest Roman town in the country. The villa was a chance discovery in 1864 by a gamekeeper digging to retrieve a lost ferret. Subsequent excavation has revealed an extensive site containing wonderfully preserved features. First built around

120AD, it was enlarged and added to over the next 300 years, and some 32 rooms have been identified, including kitchens, living and dining rooms, latrines and bath houses as well as outside courtyard and garden areas. Bathing was an important element in Roman life, a social occasion rather than simply a means of keeping clean. The baths here were obviously well used, judging by the wear on the floors, and in addition to cold plunges, there were wet and dry hot baths. The hypocaust is clearly revealed, showing how hot air circulated beneath the floors and within the walls to provide all-round heating. But perhaps the most spectacular feature is the mosaic flooring. The one in the dining room

Chedworth

GLOUCESTERSHIRE

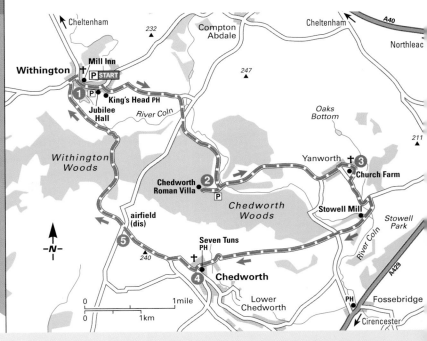

Above: Mosaic at Chedworth Roman Villa
Next page: Foundations of the Roman villa

3h00 — **10.75** MILES — **17.3** KM — LEVEL **123**

MAP: OS Explorer OL45 The Cotswolds
START/FINISH: The Mill Inn, Withington
(ask permission first); grid ref: SP 032154
TRAILS/TRACKS: country lanes throughout
LANDSCAPE: steeply rolling hills cleaved by
deep, wooded valleys
PUBLIC TOILETS: none on route
TOURIST INFORMATION: Cirencester,
tel 01285 654180
CYCLE HIRE: none locally
THE PUB: The Mill Inn, Withington
🅛 Several long, steep climbs; care on
country lanes

Getting to the start
Some 6 miles (9.7km) south east of
Cheltenham, Withington lies in the valley
of the River Coln and is most easily reached
along a minor lane from the A436. If The Mill
Inn is busy, use a car park by the Jubilee Hall
on the other side of the old railway bridge.

Why do this cycle ride?
The Coln is one of the prettiest rivers in the
Cotswolds and below Withington it winds
through a lovely, deep wooded valley. The
ride begins in Withington, climbing a
shoulder to drop back into the Coln valley,
where it passes a Roman villa. The climb to
Yanworth is rewarded by medieval wall
paintings in its church. On the other side of
the valley, the route is via Chedworth before
finally returning to Withington past a disused
wartime airfield.

Researched and written by: Dennis Kelsall

is particularly brilliant, depicting young
boys who represent the four seasons,
although sadly, autumn is missing.

the ride

1 From **The Mill Inn** car park, go left
between the abutments of a dismantled
railway bridge to rise past the entrance to
Jubilee Hall, which is on the right. At the
next turning, go right, signed 'Yanworth'
and 'Roman Villa'. After the **King's Head**,
leave the village behind, the narrow lane
climbing over a hill then falling in a long
descent into the Coln valley. There is a fine
view ahead across the wolds, although it
may be marred for some by the lines of
pylons marching over the hills. Cross
the river at the bottom and climb to a
crossroads. Ahead the lane undulates
easily along the wooded edge, shortly
reaching a junction where the **Roman
villa** is signed off on the right.

2 Rejoin the lane at this point after visiting the villa and re-cross the river, the way signed to Yanworth and Northleach. After another stiff pull, the lane runs more easily over Yanworth Common, eventually reaching a junction. Keep ahead towards **Yanworth**. Pedal through the village, but at the far side where the road bends to Northleach, go left. The lane winds around and down to the church.

3 Carry on down the hill below **Church Farm,** swinging beneath paddocks to a junction. Go left and drop across the bottom of the valley, pulling away steeply beyond to a junction. Turn right towards **Chedworth**, descending back into the vale to re-cross the river by **Stowell Mill**. Another short climb follows, soon levelling to reach a crossroads. Keep ahead, still towards Chedworth, the way rising steadily away. Eventually the lane begins to fall, the

gradient increasing as it twists through sharp bends into Chedworth. Over a stream at the bottom, it is up again, to the **Seven Tuns pub**, opposite which is the church.

4 Continue past the pub and take the lane ahead at the junction above, signed to Withington. At the top of the hill, go right, shortly passing the runways of a **disued airfield**.

5 Carry on at the crossing and then bear right to join a busier road, still following signs to **Withington**. Entering woodland there begins a long descent, which later steepens to a sharp right-hand bend. Emerging from the trees, the way undulates for another 0.75 mile (1.2km) into Withington. Keep with the main lane as it winds through the village, turning right opposite the church to return to The Mill Inn.

The Mill Inn

Splendid low-beamed ceilings, large open fireplaces, stone- and oak-panelled walls and worn flagstone floors combine with simple rustic furnishings and country style artefacts to re-create the original atmosphere of this 400-year-old former corn mill and local brewhouse. Right up until 1914 the landlord was listed as an innkeeper and keeper of the watermill. The pub stands in a deep valley on the banks of the River Coln, surrounded by beech and chestnut trees, and it has a lovely riverside garden, complete with ducks, providing an idyllic post-ride setting for peaceful summer drinking. It is one of the few country pubs in the south where you can quaff Samuel Smith's beers.

about the pub

The Mill Inn
Withington, Cheltenham
Gloucestershire GL54 4BE
Tel: 01242 890204

DIRECTIONS: see Getting to the start
PARKING: 60
OPEN: daily
FOOD: daily
BREWERY/COMPANY: Samuel Smith Brewery
REAL ALE: Samuel Smith Best & Old Brewery Bitter
ROOMS: 3 en suite

Food
Menu choices include minty lamb casserole, creamy pork and mushroom pepperpot, steak and ale pie, home-baked crusty baguettes, ploughman's lunches, and a range of 'basket meals' – a food concept said to have originated here in the 1950s.

Family facilities
Families can expect a warm welcome and good provision for children. There's a family area in the pub, youngsters have their own menu and the toilets are equipped with baby-changing facilities. Children should be well supervised in the riverside garden.

Alternative refreshment stops
On the route you will pass the Seven Tuns in Chedworth village and the King's Head at Withington.

☛ Where to go from here
Explore Chedworth Roman Villa, one of the finest Romano-British villas in Britain, or head for Northleach to visit Keith Harding's World of Mechanical Music, a living museum of self-playing musical instruments (www.mechanicalmusic.co.uk).

Chedworth GLOUCESTERSHIRE

The Leach and Coln valleys

Wander the wolds between rivers that feed the upper reaches of the River Thames.

Ancient trackways

Salt was once a highly valued commodity, attracting taxes and being paid as wages. Important not only as a condiment, it was demanded in large quantities during the Middle Ages to preserve meat and fish for use during the winter. Produced at certain spots along the coast, where seawater could be panned and concentrated into brine, salt was also found naturally as geological deposits, such places often incorporating 'wich' within their name. The salt was traded across the country, carried by packhorse along routes which became known as 'Salt Ways'.

It is often assumed that Britain had no roads before the Romans arrived, but this is far from the truth and there is abundant evidence of a complex pattern of prehistoric paths and trackways. But the stability of the Roman Empire depended upon efficient communications, and it was they who first laid out a formal network of paved roads throughout the country. The pattern radiated from Londinium, linking the major military bases, but other routes quickly followed connecting the various towns and settlements as local trade developed. Akeman Street ran for more than 75 miles (121km) between Verulamium (St Albans) and Corinium (Cirencester), and at least in part followed a pre-existing British trackway. As with many Roman roads, it continued in use after the occupation and large sections are incorporated into today's road system.

the ride

1 The crossroads in the middle of Coln St Aldwyns is marked by a sturdy spreading chestnut tree. Begin the ride along the lane signed to Quenington and Fairford, passing the **New Inn**. Leaving the village, cycle over the River Coln and climb to a crossroads at the edge of **Quenington**. Go left onto **Fowlers Hill** and drop back into the valley, following signs to Southrop and Lechlade as you bend past a junction to re-cross the Coln. After a bit of a pull, the lane gently rises over open down, following the line of an ancient **salt way**. Pedal on for some 2.5 miles (4km), following signs for Southrop past junctions, before eventually losing height to a 'Give Way' junction.

2h30 — **11.25 MILES** — **26.9 KM** — **LEVEL 1 2 3**

2 Go left, gaining height along a gentle fold in the rolling hillside. Stay with the main lane as it later turns to rise over the hill, winding down on the other side into **Southrop**. Carry on past the village hall and **The Swan**, the street slotted between high-kerbed pavements and now signed to Filkins.

3 After dropping away and crossing the second river of the journey, the Leach, turn off left to Fyfield and Eastleach. Keep left again as the lane splits at **Fyfield**, following the gently rising valley to Eastleach. There are two separately named halves to the village and the lane ends at a junction by the church in **Eastleach Martin**. Go left, and re-cross the Leach to enter

A Highland cow paddling at Coln St Aldwyns

MAP: OS Explorer OL45 The Cotswolds

START/FINISH: Coln St Aldwyns; grid ref: SP 145052

TRAILS/TRACKS: minor lanes

LANDSCAPE: gently rolling Cotswold hills

PUBLIC TOILETS: none on route

TOURIST INFORMATION: Cirencester, tel 01285 654180

CYCLE HIRE: none locally

THE PUB: The Swan at Southrop, Southrop

🔵 Care on the narrow lanes is required

Getting to the start

The small village of Coln St Aldwyns nestles in the Coln Valley some 8 miles (12.9km) east of Cirencester. The nearest town is Fairford on the A417, just over 2 miles (3.2km) to the south along the vale. Park in a cul-de-sac at the centre of the village.

Why do this cycle ride?

Cotswold villages are famed the world over for their quintessential English beauty, but in reality, only a handful have become a fixture of the tourist trail. There are many others, content in their anonymity, which have no less charm, and which offer a quiet escape from hectic modern life. It is through villages such as these that this pleasant ride meanders, crossing the rolling downs between the pretty valleys of the Coln and Leach.

Researched and written by: Dennis Kelsall

Coln St Aldwyns

GLOUCESTERSHIRE

Coln St Aldwyns

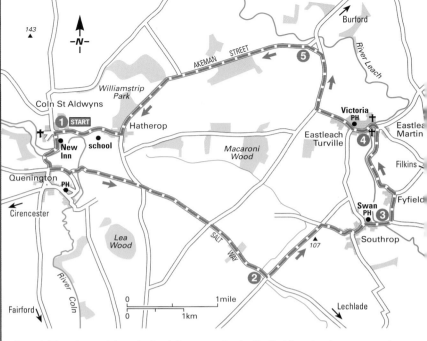

the neighbouring parish, swinging left again beneath a massive **willow tree**, from which a track leads off to **Eastleach Turville's church**.

4 The main lane winds on past the village cross and then a row of **almshouses** to reach a junction below The Victoria pub. Keep ahead, the way signed 'Hatherop and Burford', climbing shortly to a second junction where you should go right in the direction of **Burford and Westwell**. Undulate onwards across open hills that are interspersed with clumps of copse. Stay left at successive turnings to curve above the higher reaches of the Leach valley, signs now directing you to **Hatherop and Coln St Aldwyns**.

5 For 1.25 miles (2km), the way follows the course of **Akeman Street**, a Roman road, passing a turn off signed to **Dean Farm** before breaking away from line of the ancient thoroughfare into **Hatherop**. At a junction, go right towards Coln St Aldwyns, winding down to leave the village past **Hatherop School**. It is then only a short ride back to the start at Coln St Aldwyns.

A pretty cottage in Coln St Aldwyns

The Swan at Southrop

The Swan stands at one end of the tiny green in this quintessential Cotswold village, its old stone walls absolutely covered in creepers. This cosy village pub dates back to 1645 and has a mixed history – at one time it was the premises of the local coffin maker. John Keble, the poet and clergyman, frequented the pub when he lived at the Old Vicarage. Today's Swan has been attractively smartened up and, despite offering some classy modern pub food, it successfully retains its pubby charm with a stone-floored locals' bar dispensing pints of Hook Norton, and a well-used skittle alley. Flagstones, open fires and chunky furnishings characterise the low-beamed dining room. Watch the world go by on a summer's day at pavement tables.

about the pub

The Swan at Southrop
Southrop, Lechlade
Gloucestershire GL7 3NU
Tel: 01367 850205

DIRECTIONS: village signposted off the A361 Lechlade to Burford road, 2 miles (3.2km) north of Lechlade. Pub is located adjacent to the village green.

PARKING: roadside

OPEN: daily

FOOD: daily

BREWERY/COMPANY: free house

REAL ALE: Hook Norton Bitter, Greene King Abbot Ale, Morland Original

Food
Food at The Swan cleverly mixes British and European classics. Menus in the bar offer potted shrimps, goujons of fresh plaice, steak sandwich and home-baked ham, egg and chips alongside linguine carbonara and a plate of Spanish cured meats with pickled chillies. The separate dining room menu offers the likes of confit of duck and foie gras terrine, steak with béarnaise, and pannacotta with poached rhubarb.

Family facilities
Children of all ages are welcome. Small portions from the menus are available and activities (colouring pads) can be provided.

Alternative refreshment stops
In Coln St Aldwyns you'll find the New Inn along the way, or try The Victoria at Eastleach Turville (see Route 31 for details).

☛ Where to go from here
Experience the clack of loom-shuttles and the evocative smell of wood-oil while you watch age-old skills of spinning and weaving transform fleece into woollen fabric at the Cotswold Woollen Weavers at Filkins. Head off into Cirencester to visit the Corinium Museum (www.cotswold.gov.uk), or enjoy the rare and endangered animals, the children's farmyard, and the adventure playground at the Cotswold Wildlife Park near Burford (www.cotswoldwildlifepark.co.uk).

The Oxford waterway

Follow a quiet canal to meet the Thames in Britain's most famous university city.

Oxford Canal

OXFORDSHIRE

Oxford Canal

The Oxford Canal took over 30 years to build, its 91 miles (146km) running up £307,000 by the time it finally opened in 1790. Begun by James Brindley, it took a sinuous contour-hugging route to minimise the locks and aqueducts required. But the economy was double-edged, for although construction costs were reduced, passage time increased, and to stave off competition in the 1820s, Brunel was asked to straighten some of the bends. Financed by a consortium that included Oxford University, the City Corporation and the Duke of Marlborough, the canal brought coal from pits at Hawkesbury near Coventry. It quickly became profitable and managed to survive the steam revolution of the 19th century, carrying materials for the construction of the Midland railways and then reducing its tolls to maintain its share of traffic. Decline, however, was inevitable and by the early 1950s commercial traffic had all but ceased.

Oxford's university is thought to date from Henry II's reign, set up to accommodate English students thrown out of Paris by Louis VII. It comprises 41 separate colleges, many of them founded by rich monastic houses and bishops; Magdalen College was established by a Bishop of Winchester in 1458 and Queens College in 1540 by the chaplain of Queen Philippa, Edward III's wife. A tradition of museums stems from this great seat of learning, with collections on every possible theme. The Museum of History of Science has one of Einstein's blackboards – complete with equations – while the Ashmolean collection includes Guy Fawkes' lantern and Henry VIII's stirrups.

the ride

1 Turning right from the car park, pedal back through the village to reach a pair of consecutive **bridges**. Leave the road immediately over the first, dismounting to negotiate a flight of downward **steps** on the left to the tow path.

2 Oxford lies to the right, the way shortly bridged by the railway and then running tree-lined past house gardens on the far bank. The residential suburbs of Oxford spill onto the canal itself, and many boats are

A houseboat on the Oxford Canal

permanently moored and serve as accommodation. Further on, wetland and marsh on the right, **Trap Grounds**, is managed as a **nature reserve**. Such marshy areas were once common around the old city where willows and osiers provided withies for basket-making. The reserve provides a last local refuge for the elusive water rail, where the timid bird finds secluded nest sites amongst the thick vegetation. Further on, although the surroundings become increasingly urban, the corridor of the canal retains a pleasant isolation.

3 Before long, a **cast-iron bridge** appears ahead where there is a choice of paths. Take the middle one crossing the bridge and continue on a narrow strip of land separating the canal from the **River Thames**. The path carries on for a little over 0.5 mile (800m) before reaching the canal's abrupt end at **Oxford**. Oxford's heart lies to the left, and there is much to see in this distinguished ancient city. However, as some of the streets are very busy, you may prefer to secure your bike and wander around on foot. Return along the canal to **Wolvercote** after your visit.

4 Following the canal in the other direction from Wolvercote takes you away from the city, passing beneath a couple of starkly functional bridges supporting the main roads. The tow path then crosses Duke's Cut, a short arm that connects to the River Thames. Keep ahead beside the main canal past **Duke's Lock**, pedalling beyond a disused railway bridge and another road bridge (where National Cycle Route 5 leaves for Woodstock), later reaching **Kidlington Green Lock**.

| 2h00 | 9.5 MILES | 15.3 KM | LEVEL 1 2 3 |

SHORTER ALTERNATIVE ROUTE

| 1h30 | 6 MILES | 9.5 KM | LEVEL 1 2 3 |

MAP: OS Explorer 180 Oxford
START/FINISH: car park in Wolvercote; grid ref: SP 487094
TRAILS/TRACKS: surfaced canal tow path , short road section
LANDSCAPE: canal through Oxford's fringes
PUBLIC TOILETS: at car park
TOURIST INFORMATION: Oxford, tel 01865 726871
CYCLE HIRE: Bee-Line, 61–63 Cowley Road, Oxford, tel 01865 246615
THE PUB: The Trout Inn, Lower Wolvercote
🛈 Steps down to tow path at start (unless you start at Thrupp); unguarded canal tow paths shared with pedestrians; low-arched bridges; busy roads in Oxford.

Getting to the start
The ride begins from Wolvercote, which lies just north of Oxford near the junction of the A40 and A44 roads. Follow a minor road from the roundabout through the village to find a car park at a bend on the left.

Why do this cycle ride?
Oxford is best approached by bike. This uncomplicated ride takes you along the canal from one of its quiet suburbs, where there is a splendid Morse pub on the very banks of the Thames, almost to its heart. For a rural ride, follow the canal in the other direction to the attractive canal-side hamlet of Thrupp.

Researched and written by: Dennis Kelsall

Oxford Canal

OXFORDSHIRE

5 Another mile (1.6km) lies between you and **Roundham Lock** as the canal slowly climbs from the upper Thames valley towards Banbury and the Midlands. Later on a small **industrial area** unobtrusively stands away from the canal, beyond which is a handful of cottages. After passing beneath the A4260, the tow path briefly follows the main road to the **Jolly Boatman pub**.

6 The waterway then swings away beside the tiny hamlet of **Thrupp**, where there is another pub and, opposite it, a much-weathered ancient cross. At the top end of the street, the tow path switches banks and the canal makes an abrupt turn in front of a maintenance yard. You can, of course continue north along the canal, but the hard surface later deteriorates making passage difficult. The way back to Wolvercote retraces your outward route.

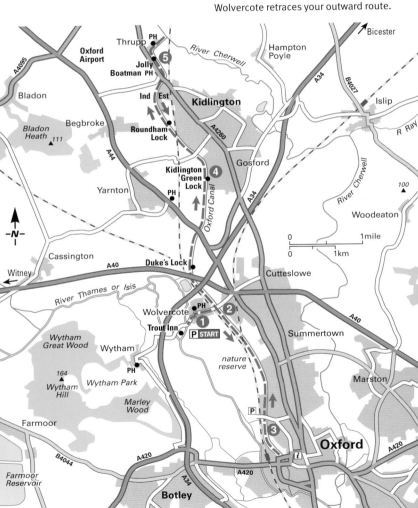

Oxford Canal — OXFORDSHIRE

The Trout Inn

about the pub

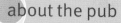

The Trout Inn
Godstow Road, Lower Wolvercote
Oxford, Oxfordshire OX2 8PN
Tel: 01865 302071

DIRECTIONS: continue on from the car park to find the pub on the banks of the River Thames

PARKING: 95

OPEN: daily; all day

FOOD: daily; all day

BREWERY/COMPANY: Mitchells & Butler

REAL ALE: Bass, guest beer

Constructed in the 17th century from the ruins of Godstow Abbey, with a history that includes being torched by Parliamentarian troops, this famous medieval pub is serenely situated beside the River Thames and attracts thousands of visitors every year. In summer, the cobbled terrace beside the fast-running river with its weir makes a restful place for a quiet pint while watching the peacocks wandering round the terrace and catching a glimpse of the chub in the clear water. Inside, you'll find flagstones, beamed ceilings, bare boards and welcoming log fires throughout the several linked rooms, all adorned with hops, attractive pictures and country bric-a-brac. It has associations with Matthew Arnold, Lewis Carroll and Colin Dexter's Inspector Morse – numerous scenes from the TV series were filmed at the pub.

Food

A good choice of food offers baked whole trout with garlic mushrooms and cheddar mash, lemon chicken, beef, mushroom and Bass pie, or Cumberland sausage wrapped in Yorkshire pudding, with liver and bacon. Sandwiches and specials are listed on the blackboard.

Family facilities

Children are welcome in the pub if eating and there are smaller portions of some adult dishes. Supervised children will love the peacocks on the terrace and looking for the fish in the river.

Alternative refreshment stops

Choice of pubs in both Wolvercote and Oxford (and cafés) and two pubs beside the tow path at Thrupp.

☞ Where to go from here

Linger longer in Oxford, for there's plenty to see and do. In particular, some fascinating museums to visit: the Museum of Oxford (www.oxford.gov.uk/museum); the Ashmolean Museum of Art and Archaeology (www.ashmol.ox.ac.uk); the Pitt Rivers Museum (www.prm.os.ac.uk); the Oxford University Museum of Natural History (www.oum.ox.ac.uk); and the Museum of the History of Science (www.mhs.os.ac.uk). Why not visit the university and its various colleges (www.visitoxford.org) or take in the oldest botanic garden in the country with its collection of more than 8,000 species of plant (www.botanic-garden.ox.ac.uk)?

Oxford Canal

OXFORDSHIRE

17

Caernarfon and Dinas Dinlle

An old railway trail and country lanes lead you through gentle countryside south of Caernarfon.

Caernarfon and Dinas Dinlle

The centrepiece of this medieval walled town is the magnificent 13th-century castle built by King Edward I, splendidly sited by the lapping waters of the Menai Straits. The Slate Quay and Harbour Offices nearby are reminders of later centuries when the port bustled with commercial vessels loading Welsh slate for distant shores. There are several other attractions in the town, such as the Seiont II Martime Museum at Victoria Dock, the Regimental Museum of the Royal Welsh Fusiliers, the Roman fort of Segontium, and Welsh Highland Railway, which runs parallel with Lon Eifion between Caernarfon and Dinas station.

Lon Eifion is a splendid cycle trail, forming part of the National Cycle Network and route number 8 that traverses Wales. It is a long stretch of dismantled railway, a green avenue of native trees and plants that stretches for 12 miles (18.2km) to Bryncir. This was the former Caernarfon to Afon Wen line, which was opened as standard gauge in 1867.

The large mound known as Dinas Dinlle is a natural deposit dating from the Ice Age, which has evidently been used several times as a fortification by different peoples. Roman coins, dating from the time of Emperor Alectus (AD293), have been found here. It is also a site rich in legend, a place woven into the tales of the Mabinogi.

Foryd Bay is a large shallow estuary rich in wildfowl which love the habitat of mud and reeds and saltmarsh. It is now a local nature reserve where you will see shelduck, oystercatchers, dunlin, and many other birds, including the curlew with its distinctive beak and haunting call.

Above: Dinas Dinlle
Right: Caernarfon Castle

the ride

1 From Slate Quay car park, pass the Harbour Offices to join a road between the railway line and warehouses. In 300 yards (274m) join the old trackbed on the left and pass beneath the impressive Lon Eifion cycle route sign. With the Welsh Highland railway to your left, gradually climb above the harbour and leave the town. Cross a lane by a house, signposted 'Hendy', continue to cross another road and keep to the trail to reach **Bontnewydd**, where you cross the Afon Gwyrfai. Gently ascend through a cutting, pass **Dinas station** to reach a road at **Llanwnda**, with the village church to your left.

2 Go right along the narrow lane for two miles (3.2km), ignoring a turning on the right and soon drop down to the waters of the **Afon Carrog**. Climb to a junction, go right and then left at the next junction to reach **Llandwrog**. Turn right by the Harp Inn; the road descends to a junction in 0.5 mile (0.8km). Go right for **Dinas Dinlle** and soon reach the seafront.

3 Retrace your route to **Llandwrog** and turn left before the Harp Inn, still on your outward route. Keep to this lane for

| 2h30 | 14 MILES | 22.8 KM | LEVEL 1 2 3 |

MAP: OS OL Explorer 17 Snowdonia _ Snowdon & Conwy Valley

START/FINISH: Slate Quay car park, Caernarfon; grid ref: SH 477627

TRAILS/TRACKS: gravel cycle trail, quiet country lanes

LANDSCAPE: gently undulating farmland, level coastline, views of mountains

PUBLIC TOILETS: Slate Quay, Dinas Dinlle

TOURIST INFORMATION: Caernarfon, tel 01286 672232

CYCLE HIRE: Beics Menai Cycles, Slate Quay, Caernarfon, tel: 01286 676804

THE PUB: The Harp Inn, Llandwrog

🛈 Short stretch of busy road linking Slate Quay and the start of the cycle trail. A few short climbs and a couple of blind bends on the lanes. An easy ride for older children

Getting to the start

Caernarfon lies south west of Bangor on the A487. Follow signs to Caernarfon Castle and the car park beneath (pay on entry) on Slate Quay.

Why do this cycle ride?

For mountainous North Wales this ride is a delight for family cyclists looking for few hills and gentle pedalling. You can enjoy exceptional views across the mountain range of Snowdonia to the east and to the island of Anglesey in the west. You begin by riding the traffic-free Lon Eifion trail (former railway) out of Caernarfon, then follow narrow back lanes to Llandwrog and the Harp Inn, with an optional out-and-back ride to the nearby golden sands of Dinas Dinlle. Highlights are Foryd Bay and the lane that hugs the shores of the Menai Straits back to Caernarfon.

Researched and written by: David Hancock

0.75 mile (1.2km) to cross the Afon Carrog and pass a small cluster of buildings (telephone box). Continue to a sharp right bend and bear off left along a quiet narrow road leading to **Foryd Bay**. The lane bears right close to the water's edge, eventually reaching a crossroads. Go left here through the hamlet of **Saron**.

4 The road descends to a bridge at Pont Faen, crossing the **Afon Gwyrfai**, and rises to a junction, just before the

Llanfaglan village sign. Turn left and continue for less than 0.5 mile (0.8km) to the water's edge at Foryd Bay, with excellent views across to the Isle of Anglesey. This delightful lane hugs the coast and passes the small windswept **Llanfaglan church**, isolated in a field to your right. The road bears right and runs along the front of the harbour at Caernarfon. Wheel your cycle across the Aber footbridge and return to the **castle** and the start point of the ride.

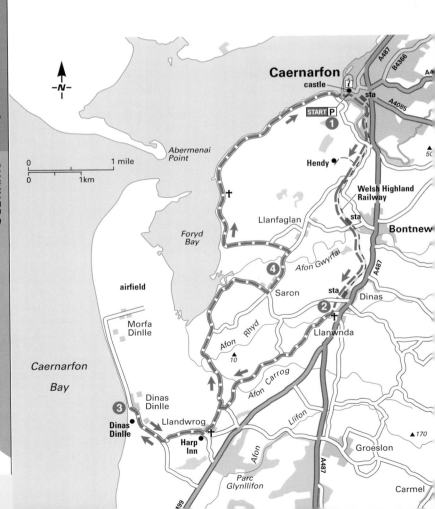

The Harp Inn

A long established haven for travellers, this stone Georgian building is located in the historic home village of the nearby Glynllifon Estate, close to the beautiful beaches of Dinas Dinlle. An inn has existed on the site since Roman times, as Llandwrog was on the pilgrim route from Holyhead to Bardsey Island. The traditional interior comprises a cheerful bar area, where you will find a good range of real ales and ciders, a comfortable restaurant and a popular games room. Note the tablet on the wall of the pub featuring a poem by the well-known Welsh poet Evan Fardd.

Food

A proudly Welsh menu offers lob scouse with roll and red cabbage, Welsh mackerel rarebit on toast, trio of local bangers and mash, Welsh lamb steaks with a laverbread and citrus sauce, and local sea bass with ginger and sesame seeds. There's also lasagne, cod and chips and filled baked potatoes and homemade hoggies filled with hot beef. Sunday roast lunches.

Family facilities

Children are welcome in the eating areas and the games room. There are healthy eating options for "little people" on the menu, a safe garden and overnight accommodation in one large family room.

Alternative refreshment stops

There are pubs and cafés in Caernarfon and at Dinas Dinlle, and a pleasant picnic site by Foryd Bay.

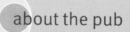

☛ Where to go from here

Just a short ride away from the Harp Inn is Parc Glynllifon, a 70-acre country park with exotic gardens, 18th-century follies, contemporary sculptures, a restored steam engine, a craft centre and signed walks. It is also home to a rich and diverse wildlife, including the largest roost in Europe for the Lesser Horse Shoe Bat.

Caernarfon GWYNEDD

about the pub

The Harp Inn
Tyn'llan, Llandwrog
Gwynedd LL54 5SY
Tel: 01286 831071

DIRECTIONS: village and pub signposted off the A499 south of Caernarfon
PARKING: 20
OPEN: all day in summer and Saturday in winter. Closed Monday except Bank Holidays
FOOD: daily; all day Sunday in summer
BREWERY/COMPANY: free house
REAL ALE: Bass, Black Sheep Best, Plassey Bitter, guest beers
ROOMS: 4 bedrooms (1 en suite)

Along the Elan Valley Trail

A spectacular traffic-free ride past dams and reservoirs into the heart of the mid-Wales mountains.

The Elan Valley

"No sound is here save the stream that shrills and now and then a cry of faint wailing when the kite comes sailing o'er the crags", so wrote the 18th-century poet William Lisle Bowles in his poem Cwm Elan. Today, thanks to Welsh Water, which owns the 180 square kilometres of moorland, valley, woodland and reservoirs which make up the Elan Valley Estate, this beautiful area of mid Wales remains peaceful and unspoilt, although a little different in appearance from when Bowles wrote his poem. In between times, from 1893 to 1904 and later from 1946 and 1952 to be precise, the serenity of the Elan Valley and the glorious surrounding uplands was shattered by the construction of a railway and four huge dams.

In the mid-19th century Birmingham's growing need for water prompted a search for a reliable supply and the Elan Valley and Claerwen area of mid-Wales 73 miles (116km) away, with its 1800mm of rain per year and easily dammed valleys, provided the ideal solution to the problem. To facilitate the construction of the dams the Elan Valley Railway had to be built. Work began on the standard width railway, one that connected with the Cambrian Railway at Rhayader, in 1893 and eventually had 33 miles (53km) of track. Special short-wheelbase locomotives were required to negotiate the sharp curves and steep gradients, and they moved 1,000 tons of

building material a day to the dam construction sites.

Around 100 occupants of the Elan Valley had to move and many buildings were demolished, while 18 farms, the remains of two fine mansions, once homes to the poet Shelley, and a school now lie under millions of litres of water. Close to the Elan Valley Visitor Centre a new village was built to accommodate the hundreds of workers. There were two hospitals, a bath house, pub, library, hall, shop, canteens, and a school for children under the age of eleven. After that they were expected to work. Little remains of the village, save for the school and a few riverside buildings beneath the Caban Coch dam.

The four Elan Valley dams (Caban Coch, Garreg Ddu, Pen y Garreg and Craig Goch), were opened by King Edward VII and Queen Alexandra in 1904. The large Claerwen dam was completed in 1952 and today some 365 millions litres of water daily can be extracted from the Elan Valley reservoirs to supply Birmingham.

the ride

1 The start of the Elan Valley Trail, an impressive **sculptured gateway**, can be located away to your left on the opposite

The Elan Trail and Caban Coch reservoir

3h00 | **16 MILES** | **26 KM** | **LEVEL 1 2 3**

MAP: OS Explorer 200 Llandrindod Wells & Elan Valley

START/FINISH: Cwmdauddwr, west of Rhayader grid ref: SN 966677

TRAILS/TRACKS: railway path - part tarmac, part gravel, with plenty of gates

LANDSCAPE: lush river valley, wooded shores of reservoirs and open mountain scenery

PUBLIC TOILETS: Elan Valley Visitor Centre; beside Craig Goch Dam

TOURIST INFORMATION: Elan Valley Visitor Centre, tel 01597 810898; Rhayader, tel 01597 810591

CYCLE HIRE: Elan Cyclery, West Street, Rhayader, tel 01597 811343; www.clivepowell-mtb.co.uk

THE PUB: Elan Valley Hotel, Elan Valley

🛈 Short, sharp climb at the start, steady climb from the visitor centre, gradual uphill from the start to top reservoir. Plenty of gates to negotiate and take care where the trail crosses roads

Getting to the start
The hamlet of Cwmdauddar lies just west of Rhayader on the B4518. The Elan Valley Trail car park is signposted on the right.

Why do this cycle ride?
The Elan Valley Trail is one of the most spectacular off-road trails in Britain. It climbs gradually and is suitable for the whole family. From the lush valley meadows bordering the Afon Elan, you follow the route of the former railway to Caban Coch Dam, then cycle beside reservoirs through a wild moorland landscape. Views are far-reaching and there is plenty of wildlife to see.

Researched and written by: David Hancock

side of the B4518. The trail is waymarked with Red Kite discs. The first 0.5 mile (0.8km) of smooth tarmac path climbs steadily away from the old railway line to avoid using Rhayader Tunnel, which was closed for bats in 1993 and is now a favoured hibernating site for brown long-eared, Daubenton's and Natterer's bats. You can see the tunnel and the route of the old line as you pass through the Wildlife Reserve, an area managed to encourage butterflies and other invertebrates.

2 Drop downhill and join the route of the Elan Valley Railway, at the point where it joined Cambrian Railway. The trail levels out and you have to negotiate a number of double gates at farm and field drives before it merges with the B4518 (steep hill down to a gate). Cross a road, proceed along the **cycle pavement**, and soon dog-leg left, then right beyond a house as the trail runs parallel yet well away from the road. Gently climb through trees, with views across the Afon Elan to your left, for just over a mile (1.6km) to reach the **Elan Valley Hotel** (across the road to your right).

3 Continue along the trail, enter the Elan Valley Estate and reach the access road to the **Elan Valley Visitor Centre**. It's well worth the 0.25 mile (0.4km) detour for the informative displays, riverside picnic area, and views of Caban Coch Dam. Return to the junction, bear left with the **Red Kite disc** and steadily ascend the metalled path above the valley and Visitor Centre to reach **Caban Coch Dam**. Pause here for super views back down the Elan Valley and across the reservoir.

4 From here you pedal the tarmac trail above the reservoir and just below the road. In summer rosebay willow herb and foxgloves line the route which bears right to reach Garreg Dhu Dam. You can cross the viaduct for a closer look at **Nantgwyllt Church**, built to replace the local church that was submerged.

5 Cross the road and pass **Foel Tower**, where water destined for Birmingham begins its 120km-long journey by gravity. The surface of the trail now becomes hard gravel and remains level for 2 miles (3km)

alongside **Garreg Ddu Reservoir**. At intervals you will see sculptural benches created by artist Dominic Clare, and more conventional picnic benches – take time to pause and savour the views. Look out for goosanders on the reservoir, and red kites and buzzards soaring high above the surrounding hills. Eighty species of bird breed annually on the estate.

6 Cross the road and climb up the gradual incline through the trees to reach the top of **Pen y Garreg Dam**. The track levels out alongside Pen y Garreg Reservoir until you reach a cutting called **Devil's Gulch**. This cutting through the rock had to be blasted away and held up construction of the railway for three months. From here you climb gradually, high above the reservoir to Craig Goch Dam and the end of the Elan Valley Trail. This was also the terminus of the railway.

7 Return along this spectacular trail and enjoy the long, invigorating descents back to the start.

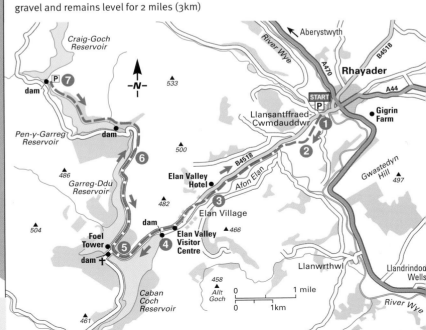

Elan Valley Hotel

Formerly a Victorian fishing lodge, this rejuvenated hotel and pub stands in the heart of stunning mid-Wales scenery, just below the last of the four reservoirs in the Elan Valley. Not only is the hotel the perfect base from which to explore this beautiful area, it provides welcome refreshment to walkers and cyclists on the Elan Valley Trail. Summer bar lunches are served in the rustic, simply furnished Farmer's bar and in the tree-shaded front garden. Striking colours brighten up the informal Dish Dash restaurant, where locally sourced fruit and vegetables, organic meats and trout are featured on daily changing menus. The hotel also offers off-road Biking Breaks.

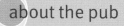

about the pub

Elan Valley Hotel
Elan Valley, Rhayader
Powys LD6 5HN
Tel: 01597 810448
www.elanvalleyhotel.co.uk

DIRECTIONS: on the B4518 2 miles (3.2km) west of Rhayader. Accessible from the Elan Valley Trail which runs parallel with B4518, look out for the hotel on the right

PARKING: 30

OPEN: daily in summer, closed weekday lunchtimes in winter

FOOD: no food winter weekday lunchtimes

BREWERY/COMPANY: free house

REAL ALE: Timothy Taylor Landlord, Hancocks HB, Brains Rev James, guest beer

ROOMS: 10 en suite

Food

In the bar, choose from snacks like hot filled baguettes, ploughman's lunches and specials such as aromatic coriander and mixed bean curry. Restaurant meals may take in grilled Pencerrig goat's cheese with apple chutney, whole stuffed sea bass, or Welsh lamb cooked with red wine and rosemary, followed by bread-and-butter pudding.

Family facilities

Children are welcome at the hotel. A varied children's menu is available in the bar and under-4s stay free.

Alternative refreshment stops

Good café with riverside terrace at the Elan Visitor Centre and various pubs and cafés in Rhayader near the start of the ride. Take a picnic and enjoy it at one of the many picnic benches beside the reservoirs.

☞ Where to go from here

Visit the Red Kite Centre at Gigrin Farm (www.gigrin.co.uk), just south of Rhayader off the A470. Here you can learn about the successful breeding of red kite in mid Wales, follow a 2-mile nature trail and, at 3pm (2pm winter), watch up to 200 kites feeding at close quarters.

Elan Valley

POWYS

Through the Teme Valley

Teme Valley

SHROPSHIRE

Seeking out the valleys amongst the Shropshire Hills.

Leintwardine

The lane out of Leintwardine takes you below a prominent hill on the right, on which there are the earthbank remains of a large Iron Age stronghold. When the Romans arrived in the area around 50AD, they too recognised its importance and, in addition to taking it over, established another camp, Bravonium, by the river where the village now stands. In fact the church actually straddles one of the ramparts. The camp lay on a Roman road, Welsh Watling Street, between Wroxeter (near Shrewsbury) and Caerleon (outside Newport), and was an important military route to help maintain order amongst the British tribes that still held strong in Wales. The road was also an imperial post road, and the camp was the equivalent of a stage post, supplying fresh horses and refreshment to speed the messengers on their way. During the calmer period of the 3rd century, the military presence declined, but by then, a civilian settlement had already sprung up, thriving on the trade that passed up and down the road.

Leintwardine's large church is known locally as the 'Cathedral of North Herefordshire'. It contains early 15th-century choir stalls with interestingly carved misericords, said to have come from the Augustinian Wigmore Abbey, which stood close to Paytoe Hall. In the churchyard of Burrington Church are a number of unusual cast-iron grave slabs, marking the burials of local iron-founding families. During the 17th and early 18th centuries, iron was smelted using charcoal, and the surrounding forests were managed to provide abundant supplies of fuel.

the ride

1 Leaving **Petchfield Farm**, go right towards the hamlet of Elton, shortly passing a narrow lane off on the right, **Killhorse Lane**. You will discover the appropriateness of its name if you turn up it, for it has just about the steepest gradient in the area. Thankfully your route bends left, signed to Ludlow, soon taking you past a splendid manor house, **Elton Hall**.

2 At the next junction, turn off left, signed '**Burrington and Leintwardine**', along a narrower lane, where occasional breaks in the hedges allow views across the valley to a backdrop of rolling hills. Before long the road begins to lose height, soon passing a lane off to the right, some 150yds (137m) along which you will find the entrance to **Burrington Church**. The route, however continues ahead, the lane by now a leafy tunnel formed by a profuse growth of hazels on either side. Keep ahead past a turning to Leinthall Starkes to cross a bridge over the **Teme**, ignoring successive turnings to Downton a little later on and eventually reaching a junction by **Nacklestone Farm**.

3 **Leintwardine** is signed to the right, the way falling easily and soon affording a view to the village, the church

MAP: OS Explorer 203 Ludlow, Tenbury Wells & Cleobury Mortimer

START/FINISH: Petchfield Farm, Elton; grid ref: SO 454704 (small charge for parking)

TRAILS/TRACKS: quiet lanes throughout

LANDSCAPE: gentle valley amidst rolling hills

PUBLIC TOILETS: none on route

TOURIST INFORMATION: Ludlow, tel 01584 875053

CYCLE HIRE: Wheely Wonderful Cycling, Petchfield Farm, Elton, Ludlow, tel 01568 770755 (www.wheelywonderfulcycling.co.uk)

THE PUB: The Lion Hotel, Leintwardine

⦿ Narrow country lanes, be aware of traffic and pedestrians

Getting to the start

Petchfield Farm, some 5 miles (8km) south west of Ludlow, is most easily approached from the A4110 at Wigmore along a minor lane east through Leithnall Starkes. You will find the entrance to Petchfield Farm on the right after a mile (1.6km). Park in the yard beside 'Wheely Wonderful Cycle Hire'.

Why do this cycle ride?

The country lanes around Ludlow offer superb cycling, and although the general landscape is quite hilly, there are many easy routes that follow the base of the valleys. This one explores the valley of the River Teme between Elton and Leintwardine, and at one point follows the line of an important Roman road.

Researched and written by: Dennis Kelsall

Teme Valley

SHROPSHIRE

The 14th-century clock tower of the Church of St Mary Magdalene at Leintwardine

with its sturdy tower an obvious feature. At a **T-junction**, sweep left with the main lane, and carry on to the end where there is a riverside green opposite **The Lion Hotel**.

4 Turn left over an arched bridge to re-cross the River Teme, and then go left again just beyond onto a narrow lane signed to **Paytoe**. After passing a couple of **yards** on the outskirts of the village, the way continues in an almost dead-straight line along the flat valley floor following the line of a Roman road.

5 When you reach a junction, turn left in front of the splendid black-and-white **Paytoe Hall**, and pedal across the width of the valley, directed towards Ludlow. After crossing the Teme once more, go right and for a short while retrace your outward route. Just after the next bridge, turn off right to **Leinthall Starkes** and begin a short climb out of the valley that levels off to offer a view ahead to a **windmill** on the hillside above Leinthall. The lane then bends sharply right and later left to drop towards the village.

6 When you reach a T-junction at the end go left, the lane undulating gently downwards along the valley side to take you back to **Petchfield Farm**.

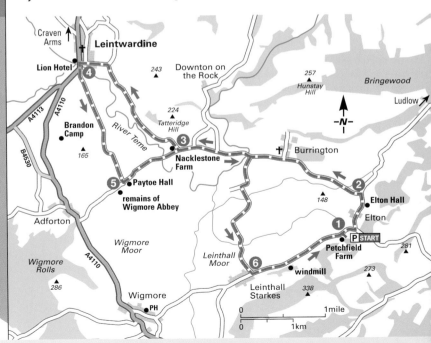

The Lion Hotel

The Lion enjoys an attractive riverside location by the bridge opposite the village green, and at the back has a peaceful, landscaped garden overlooking the River Teme and Brockley Meadow. It dates back to the 18th century when it was a thriving hotel and, although no longer residential, the building retains much of its character both in appearance and in the traditional hospitality offered by the hosts.

Food

Wide-ranging menus take in lunchtime sandwiches, baguettes and filled jacket potatoes, standard bar snacks, various pies and grills, and daily specials like lamb pie, Somerset pork and cauliflower cheese. On Sundays, you'll find a choice of roasts, and there is a regular barbecue on summer Friday evenings.

Family facilities

Children of all ages are welcomed inside and there's a children's menu and an area set aside for families.

about the pub

The Lion Hotel
High Street, Leintwardine, Ludlow
Shropshire SY7 0JZ
Tel: 01547 540203

DIRECTIONS: close to Leintwardine Bridge over the River Teme on the A4113 (see Point **3**)	
PARKING: 40	
OPEN: daily; all day Saturday	
FOOD: no food Sunday evening	
BREWERY/COMPANY: Enterprise Inns	
REAL ALE: changing guest beers	

Alternative refreshment stops
The Sun at Leintwardine (Rosemary Lane) is an unspoiled gem and worth a visit for Woods tapped from the barrel, but no food is available.

☞ Where to go from here

Spend some time exploring the extensive range of ruined buildings at Ludlow Castle (www.ludlowcastle.com), where audio guides bring the castle to life. Discover the secrets of the Shropshire Hills at the Discovery Centre in Craven Arms, where the history, nature and geography of the area is explored through a series of interactive displays and simulations, all housed in a striking building set in 25 acres (10ha) of meadows (www.shropshireonline.gov.uk/discover.nsf). Visit Stokesay Castle, a perfectly preserved 13th-century fortified manor house – stroll through the great hall and delightful cottage gardens.

Teme Valley

SHROPSHIRE

The Silkin Way to Ironbridge

Coalbrookdale

SHROPSHIRE

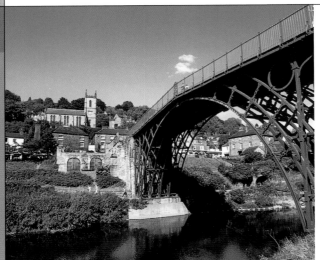

a massive ceramic industry, with tile, pottery and china factories being set up beside the river. Indeed, Coalport was the new town of its day, established to house the families working in the potteries. To service the industries, a canal was built to Shrewsbury in 1793, with a link being built later to Norbury that gave access to the Shropshire Canal, some 18 miles (29km) away. In such hilly country, the use of locks was totally impractical, but William Reynolds, who owned ironworks here, invented the inclined plane whereby the tub-like boats could be lowered and raised on tracks between the different levels.

Pedal back in time to discover what a 'Saggar-maker's Bottom Knocker' did.

Coalbrookdale

Although the gorge's natural resources had been exploited since medieval times, the industrial boom only began in 1709 with Abraham Darby's invention at Coalbrookdale that used coke rather than charcoal to produce large quantities of cast iron cheaply. It was his grandson who was responsible for the graceful cast-iron bridge that spans the gorge, erected between 1777 and 1779. Its 400 tons of castings represented nearly 4 months' output from a blast furnace and was the first structure of its kind to be erected.

But it was not only the blast of iron furnaces that lit up the gorge, for the abundant clay deposits in the area spawned

The most spectacular example is the Hay Inclined Plane, which moved the boats a vertical distance of over 200 feet (61m) in a matter of minutes, an operation that would otherwise have taken hours had the equivalent 27 locks been used.

The railways inevitably followed, the LNWR branch to Coalport (now the Silkin Way) being built in 1861 and the Severn Valley Railway the year after. A large goods yard grew up at Jackfield where coal, pottery, iron, tar and many other commodities were marshalled for transport to the various industrial centres and seaports around the country. Yet, even the railways lasted barely a century, for the decline had set in long

The cast-iron bridge that spans the gorge and the River Severn at Coalbrookdale

before Beeching recommended his sweeping cuts to the rail system, as a result of under-investment after the War and competition from the greater flexibility offered by road transport.

the ride

1 Leaving the car park, cross the road and climb shallow steps to a tarmac track, the **Silkin Way**. Follow it left, passing **Station Road** and dropping to curve beneath the main road. Swing right as you emerge and carry on at the edge of a **park**, later joining the pavement to reach **Blists Hill Victorian Town**. Keep going down the hill, the cycleway shortly diverging from the road on a gradual tree-lined descent along the line of an old railway. Through a **short tunnel**, the way courses enjoyably down, later passing beneath the ingenious **Hay Inclined Plane**. The track eventually ends in front of the **Brewery Inn**.

2 Cross the road to a gated track left of the pub, that descends past **cottages** to the **riverbank**. Bear right as it forks, rising to meet a road. Follow that over the Severn, and then leave immediately down **steps** on the right to reach a riverside path. It skirts a **picnic area** and climbs around to a gate, there joining the line of another disused railway. The track continues above the river for just over half a mile (800m) before passing **Maws Craft Centre**, once the site of a booming tile industry. A little further on as the track ends, keep ahead on the right-most of two roads, which leads past more tile works at **Jackfield**. These were built by

2h00 — **7.5 MILES** — **12.1 KM** — **LEVEL 1 2**

MAP: OS Explorer 242 Telford, Ironbridge & The Wreakin

START/FINISH: Legge Road car park, Madeley; grid ref: SJ 700043

TRAILS/TRACKS: off-road tracks (can be muddy) and lanes, gentle descents and gradual climbs

LANDSCAPE: wooded valley

PUBLIC TOILETS: main car park at Blists Hill, at Maws Craft Centre and in Ironbridge

TOURIST INFORMATION: Ironbridge, tel 01952 884391

CYCLE HIRE: None locally

THE PUB: The Swan, Ironbridge

🛈 Although an easy ride, there are long, but gentle gradients, an unlit tunnel, short stretches of loose pebbles, steps, and poorly surfaced roads

Getting to the start

Ironbridge Gorge lies south of Telford New Town. From the M54, follow the A442 south for 3 miles (4.8km), to its junction with the A4169. Turn right for Madeley, then at a roundabout as you approach the town, go left towards Blists Hill, Coalport and the Ironbridge Gorge Museums. The entrance to the car park is a short way along on the left.

Why do this cycle ride?

The gorge's tranquillity is deceptive, for here began a world-changing revolution. The ride takes you past the spectacular remains of its once-booming industry.

Researched and written by: Dennis Kelsall

Coalbrookdale **SHROPSHIRE**

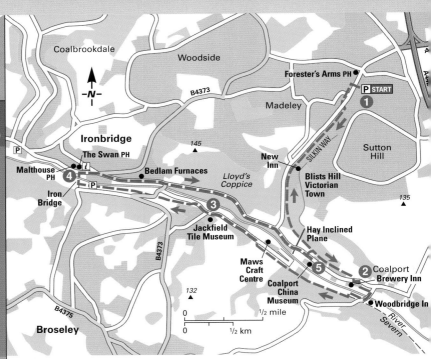

Charles Lynam between 1871 and 1874 for Craven Dunnill & Co. and now house a fascinating museum.

3 Go forward at a **junction**, but as the road then bends to a reconstructed level crossing, turn off left to regain the line of the railway through **Jackfield Sidings**. Further on, beyond the Black Swan, pass beneath a skew bridge carrying the road to the **Jackfield suspension bridge**. It is then not far to the main car park at Ironbridge. Pedal through to the far side and dismount to cross the famous **Iron Bridge** into the town, where you will find the Malthouse a little way to the left.

4 The route from the bridge, however, is along the main street to the right. At a mini-roundabout, take the right fork ahead,

Right: A character in Blists Victorian Town

the B4373 to **Jackfield and Broseley**, leaving the town past the ruins of the **Bedlam Furnaces**. Where the road later bends to Jackfield Bridge, keep ahead on a narrow, bumpy lane, which undulates along the valley to **Coalport**. Keep going forward at a later junction, a bridge taking you over the **Hay Inclined Plane**, just beyond which, opposite the Shakespeare Inn, you will find the entrance to the **Tar Museum**. A little further on is the **Coalport China Museum**.

5 From the museum, go back along the lane a few yards/metres, turning off right onto a track that winds around **Coalport Village Hall** to an overflow car park. Pass through it right to find a track climbing to meet the **Silkin Way**. Turn left and retrace your outward route past **Blists Hill** to the car park from which you began. The way is steadily uphill, but the track is well-graded and the climb relatively easy.

The Swan

An 18th-century former malthouse set on the riverfront close to the heart of Ironbridge. This was an inn during Darby's time and it is rumoured that site meetings were held at The Swan from time to time. The inn has been developed in recent years by Malthouse Pubs to create a modern pub but with traditional home-cooked food, a buzzy all-day bar, a summer courtyard, and a warm welcome.

Food

Expect a varied menu of freshly prepared dishes ranging from home-made pork pie with chutney, smoked fish mousse with garlic toast, and confit chicken with salad. Substantial main meals take in braised lamb shank, bubble & squeak with port and redcurrant sauce, Cajun beefburger, and wild mushroom and basil risotto.

Family facilities

Children are welcome throughout the pub. There's a children's menu, smaller portions of adult dishes and crayons and colouring books to keep youngsters amused.

Alternative refreshment stops

Along the way you have the Foresters' Arms at Madeley, a café at the entrance to Blists Hill Victorian Town and at Maws Craft Centre and pubs and cafés in Ironbridge.

☛ Where to go from here

There is so much to see and do as the whole area here is a World Heritage Site with a remarkable series of nine museums relating the story of the bridge, re-creating Victorian times and featuring ceramics and social history displays. Explore Blists Hill Victorian Town, the Museum of the Gorge, Coalport China Museum, Jackfield Tile Museum, the Museum of Iron, and the Broseley Pipeworks, among others (www.ironbridge.org.uk).

Coalbrookdale SHROPSHIRE

about the pub

The Swan
The Wharfage, Ironbridge
Shropshire, TF8 7NH
Tel: 01952 432306

DIRECTIONS: just east of the Iron Bridge, see Point **4**	
PARKING: 10	
OPEN: daily; all day	
FOOD: daily; all day Sunday	
BREWERY/COMPANY: free house	
REAL ALE: four changing guest beers	
ROOMS: 8 en suite	

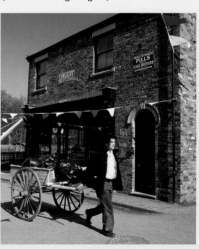

The Shropshire Canal

With more miles of canal than any other county, what better way to discover Staffordshire's countryside?

Shropshire Canal

The Shropshire Canal was built between 1830 and 1835 under the direction of Thomas Telford, creating a more direct link than hitherto between the industrial towns of England's heartland and the seaports along the Dee and Mersey rivers. A branch from Norbury ran to Wappenshall Junction on the edge of Telford where, via the Shrewsbury Canal and the Hay Inclined Plane, boats could reach the ironworks and potteries of the Ironbridge Gorge. From the very beginning, canals proved their worth in moving heavy and bulky cargoes cheaply and quickly, and the late 18th and early 19th centuries saw a period of spectacular industrial growth as the network spread across the country. All operated on a system of tolls to cover the cost of construction and maintenance and there was intense competition between rival routes to attract trade. Junctions like that here at Norbury would have been controlled with a toll bar, where charges were levied on the type of goods and weight carried. There would also have been a certain amount of reloading too, as cargoes were split or combined for the various destinations served by the separate branches. Alongside the canals, inns, stables and blacksmiths sprang up to provide sustenance for the bargees and the horses that pulled the boats. Workyards were also necessary to undertake repairs on the barges as well as to provide depots for the gangs maintaining the canal itself.

The branch to Wappenshall and Telford fell into disuse during the 1930s, the trade having been taken over by the railways. By the end of the war, it had been completely abandoned and much of it was filled in. You can still trace its ghostly course on the map, where odd short stretches are shown as pools. The main Shropshire Canal

The Shropshire Canal at Gnosall Heath

A barge on the Shropshire Canal

1h30 — **6.5 MILES** — **10.6 KM** — **LEVEL 1**

MAP: Explorer 243 Market Drayton, Loggerheads & Eccleshall
START/FINISH: Norbury Village Hall; grid ref: SJ 782235
TRAILS/TRACKS: canal towpath (one short grass section) and quiet lanes
LANDSCAPE: open countryside and woodland
PUBLIC TOILETS: none on route
TOURIST INFORMATION: Stafford, tel 01785 619619
CYCLE HIRE: none locally
THE PUB: The Navigation Inn, Gnosall
🛑 One main road crossing, two dark bridges, tow paths (can be muddy after rain)

Getting to the start
Norbury lies 8.5 miles (13.7km) west of Stafford. An unclassified road off the A519 3 miles (4.8km) north of Newport leads into the village.

Why do this cycle ride?
An easy uncomplicated ride along quiet and gently undulating country lanes to the village of Gnosall Heath, where there is a splendid canalside pub. The return is along the canal, often busy with colourful boats plying their way through the Heart of England.

Researched and written by: Dennis Kelsall

Shropshire Canal

STAFFORDSHIRE

survived and is today busy with leisure boats. Set against the backdrop of buildings at Norbury Junction, it takes little imagination to envisage how the waterway might have looked during its heyday.

the ride

1 Out of the car park go right and then left to pedal through the village, signed to **Oulton and Norbury Junction**. Keep with the main lane as it bends right past a track leading to the striking village **church**, a large building, dedicated to St Peter, of much weathered sandstone that nestles below a massive brick tower. Leaving the village, go left at a fork signed to **Norbury Junction and Gnosall**.

2 You will be passing through **Norbury Junction** on the way back, so for the time being, carry on over the canal bridge and continue along the lane behind the old canal offices and **workshops**. Beside the lane is a **millennium boulder**, similar to one beside the village hall, an erratic stranded as the vast ice sheets that covered this part of the country melted at the end of the last ice age, some 10,000 years ago. Beyond **cottages,** the lane falls towards a wood, there bending sharply right to pass under a **bridge** (beware of traffic).

3 At the junction beyond, go left towards **Gnosall**, the lane rising gently along the base of a high **wooded embankment** upon which the canal runs. After a mile (1.6km), it twists beneath the canal once more (again watch out for traffic) and climbs to a bend beyond. Keep going with the undulating lane, eventually passing beneath a bridge that once carried the Stafford Newport Railway to a **T-junction** with the main road at the end.

4 Turn right, crossing the canal to find **The Navigation** on the right. If going to the pub, there are steps to the canal towpath from the car park, but an easier way lies down a **ramp** on the left-hand side of the road. Double back under the bridge and cycle away past the pub beside the canal, shortly going beneath the railway

again. The **bridge** here is very wide, the passage almost tunnel-like, not due to carrying several tracks, but because it is skewed across the canal. Such bridges were disproportionately expensive if built in brick or stone, and it was only the invention of the skew arch that allowed the bridge to be preserved within the width of the upper passage. Shortly emerging from a **cutting**, there are pleasing views across the open countryside. The way continues to **Shelmore Wood**, where there is a **stop lock**, a device inserted periodically along the canal for isolating individual sections so that they could be drained for maintenance. Carry on in trees for another 1.25 miles (2km) to **Norbury Junction**, there crossing a bridge over the abandoned Wappenshall Branch to reach **The Junction pub**.

5 Leave the canal for the lane, and retrace your outward route left back to the car park by the village hall in Norbury.

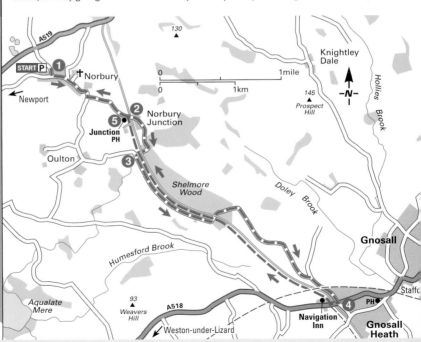

The Navigation Inn

Constructed to serve the needs of the workers building the Shropshire Canal in the 1830s, the Navigation is a traditional, cream-painted pub smack beside the canal, with several cosy rooms adorned with brassware. There's also an airy conservatory dining area which overlooks the garden and passing canal boats.

Food

Standard pub food is available, the snack menu listing ploughman's lunches, a good range of sandwiches and various basket meals. The carte extends the choice to include steak and kidney pie, jumbo haddock and lamb shank, while the specials board may add wild boar, liver and bacon and fresh fish dishes.

Family facilities

Families can expect a good welcome here as children are allowed throughout the pub. Youngsters have a standard children's menu and they will love exploring the play area in a canal-side garden.

Alternative refreshment stops

The Junction pub at Norbury Junction.

☞ Where to go from here

At Weston-under-Lizard you'll find Weston Park (www.weston-park.com), a fine mansion built in 1671. It stands in elegant gardens and a vast park with three lakes, a miniature railway, a woodland adventure playground, an animal centre and deer park. The house contains a magnificent collection of pictures, furniture and tapestries. Take a self-guided tour of the Wedgwood Ceramic Factory at Barlaston (www.wedgwood.com) and learn about the story of Wedgwood. The visitor centre has a film theatre, exhibition area and a demonstration/hands-on area.

about the pub

The Navigation Inn
Newport Road, Gnosall
Staffordshire ST20 0BM
Tel: 01785 822327

DIRECTIONS: beside the canal and A518 Newport road just west of the village; Point **4** of the route	
PARKING: 50	
OPEN: daily; all day Sunday	
FOOD: daily; all day Sunday	
BREWERY/COMPANY: Banks Brewery	
REAL ALE: Banks Bitter & Original, Greene King Old Speckled Hen, guest beer	

Baddesley Clinton and Packwood House

Ride along tow paths that connect two old houses.

Ancient houses

The Stratford-upon-Avon Canal created a route between the Worcester Canal at Kings Norton Junction, just south of Birmingham, and the River Avon at Stratford. Authorised by an Act of Parliament in 1793, the upper section to Hockley Heath was soon completed, but a shortage of funds delayed construction of the costly locks taking the canal downhill into the Avon valley. The waterway only reached Kingswood in 1802 and was not finally completed until 1816. A cut at Kingswood joined the Stratford to the Warwick and Birmingham Canal, which lay just to the east and was absorbed within the Grand Union system during the 1920s. Although commercial traffic continued on the Grand Union into the 1960s, the closure of the Avon Navigation in 1873 dealt a harsh blow to the Stratford Canal's fortunes and by the 1930s the section below Lapworth was derelict.

Centred like a jewel within its 13th-century moat, Baddesley Clinton has one of the most picturesque settings in the country. Slender Tudor chimneys of ornate brick rise above the roof, while below, the stonework of the inner sanctum gives way to half-timbering overlooking a delightful courtyard garden secluded from the world. Inside is no less a delight; elaborately carved chimney pieces and wood-panelled walls decorate rooms that are elegantly furnished to represent different periods in the life of the house, whilst shimmering reflections dance off the water through mullioned windows onto the ceilings.

Formerly held by the Benedictine priory of Coventry, Packwood passed into secular ownership following Henry VIII's Dissolution of the monasteries in the 1530s. The splendid many-gabled and chimneyed manor house was erected by the Fetherstones towards the end of the 16th century, originally a timber-frame building, but subsequently 'modernised' with a rendered brick façade. Inside, however, it is infused with the charm of its early period. Its last owner, Graham Ash, carefully restored the building and scoured the neighbourhood rescuing authentic furnishings and fittings from the break up or demolition of other ancient houses. He, too, is partly responsible for the yew garden, for which the house is famous, extending the mid-17th-century topiary towards the house in an arrangement that has since become known as 'The Sermon on the Mount'.

2h00 | **9.75 MILES** | **15.7 KM** | **LEVEL 123**

the ride

1 Join the Stratford-upon-Avon Canal behind the car park, turn right past a lock to a **bridge** where the canal splits. Cross to the spur, which drops through a second lock to another bridge, there dismounting to descend **four steps** on the far side. Follow the **tow path** away from the junction, passing a picnic site and going beneath a railway bridge to meet the **Grand Union Canal**.

2 Cycle along the tow path to the right for some 0.75 mile (1.2km) to the second **bridge (No. 63)**, leaving immediately beyond it for the lane above. Over the bridge, climb away past the Tom O' The Wood pub. At a **'Give Way'** crossroads, keep ahead over the **B4439**, enjoying easy pedalling for a little over 0.5 mile (800m) to the end of the lane.

3 To the left, the way leads past **Hay Wood**, eventually meeting another junction. Go left again towards Lapworth and **Baddesley Clinton**, the lane shortly falling to pass the entrance of Baddesley Clinton, which lies opposite Netherwood Lane. Turn in beside the **lodge** and follow the winding drive to a car park at its end. The National Trust has provided separate facilities for cycles, enabling you to explore the house and nearby church on foot.

4 Returning to the main lane, turn left towards **Hockley Heath**, soon dropping to a blind humpback bridge spanning the

Top right: The Stratford & Avon Canal
Left: Packwood House

MAP: OS Explorer 220 Birmingham & Explorer 221 Coventry & Warwick
START/FINISH: Kingswood; car park in Brome Hall lane; grid ref: SP 185710
TRAILS/TRACKS: quiet lanes and canal tow paths with predominantly gravel surfaces
LANDSCAPE: hedged lanes and canals winding through rolling agricultural countryside
PUBLIC TOILETS: at the start
TOURIST INFORMATION: Solihull, tel 0121 704 6130
CYCLE HIRE: Clarkes Cycle Shop, Henley Street and Guild Street, Stratford-upon-Avon, tel 01789 205057, www.cycling-tours.org.uk
THE PUB: The Boot Inn, Lapworth
🛑 Traffic on country lanes, one awkward right-hand turn, low bridges and overhanging branches along tow path

Getting to the start
From M42, junction 4, follow the A3400 south in the direction of Stratford. Passing through Hockley Heath, bear left onto the B4439, continuing for 2.5 miles (4km) to Kingswood. Shortly after passing The Boot Inn turn right into Brome Hall lane. The car park entrance is on the left.

Why do this cycle ride?
At Kingswood, two separate canals came within yards of each other. Their tow paths provide an off-road link in this enjoyable ride that visits two nearby ancient houses.

Researched and written by: Dennis Kelsall

Baddesley Clinton   WARWICKSHIRE

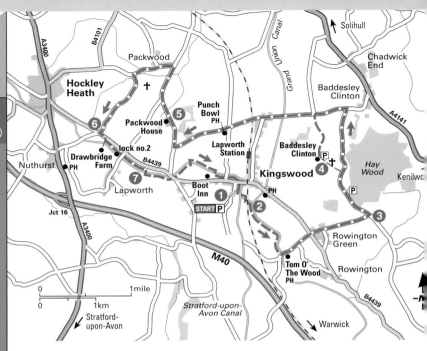

Grand Union Canal. Beyond there, keep going over a railway bridge and later, ahead at a crossroads beside the **Punch Bowl**. About 0.5 mile (800m) further on, the road turns sharply left. Exercising caution, turn off right onto a narrow lane leading past **Packwood House**, which stands beside the road only a short distance along.

5 Resuming your ride, carry on for almost another 0.75 mile (1.2km) to the second lane leaving on the left, **Vicarage Road**. It is signed to Packwood and Hockley Heath. Follow that for 0.5 mile (800m) and then turn left at an unsigned junction. Winding past Packwood's church, **St Giles**, the lane eventually ends at a main road, the B4439.

6 Turn left towards **Lapworth and Warwick**, but after 200 yards (182m) and just before some **white cottages**, swing off right onto a gravel track, the entrance to **Drawbridge Farm**. Meeting the canal a few

yards/metres along, follow the tow path left to the first of a long series of **locks** (No 2) heralding the canal's descent to **Kingswood**. Prudent cyclists will then dismount to negotiate the sharp dip and low ridge immediately beyond the lock.

7 The path crosses to the opposite bank over a bridge below **lock No 4**, remaining on that side to pass beneath a road bridge and shortly reaching **lock No 6**. Beyond, locks then follow in quick succession, forming a staircase that drops the canal some 70ft (21m) in little over 0.5 mile (800m). The tow path reverts to the north bank below **lock No 7**, recrossing once more after lock No 14, where **The Boot Inn** lies, just along a track south of the canal. The final stretch continues along the tow path beneath a road bridge, bending past four more locks and under a final **bridge** to return you to the car park.

The Boot Inn

Barely a stone's throw from the Grand Union Canal, the 16th-century Boot is a rustic and rambling brick building that became a pub when the canal was built some 200 years ago. Much of its early trade came from the canal, busy with cargo to Birmingham. Today it is a lively and convivial place, the smart refurbished bar with timbered ceilings, quarry-tiled floors and glowing fires, drawing diners from far and wide for modern brasserie-style food and interesting global wines. There's an attractive summer garden with a canopy and patio heaters for those cooler evenings. The inn sign depicts a caricature by renowned artist, Jim Bulmer, known for his humorous cartoons of local characters.

about the pub

The Boot Inn
Old Warwick Road, Lapworth,
Warwickshire B94 6JU
Tel: 01564 782464
www.thebootatlapworth.co.uk

DIRECTIONS: See Getting to the start and point **7** of the ride	
PARKING: 60	
OPEN: daily; all day	
FOOD: daily	
BREWERY/COMPANY: Enterprise Inns	
REAL ALE: Bass, Wadworth 6X, Greene King Old Speckled Hen	

Food

Food is freshly prepared and both the main menu and blackboard specials take in 'first plates' like rustic breads with roast garlic and olive oil or onion tart with parmesan and rocket, with main dishes ranging from leek, spinach and smoked mozzarella risotto to haddock in tempura batter with pea purée. Sandwiches are served at lunchtime.

Family facilities

Children are most welcome inside the pub. There's a children's menu and both smaller portions of adult dishes and high chairs are available.

Alternative refreshment stops

The Punch Bowl and Tom O' The Wood pubs are along the route and there's a restaurant and tea room at Baddesley Clinton.

☛ Where to go from here

In addition to Packwood House and Baddesley Clinton (www.nationaltrust. org.uk), the area has two grand castles, Kenilworth and Warwick. The latter dominates the town and attractions include the gloomy dungeon and Torture Chamber, the grand State Rooms and Great Hall (www.warwick-castle.com). Shakespeare enthusiasts should head south to Stratford-upon-Avon and the surrounding villages – Mary Arden's house in Wilmcote and Anne Hathaway's Cottage in Shottery (www.shakespeare.org.uk).

Baddesley Clinton WARWICKSHIRE

Stratford Greenway

Explore the quiet countryside in which England's greatest bard grew up.

Stratford-upon-Avon

Whilst Stratford was already a prosperous town before Shakespeare's day, it is probably due to his association that so many of the town's splendid 16th-century buildings have survived. Some of the best line Church Street, along which the ride finishes. Buildings include a splendid row of almshouses, the early 15th-century Guild Hall and Grammar School (where Shakespeare is said to have been educated), some impressive inns and the site of New Place, where the poet died in 1616. Stop off too to look in Holy Trinity Church, where he was both baptised and buried.

The ride out follows the route of the Oxford, Worcester and Wolverhampton Railway, built in 1859 to link the Midlands with the south west of England. A decade and a half later, another line was constructed to the town from the south east, with junctions and sidings in the area now occupied by Swan Meadow car park and a separate station to service the racecourse. As the country's rail network developed, the smaller lines were absorbed, the Great Western buying up the Midlands line whilst the London, Midland and Scottish Railway took over the other. Bringing tourists to the town from the capital, the latter became known as the 'Shakespeare Route', but closed in 1965 as part of Beeching's rationalisation programme. The GWR, along which the Greenway now runs, was taken up in 1976, leaving only the route from the north into the town.

the ride

1 Leave Clopton Bridge along Waterside, passing the **Royal Shakespeare Theatre** and famous Dirty Duck pub. Turn left at the end to wind past Holy Trinity Church and then go left again into **Mill Lane**. It finishes in a narrow alley, usually busy with pedestrians, that leads to the river. The continuing path swings beneath a **bridge** to shadow the main road, shortly passing **Seven Meadows car park**.

2 If joining the **railway track** at Seven Meadows, turn right to **Milcote picnic area**. The way runs beside Stratford's **racecourse** where, on race days, horses gallop along the back straight. The track then crosses the Avon by a riverside picnic area and later, the River Stour. Pedal on beyond **Chambers Halt** and Pearces Crossing to the pine-grown platform of **Milcote Station**.

3 Through barriers and a parking area, cross a road to a **picnic site** where an old railway coach houses a café. The track continues for a further 2 miles (3.2km), passing crossings at **Knobbs Farm** and the **Airfield** before ultimately reaching **Wyre Lane Crossing**. Leave there, going right along Wyre Lane into **Long Marston**. The

Mason's Arms is just a short way along the main road to the right.

4 To return, either retrace your outward route, or alternatively, instead of going back along Wyre Lane, keep ahead on the road to the outskirts of the village. There, turn off right to **Dorsington**, passing the church of **St James the Great**. Carry on for 1.5 miles (2.4km) to a T-junction and go right, winding to another junction in the middle of Dorsington. Take the lane on the right to **Welford**, which snakes north between the fields, culminating in a short, stiff pull to give a view across the Avon valley. Drop to a road and follow that right into modern Welford. However, leave after just over 0.5 mile (800m) along **Headland Road** on the left, which ends in the old village opposite **St Peter's Church**.

5 The onward route lies to the right along **Church Street**, but first wander down Boat Lane to see its thatched black and white cottages. At the end of Church Street by the **Bell Inn**, take the main road right through the village, passing a small green where there stands a tall **maypole**. Leaving Welford, turn off left to **Weston and Clifford Chambers**, going left again after 0.5 mile (800m) on a narrow lane to **Weston-on-Avon**.

Safe family cycling on Stratford Railway Path

3h30 — **15.5 MILES** — **25 KM** — **LEVEL 1** 2 3

MAP: OS Explorer 205 Stratford-upon-Avon & Evesham

START/FINISH: Stratford: Clopton Bridge, grid ref SP 203549 or Seven Meadows car park, grid ref SP 195540

TRAILS/TRACKS: streets in Stratford and disused railway line with good gravel surface, country lanes and farm track

LANDSCAPE: patchwork fields of the Avon valley rising to a backdrop of low hills

PUBLIC TOILETS: in Stratford

TOURIST INFORMATION: Stratford, tel 0870 160 7930

CYCLE HIRE: Clarkes Cycle Shop, Henley Street and Guild Street, Stratford-upon-Avon; tel: 01789 205057; www.cycling-tours.org.uk

THE PUB: Masons Arms, Long Marston

🚫 Traffic on Stratford's busy streets and country lanes, pedestrians along the track

Getting to the start
Stratford-upon-Avon is close to junction 15 on the M40. If parking in the town, start the ride at Clopton Bridge, which brings the A422 into Stratford. Alternatively, begin from Seven Meadows car park on the A4390.

Why do this cycle ride?
Leaving Stratford-upon-Avon along the level track of a former railway line, the route leads to Long Marston, where the pub makes an excellent stop for lunch. Either return on the outward track or follow country lanes via the picturesque village of Welford-on-Avon.

Researched and written by: Dennis Kelsall

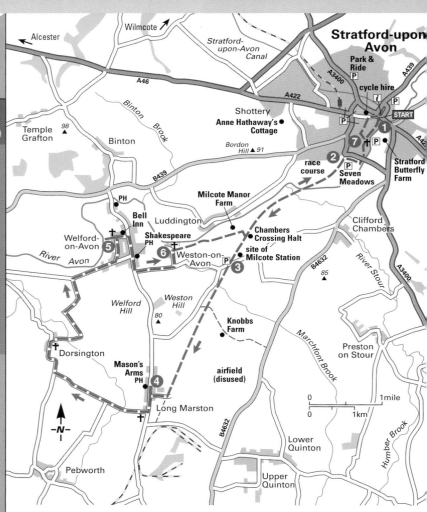

Alcester

Wilmcote

Stratford-
upon-Avon
Canal

Stratford-upon-Avon

Park &
Ride
P

A46

cycle hire
i   P

A3400

A439

A439

Binton
Brook

Shottery
**Anne Hathaway's ●
Cottage**

A422

P

START

1

Temple
Grafton   98▲

Binton

Bordon
Hill ▲ 91

P
7   †   P

Stratford
Butterfly
Farm

B439

PH

**Milcote Manor
Farm**

race
course

2

P
Seven
Meadows

Clifford
Chambers

**Bell
Inn**

Luddington

**Chambers
Crossing Halt**

River

Welford-
on-Avon

†

**Shakespeare
PH**

†

5

Avon

6   Weston-on-
Avon

site of
Milcote Station

P

3

B4632

River Stour

A3400

85 ▲

**Welford
Hill**

**Weston
Hill**

80 ▲

**Knobbs
Farm**

Marchfont Brook

Preston
on Stour

†
Dorsington

**Mason's
Arms
PH**

4

**airfield
(disused)**

0   1mile

0   1km

Long Marston

†

B4632

–N–

Lower
Quinton

Humber Brook

Pebworth

Upper
Quinton

6 At the bottom turn right past the village **church**, the way deteriorating to a farm track as it continues between the fields beyond. Keep forward as it reverts to tarmac, later passing **Milcote Manor Farm** to a couple of **cottages**. The way disintegrates to dirt as it then swings right to meet the disused railway at **Chambers Crossing Halt**. Follow it left back to Seven Meadows car park and Stratford.

7 If you began from the town, after passing **Holy Trinity Church** you must now carry on past **Riverside** and instead turn right at the next crossroads into **Church Street**. Continue ahead along Chapel Street and **High Street** to a busy roundabout in the town centre, where you might wish to dismount to return to your car park.

Masons Arms

Once part of the farm estate and a pub since 1861, this traditional pub may be small but it has bags of character, with cosy, low-beamed bars, a big inglenook with winter log fires, a worn stone-flagged floor, and a wealth of gleaming brasses for decoration. Add a popular skittle alley, summer barbecue evenings in the spacious garden, and weekly live music and you have a thriving village local.

Food

An extensive light snack menu lists a good range of sandwiches and baguettes, home-made pizzas, burgers and ploughman's lunches. Traditional main dishes include steak and ale pie, fish pie, lasagne and lamb's liver with mash and onion gravy. Specials take in ribeye steak, curries, and leek and potato bake.

Family facilities

Children are welcome inside the pub. Youngsters have their own menu and smaller portions of main menu meals are also available.

Alternative refreshment stops

There's a wide choice of pubs, cafés and restaurants in Stratford-upon-Avon, a café at Milcote picnic area, and you will also find the Bell Inn and the Shakespeare pub at Welford-on-Avon.

🕭 Where to go from here

Associations with Shakespeare (www.shakespeare.org.uk) abound in and around Stratford. You can visit Mary Arden's House and the Shakespeare Countryside Museum at Wilmcote, the childhood home of the bard's wife, Anne Hathaway's

Cottage at Shottery, and in Stratford, Hall's Croft, Harvard House and Nash's House and New Place. Europe's largest live butterfly and insect exhibit can seen at the Stratford Butterfly Farm (www.butterflyfarm.co.uk). Fine houses and parks in the area include Coughton Court, Alcester (www.coughtoncourt.co.uk), Ragley Hall, Alcester (www.ragleyhall.com), and Charlecote Park near Wellesbourne (www.nationaltrust.org.uk).

about the pub

Masons Arms
Welford Road, Long Marston
Stratford-upon-Avon, Warwickshire
CV37 8RG
Tel: 01789 720586

DIRECTIONS: village signposted off the B4632 south of Stratford-upon-Avon. On route at Point **3**

PARKING: 35

OPEN: daily; all day Saturday & Sunday

FOOD: no food Sunday evening, all Monday & Tuesday evening

BREWERY/COMPANY: Punch Taverns

REAL ALE: Boddingtons, Hook Norton Bitter

Along the Ashby Woulds Heritage Trail

Celebrate Leicestershire's rich industrial heritage on this short linear ride along a disused railway.

Ashby Woulds Heritage Trail

The Ashby Woulds Heritage Trail follows the route of the old Ashby to Nuneaton railway, and runs right through the heart of what was once an important coal-mining area. When pits were closed across the region in the mid 1980s, the landscape was left derelict and decaying, but in 1992 a forum was formed to help regenerate the local environment and boost the region's economy. The trail is a part of this initiative. It starts at the old railway station in Measham before crossing Donisthorpe Woodland Park, which was planted on the site of a reclaimed colliery. Further along is Conkers, a state-of-the-art visitor centre built on the site of Rawdon Colliery, one of the last deep mines in the Midlands to close. It finishes at Overseal sidings, where a short length of track and an abandoned signal box can still be seen. The trail also falls within the so-called National Forest, a government-backed initiative instigated in 1995 to help improve some 200 square miles of land in Leicestershire, Derbyshire and Staffordshire which have been scarred by hundreds of years of coal mining. It is hoped that 30 million trees will eventually be planted, and that 33 per cent of the total area will be wooded.

Right: A pond on the Ashby Woulds Trail

the ride

1 From the south west corner of the car park, proceed up a narrow path to reach the main bridleway, past a **heritage trail information board**. Bear right along the gravel bridleway, past a **picnic bench** at the top of the rise. After 750yds (686m), the bridleway veers to the left and goes through some **wooden bike stiles** to reach a main road. At the main road turn right along the pavement and go under the **A42**.

2 Straight after the A42, turn right to regain the **main bridleway** (there is another right turn just before this which also looks like a bridleway, but this is clearly a dead end). Continue under a pair of **road bridges**. Much of this section, and indeed the whole trail, is raised up above the surrounding landscape, but because it's enclosed by trees and bushes, it feels quite secluded and peaceful. There are numerous **signposts** and **picnic benches** along the route.

3 Just beyond the next bridge, bear left up the first short climb of the ride to reach a **main road**. Turn right along the pavement and then cross the road with care to continue along the **heritage trail** (signed). Here the trail is wider and more open as it crosses **Donisthorpe Woodland Park**. On the way it drops down a long gentle hill to a bridge and a small stream before heading back up the far side.

4 At the northern corner of the park, keep going in the same direction (frustratingly enough, you may have to dismount here to negotiate a pair of **wooden bike stiles**). The trail becomes enclosed and shaded again

1h30 · **6.8 MILES** · **11 KM** · **LEVEL 123**

MAP: OS Explorer 245 The National Forest
START/FINISH: Measham Country Park car park; grid ref SK 332119
TRAILS/TRACKS: mostly gravel, with a short section of pavement
LANDSCAPE: railway embankment
PUBLIC TOILETS: at the start
TOURIST INFORMATION: Ashby-de-la-Zouch, tel 01530 411767
CYCLE HIRE: none locally
THE PUB: Navigation Inn, Overseal
❶ Take care when riding along the pavement under the A42, and also when crossing the road in Donisthorpe. Keep an eye on young children when approaching the road at the Navigation Inn

Getting to the start
Park at a free car park just off the B5006 in the middle of Measham, which is signposted off the A42 1.5 miles (2km) south west of Ashby-de-la-Zouch. Go to the left-hand parking area, where the public toilets are situated

Why do this cycle ride?
This gentle ride is almost completely flat, and what it lacks in terms of views it more than makes up for in terms of peace and solitude. The family-friendly pub at the halfway point is an ideal spot for a rest, and kids will love the attractions at Conkers Visitor Centre, a short detour off the main route.

Researched and written by: Paul Grogan

Measham

LEICESTERSHIRE

On the Ashby Woulds Trail

as you pass over a number of roads before eventually getting to a string of **ponds** at the end of the trail; just beyond these ponds is the B5004 and, off to your left, **the Navigation Inn**.

5 To reach the **National Forest Visitor Centre (Conkers)**, go back along the trail and at the far end of the **ponds** turn left, following a sign to the **Bath Yard**. When you come to another **sign** and information board turn right, into a field, and cross it on

a well-trodden track. Turn right at the far end of this track, under a bridge, and continue as far as a **railway crossing**. Just beyond this crossing is the visitor centre.

6 To get back to the start, retrace your tracks from the Navigation Inn or the visitor centre. At the main road in Donisthorpe turn right and then left to stay on route, and at the main road into **Measham**, turn left along the pavement to go under the A42 and then left again, back into the woods.

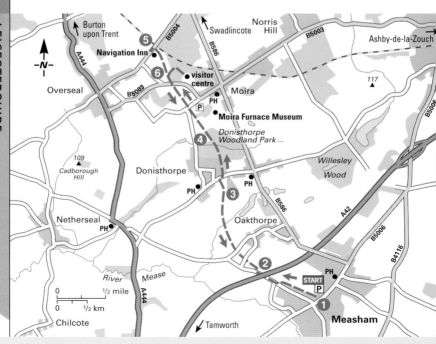

Navigation Inn

Interesting black and white prints of the local area adorn the walls of this big, family orientated pub in Overseal village. Bar and dining areas are open-plan in layout, light, spacious and immaculately maintained, and decorated in traditional style with dark wood tables and chairs laid out on bright red carpets. In summer the big garden is very popular with families and kids can let off steam in the huge adventure play area.

Food

An extensive menu offers light meals like sandwiches, wraps and paninis, standard pub main courses, and dishes like Mediterranean trout, Hawaiian chicken, salmon salad and a daily carvery.

about the pub

Navigation Inn
166 Spring Cottage Road, Overseal
Swadlincote, Derbyshire DE12 6ND
Tel: 01283 760493

DIRECTIONS: on B5004 east of Overseal (Point 5 on the route)	
PARKING: 50	
OPEN: daily; all day	
FOOD: daily; all day	
BREWERY/COMPANY: Hardy & Hanson's	
REAL ALE: Hardy & Hanson's Bitter, Marston's Pedigree	
ROOMS: 3 bedrooms	

Family facilities

Children of all ages are welcome throughout the pub and there's a safe, enclosed adventure play area in the large lawned garden. The 'young adults' menu includes lasagne, burgers and ice creams.

Alternative refreshment stops

There's a café at Conkers that serves hot and cold drinks, snacks and main meals throughout the day.

☞ Where to go from here

Aside from Conkers, other local attractions worth visiting include the superb Moira Furnace Museum, just off the route, which boasts a host of displays and interactive exhibits on the history of the furnace, and Ashby Castle in Ashby-de-la-Zouch, which offers great views of the surrounding countryside. There's also a dry-slope ski centre in nearby Swadlincote just 2 miles (3km) to the north of the Navigation Inn (www.jnll.co.uk).

A circuit from Sulgrave

This scenic ride on smooth and quiet country lanes encircles a major battlefield from the War of the Roses.

Battle of Edgecote Moor

The Battle of Edgecote Moor (1469) was one of the many skirmishes fought during the so-called Wars of the Roses (1455–1487). This involved an on-going struggle for the throne of England between rival royal families: at the time of the battle Edward IV (represented by the white rose of York), was king, having successfully ousted Henry VI (represented by the red rose of Lancaster), some eight years previously. The battle itself centred on control of a ford over the River Cherwell and was fought between the Earls of Pembroke and Devon (loyal to Edward), and Robin of Redesdale (loyal to Henry). Although heavily outnumbered, Pembroke and Devon appeared to win the first round of fighting, but the late arrival of some 15,000 Lancastrian soldiers (led by the Earl of Warwick) proved to be decisive.

Devon panicked and his men were duly routed, and although Pembroke continued to put up a spirited fight, he too was eventually defeated and executed. Devon was later captured by commoners and murdered for his cowardice. Despite the outcome of the battle, Edward IV remained on the throne for more than a year, before being forced to seek exile in Burgundy by an overwhelming tide of Lancastrian support. After rallying his own allies from abroad, however, he returned in 1471 to defeat the Lancastrians at Barnet and Tewkesbury, and had Henry VI executed. He continued to reign until his death in 1483.

the ride

1 From the Star Inn car park, turn left and continue past **Sulgrave Manor**. At the end of this road bear slightly left and continue along a narrow country lane. After a couple of gentle rises and then a steeper hill, follow the road round to the left to reach a T-junction. Turn left here along **Banbury Lane**, and at the next crossroads continue straight on towards **Culworth**.

2 Just after you enter the village of Culworth you come to a T-junction. Bear right here to continue through the village. Take care on the long, fast descent as you leave the village. Carry on along this winding road until you get to **Trafford Bridge**, the scene of a bloody battle during the War of the Roses. Go straight on here, ignoring the lane going over a little bridge to your right. Stay on this rolling section of the route as far as the **Hare & Hounds** pub.

3 Cross the road directly opposite the pub to reach the pavement on the far side, and walk your bikes right, towards the **A361**. At this busy A-road turn left, continuing

Quiet lanes around Sulgrave

2h00	11.5 MILES	18.5 KM	LEVEL 123

MAP: OS Explorer 206 Edge Hill & Fenny Compton

START/FINISH: on-street parking in Sulgrave grid ref: SP 558455

TRAILS/TRACKS: tarmac roads all the way

LANDSCAPE: country lanes and villages

PUBLIC TOILETS: none on route

TOURIST INFORMATION: Banbury, tel 01295 259855

CYCLE HIRE: none locally

THE PUB: The Star Inn, Sulgrave

🛈 A fairly long ride on country lanes, with some steep hills. Section where bikes have to be walked along a pavement to avoid a short stretch of busy A-road. Unsuitable for young, inexperienced children

Getting to the start

Sulgrave is signed off the B4525 between Banbury and the A43. To get to the start from Magpie Farm junction (see map), follow the main road into Sulgrave and at an obvious fork in the centre of the village, bear left, following signs to Sulgrave Manor. Park in the village street. The Star Inn is along this road on your left.

Why do this cycle ride?

This long and scenic circular route provides some superb road riding on smooth and quiet country lanes and takes in some charming villages. It avoids the worst of the region's hills, but there are still one or two steep climbs to negotiate.

Researched and written by: Paul Grogan

to wheel your bikes along a pavement for the next 440yds (402m). At the next left turn, into the village proper, wheel your bikes up to the top of a short rise and remount. Cycle as far as a **T-junction** and turn left to continue through the picturesque village of **Upper Wardington**, with its thatched roofs and its Cotswold stone buildings.

4 Beyond Upper Wardington, follow a quiet **country lane** for around 1.25 miles (2km) to reach a short but **steep hill**. At the brow of this hill, turn left along another narrow country road, which is initially paved with concrete (there are no signs here, so it's easy to miss – if you find yourself going downhill, you've gone too far). From this hilltop road you get some superb views out to your left. There are one or two little pot-holes to look out for towards the end of this section, but these are easily avoided.

5 At an obvious track crossroads continue straight across, following signs to **Thorpe**

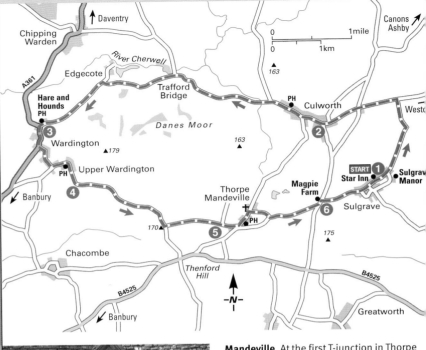

Mandeville. At the first T-junction in Thorpe Mandeville, turn left and continue as far as a squat Gothic **church** on your left (note the massive yew tree to the east of the church, which is thought to be over a thousand years old). Turn right at the church, down a long steep hill on an uneven road, to reach a wider road; turn left here to go up a short **steep hill** and continue as far as the junction at **Magpie Farm**.

6 At this junction, take care turning right towards **Sulgrave** and Sulgrave Manor. Finish on a long, gradual downhill into the village. At a fork in the centre of Sulgrave, bear left to get back to the start.

The porch of Sulgrave Manor, the ancestral home of George Washington

The Star Inn

A cosy, creeper-clad pub, created out of a 300-year-old former farmhouse a short stroll from Sulgrave Manor, where locally brewed Hook Norton ales and imaginative pub food are served in a smartly rustic and civilised bar and dining room. In the cosy bar you'll find a warm red and cream décor, a worn flagstone floor and a big inglenook with a blazing winter log fire. Separate, equally inviting dining room, a vine-covered patio and a secluded, well maintained garden for enjoying summer alfresco meals.

Food

Blackboard menus change daily and list above average pub food in the form of wild mushroom and foie gras terrine with onion marmalade and Tuscan bean soup for starters, with mains like smoked haddock fishcakes with ginger and lime mayonnaise and roast pheasant with mash, chestnuts, cranberries and game jus. Good range of sandwiches and specials and lighter meals at lunchtime.

Family facilities

Children are welcome in the dining areas. Here they can order smaller portions or opt for the children's menu choice. There are high chairs available.

Alternative refreshment stops

Pubs at Wardington (half-way) and in Thorpe Mandeville.

☛ Where to go from here

Sulgrave Manor, a short stroll to the northeast of the Star Inn, is the ancestral home of George Washington. You can take a guided tour and walk around the formal garden (www.sulgravemanor.org.uk). Nearby is Canons Ashby House, an exceptional small manor house with Elizabethan wall paintings and Jacobean plasterwork. Stowe Landscape Gardens, near Buckingham, has one of the finest Georgian landscape gardens in the country (both www.nationaltrust.org.uk). For some of the best views to be found in the area, look no further than the Burton Dassett Hills, about 10 miles to the northwest of Wardington.

about the pub

The Star Inn
Manor Road, Sulgrave
Banbury, Northamptonshire OX17 2SA
Tel: 01295 760389
www.starinnsulgrave.com

DIRECTIONS: see Getting to the start	
PARKING: 20	
OPEN: closed Sunday evenings	
FOOD: no food Monday	
BREWERY/COMPANY: Hook Norton Brewery	
REAL ALE: Hook Norton Best & Old Hooky, guest beer	
ROOMS: 3 en suite	

Sulgrave

NORTHAMPTONSHIRE

Around Rutland Water

Ride around Europe's largest man-made reservoir at the heart of England's smallest county.

Rutland Water

Rutland Water was rubber-stamped in 1970 to provide drinking water to the surrounding area. Completed seven years later, it flooded an area of 3,100 acres (equivalent to around 3000 football pitches). The dam itself is 1,312yds (1,200m) long, and the maximum depth of the reservoir is 34 metres (111ft). One of the few local landmarks to survive the flooding was Normanton Church, which had to be raised above the level of the water and joined to the shore by a causeway to protect it from ruin. Originally built in 1826, it today houses a local history museum. Other attractions include a climbing wall and marina (at Whitwell car park), a butterfly centre (at the north end of the dam), and a nature reserve (at the southwest corner of the reservoir).

The nature reserve is one of the most important bird-watching centres in the UK. Depending on the time of year, Rutland Water is home to as many as 20,000 waterfowl. Equally important are the reserve's ospreys. These impressive raptors have brown plumage, white bodies and wingspans of up to 5.6ft (1.7m). They were introduced to the region in 1996 in an attempt to encourage them to start breeding, and in 2003, after a few false starts, they were successfully bred in England for the first time since 1847. The reserve also boasts an environmental display, a viewing gallery, 22 hides and a nature trail.

the ride

1 From the car park exit opposite the bike shop and **climbing tower,** turn right and then immediately left into the **marina**. Follow the road round to the left, away from the marina buildings, and drop down to the water's edge as it becomes a **cycle track**. Turn right at the tip of the inlet and continue around the **water's edge** until you reach another car park. Continue through this car park to reach the dam.

2 After crossing the **dam**, turn right at the end, through a pair of swing gates, and continue along the obvious tarmac track as far as **Normanton Church**. Beyond the church, cross a narrow tarmac road and continue straight through an uneven gravel parking area to reach the main **Edith Weston car park**, with public toilets, snack bar and bike shop. Proceed to the far end of the car park and turn right to continue around the water's edge, past the **sailing club** and marina.

An undulating path near Rutland Water

| 3h00 | 17 MILES | 27.4 KM | LEVEL 1 2 3 |

MAP: OS Explorer 234 Rutland Water

START/FINISH: Whitwell car park; grid ref: SK 923082

TRAILS/TRACKS: largely smooth tarmac and compacted gravel and tarmac

LANDSCAPE: woodland and waterside, with the occasional village

PUBLIC TOILETS: at the start and at Edith Weston car park

TOURIST INFORMATION: Oakham, tel 01572 724329

CYCLE HIRE: Rutland Cycling (at the start), tel 01780 460705 (www.rutlandcycling.co.uk)

THE PUB: The White Horse, Empingham

🛈 There's one short, steep descent with a tight turn at the bottom (well signposted). Take care crossing the main road when you make the right turn towards Manton

Getting to the start

The north and south shores of Rutland Water are signed from the A606 between Oakham and Stamford. This route starts at Whitwell car park on the north shore. Coming from Stamford, drive through Whitwell and turn left at the top of the hill to the car park.

Why do this cycle ride?

This is a long but gentle circuit that mostly follows the water's edge. The first few miles of tarmac are ideal for younger children, while the tracks on the western half are great for older, more adventurous kids. You can walk the one or two short sharp ascents.

Researched and written by: Paul Grogan

3 A mile (1.6km) past the sailing club, the track delves into a small **wood** before dropping down a steep hill to a **tight bend** at the bottom; a sign near the top gives riders plenty of warning that this hill is coming up.

4 At the next road turn left up a steep hill to reach the B-road between **Edith Weston and Manton**. Cross the main road with care and then turn right towards Manton, following the **cycle lane**. At the first junction continue straight on into Manton. Soon after passing a **phone box** on your left, turn right, following a **Rutland Water cycling sign**. Bear left past the **Horse & Jockey** pub to reach a wide gravel track down to the A6003. Follow a narrow pavement at the bottom beneath the **railway bridge** (a sign advises riders to dismount for this bit) and stay on this pavement for a further 440yds (402m).

5 Turn right through a **swing gate** here, following the cycle track around the water's edge until it cuts across the Lax-Hill

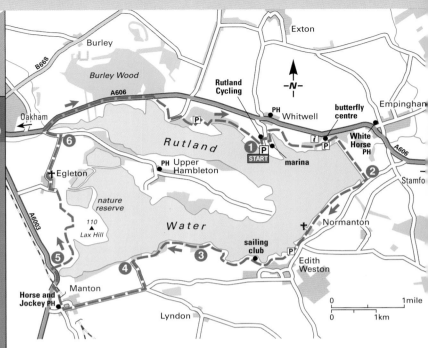

peninsula. This track eventually leads to **Egleton**. Turn left into the village and then right again after around 200yds (182m). Continue past the **church** and stay on the road to the main road into Hambleton.

Turn left, and then right after 300yds (273m) along a short **cycle track** to reach the A606. From here, stay on the rolling pavement for 1.5 miles (2km), before heading right, back onto a gravel track and around the water's edge. At the bottom of the next tarmac road, turn left up the short, sharp hill before turning right towards **Barnsdale Wood car park**. After going down and then steeply uphill to reach the car park, continue downhill again to the bottom, far right-hand corner of the car park; delve into **Barnsdale Wood** here and follow the track all the way back to the start point.

Modern sculpture above Rutland Water

The White Horse

A stone's throw from the serene Rutland Water, the stone-built, 17th-century White Horse is the centre of village life and a meeting place for the walkers, cyclists, anglers and water-sport enthusiasts exploring Europe's largest man-made lake. Originally a court house, it is now a popular inn with smart accommodation, a restaurant and a genteel, country-style bar, the latter full of traditional character, with low, beamed ceilings, dark wooden furniture and a large open log fire for cold winter days. In attempting to be all things to most callers its day stretches from morning coffee and croissants through lunches and cream teas to late evening suppers.

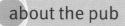 about the pub

The White Horse
2 Main Street, Empingham
Stamford, Rutland LE15 8PS
Tel: 01780 460221
www.whitehorserutland.co.uk

DIRECTIONS: load up bikes, return to Whitwell and turn right along the A606 for 2 miles (3.2km) to Empingham. The pub is at the junction with the main village street

PARKING: 60

OPEN: daily; all day

FOOD: daily; all day

BREWERY/COMPANY: Unique

REAL ALE: Ruddles Best, Adnams Bitter, Greene King Abbot Ale

ROOMS: 13 en suite

Food
Daily blackboard and printed menus provide plenty of choice and typically include giant Yorkshire pudding filled with sautéed liver of lamb, bacon and onions, beef, ale and mushroom pie, and trout with prawns, mixed pepper and spring onion sauce. Lighter meals include soups, moules and pasta dishes.

Family facilities
Children of all ages are welcome. There's a children's menu and smaller portions are also available. Small sheltered garden and two family bedrooms.

Alternative refreshment stops
Drinks, ice-creams and hot and cold snacks are available from the café at the Edith Weston Car Park. Another pub on route is the Horse & Jockey in Manton.

☛ Where to go from here
About 10 miles (16.1km) to the east of Rutland Water, on the B1443 out of Stamford, is Burghley House, a great Elizabethan palace surrounded by a fine country park landscaped by Capability Brown (www.burghley.co.uk). Head east to Oakham to view the town's castle, an exceptionally fine Norman Great Hall of a 12th century fortified manor house. Earthworks, walls and remains of an earlier motte can be seen along with medieval sculptures. Learn more about England's smallest county by visiting the Rutland County Museum in Catmos Street.

Blickling Hall and The Marriott Way

Cycle peaceful country lanes
and a former railway track
from Blickling Hall

Blickling Hall

Flanked by 17ft (5m) dark yew hedges
planted in the 17th century, Blickling Hall
(NT) is a magnificent Jacobean brick-fronted
hall and one of the great houses of East
Anglia. Dutch gabling, mullioned windows
and domed turrets characterise the
exterior. Inside there are fine collections of
furniture, pictures and tapestries, and a
spectacular Jacobean plaster ceiling in the
123ft (37.5m) Long Gallery (moulded in the
1620s) is very impressive. The gardens are
also well worth exploring.

Salle

The tiny village of Salle is the unlikely
setting for a 15th-century cathedral-like
church full of rich treasures, apparently
totally out of proportion to the tiny parish it
serves. It was built by three wealthy
families – the Briggs, the Fontaynes and
the Boleyns – who made their fortunes
from the weaving industry. Of particular
note is the unusual seven-sacrament font,
of which only 39 are said to exist. Well
worth looking at are the 26 carved oak
stalls. Some have good carvings of human
heads, others boast birds and animals;
note the swan, squirrel,
dragon and ape.

the ride

1 From the car park follow
the path to the
information board and sign
stating 'Park Only'. Turn left
along the estate road,
bearing right at a fork to
enter **Blickling Park**. In a few
yards, at a fork, take the

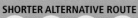

3h00	19 MILES	30.6 KM	LEVEL 1 2 3

SHORTER ALTERNATIVE ROUTE

2h00	13.5 MILES	21.8 KM	LEVEL 1 2 3

MAP: OS Explorer 252 Norfolk Coast East

START/FINISH: National Trust car park at Blickling Hall; grid ref: TG176285

TRAILS/TRACKS: parkland tracks, narrow country lanes, old railway track

LANDSCAPE: open and gently rolling agricultural countryside and parkland

PUBLIC TOILETS: Blickling Hall and Aylsham

TOURIST INFORMATION: Aylsham, tel 01263 733903

CYCLE HIRE: Blickling Hall (mid-March to October), tel 01263 738015 www.nationaltrust.org.uk/blickling

THE PUB: The Buckinghamshire Arms, Blickling

⚠ Puddles after rain along the Marriott Way, care to be taken crossing B1354 and through Aylsham

Getting to the start

Blickling Hall is located on the B1354 Aylsham to Holt road, 1.5 miles (2.4km) north-west of Aylsham and 15 miles (24.1km) north of Norwich.

Why do this cycle ride?

A level and easy-going ride, this enjoyable route begins at the splendid National Trust property of Blickling Hall, and incorporates a variety of parkland tracks, peaceful country lanes and a 6-mile (9.7km) section of disused railway track, the Marriott Way. Diversions along the way include a fascinating church and the little market town of Aylsham.

Researched and written by: David Hancock

bridleway left across the park (Weavers Way). Proceed for 1 mile (1.6km), passing a track to the Mausoleum, and keeping to the left of **Great Wood** to reach a parking area and lane.

2 Turn left, then turn left at the junction in **Itteringham Common**, following the lane uphill to a T-junction. Turn right, then left for Oulton and shortly reach the B1354. Turn right and then left in 100m, signposted Oulton. Pass **Oulton Hall**, turn left at a crossroads and pass Oulton church. Keep to the lane for a mile (1.6km) to a T-junction and turn right into Oulton Street.

3 The road crosses a **disused airfield** to reach the busy B1149. Cross straight over and follow the lane for 0.75 mile

Top: Blickling Hall fronted by its gardens
Left: Looking across to the church in Salle village

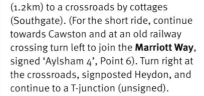

(1.2km) to a crossroads by cottages (Southgate). (For the short ride, continue towards Cawston and at an old railway crossing turn left to join the **Marriott Way**, signed 'Aylsham 4', Point 6). Turn right at the crossroads, signposted Heydon, and continue to a T-junction (unsigned).

4 Turn right, then in 0.5 mile (800m) turn left for Salle. Pass **Cherry Tree Farm** and keep left at the next junction. Take the next right turning and soon pass the impressive church at **Salle**. Pass through the hamlet to a junction and follow the road left, signposted to Reepham. Continue to **Reepham** and a T-junction on the outskirts of the village.

5 For refreshments at the old Reepham Station turn right, then right again (Kerri's). Turn left, then cross the road and pass through a gate to join the Marriott Way, a good, surfaced cycling trail along the former railway track. In 2 miles (3km) pass under a bridge and immediately fork left to climb an **embankment** (former platform of Cawston Station). Continue to a level crossing and cross a by-road.

6 Proceed for a further 4 miles (6.4km) through open country to the end of the trail in **Aylsham**, almost opposite the Bure Valley Railway (toilets). Turn left towards the town centre. Pass Budgens and follow the road left, signed to **Blickling Hall**. Pass the square and remain on the road for 0.5 mile (800m) before forking left on to a lane, signposted Abel Heath.

7 In 1 mile (1.6km) at **Abel Heath**, fork right and pass through the hamlet of Silvergate to reach the B1354, opposite Blickling Church. Turn left to return to the National Trust car park and **The Buckinghamshire Arms.**

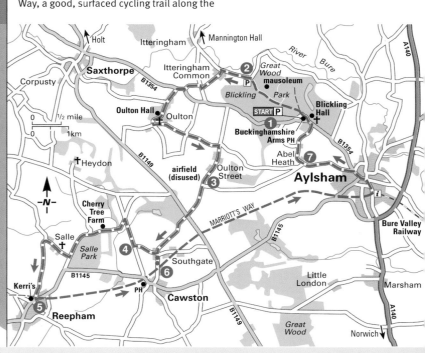

The Buckinghamshire Arms

'The Bucks', a rather stately late 17th-century coaching inn, stands by the gates of the magnificent Blickling Hall. Once the estate builder's house and later servants quarters for the fine Jacobean mansion, it has three charming and well-furnished bars with open log fires and a typically National Trust-style of décor and taste. The Victorian cellar houses ales from Norfolk, Suffolk and Kent and the spacious courtyard and gardens are popular on summer days. Bedrooms have four-posters and en suite bathrooms, and two have dramatic evening views across to the floodlit hall.

Food

Menus offer fresh local food served in both traditional and modern ways. Typically, tuck into lasagne, salmon and prawn tagliatelle, sautéed lambs' kidneys with Marsala, steak and kidney pie, Morston mussels, or local game in season. The usual bar snacks include sandwiches and ploughman's lunches

Family facilities

Well-behaved children are welcome in the dining area. No children overnight.

Alternative refreshment stops

The National Trust tea room at Blickling Hall offers good lunches and teas and a children's menu. Along the way, stop off at the café in the Old Reepham Station, or at one of the pubs in Aylsham.

☛ Where to go from here

Allow time to visit Blickling Hall (www.nationaltrust.org.uk) and its beautiful gardens. Take a trip on the Bure

about the pub

The Buckinghamshire Arms
Blickling, Aylsham
Norfolk NR11 6NF
Tel: 01263 732133

DIRECTIONS: see Getting to the start; pub beside the National Trust car park	
PARKING: 60	
OPEN: daily; all day in summer if busy	
FOOD: daily	
BREWERY/COMPANY: free house	
REAL ALE: Woodforde's Wherry & Nelson's Revenge, Adnams Bitter, guest beer	
ROOMS: 4 en suite	

Valley Railway between Aylsham and Wroxham on the Norfolk Broads (www.bvrw.co.uk), visit the outstanding gardens that surround Mannington Hall (www.manningtongardens.co.uk), or explore the timeless estate village of Heydon. The church has some remarkable 14th-century wall paintings and the village is often used at a film set.

Along Rudyard Lake

Relive the Edwardian era on this easy route beside picturesque Rudyard Reservoir, source of the water for much of the Midlands' canal network.

Rudyard Lake

You've probably passed over, or cycled beside, many a canal and taken them for granted as part of the scenery. The building of the county's canal system was a massive undertaking, but few people consider just where the water comes from to make them operate. The answer is places like Rudyard Lake. This was created in 1800 as a reservoir to supply water to the Caldon Canal, which served Leek and, more significantly, the Trent and Mersey Canal at Stoke-on-Trent, one of Britain's most important canals.

The Dingle Brook would have taken too long to fill the reservoir (and to keep it topped up) so, in addition to the dam, a feeder channel, or leat, was constructed up in the hills to the east of Rushton Spencer.

This collects water from the River Dane as it rushes down from the high Staffordshire moors and delivers it to Rudyard.

When the North Staffordshire Railway line was built between Leek and Macclesfield during the 1840s, the owners realised the reservoir was a potential leisure resource. They ran special excursion trains and laid out walks in the area. One couple had such pleasant memories of the time they spent here they named their son Rudyard Kipling after the area. Wealthy patrons built eccentric boathouses and chalets along the western shore of the lake, and these can still be seen today.

the ride

1 This is an easy there-and-back route from **Rudyard Old Station,** now the base for the little Rudyard Lake Steam Railway. This narrow gauge line follows the course of the former standard gauge line for 1.5 miles (2.4km) along the lake shore, its miniature steam engines providing endless fascination for visitors of all ages. The route follows the track north through cool woodlands to reach the **Dam Station.** As the name suggests, this is adjacent to the dam holding back **Rudyard Lake.** Make a side detour across the dam to a **visitor centre,** café and toilets – here, too, you'll find rowing boat hire and seasonal launch trips on the lake.

Left: Boathouses at Rudyard Lake
Top: View south down the lake

| 3h00 | 8.5 MILES | 13.7 KM | LEVEL 1 2 3 |

SHORTER ALTERNATIVE ROUTE

| 1h30 | 4 MILES | 6.4 KM | LEVEL 1 2 3 |

MAP: OS Explorer OL24 White Peak
START/FINISH: Rudyard Old Station, grid ref SJ 955579
TRAILS/TRACKS: old railway trackbed
LANDSCAPE: wooded lake shore, peaceful pastures and meadows
PUBLIC TOILETS: Rudyard village
TOURIST INFORMATION: Leek, tel 01538 483741
CYCLE HIRE: none near by
THE PUB: The Abbey Inn, Leek, see Directions to the pub, page 27
🚴 Take care along the banks of the lake – keep well away from the shore line

Getting to the start

From Leek take the A523 north west towards Macclesfield. Soon turn left on to the B5331, signed to Rudyard Lake. The entrance to the car park is on the left immediately under the railway bridge and before Rudyard village.

Why do this cycle ride?

Rudyard Lake is surrounded by wooded hills, pleasant hay meadows and cow pastures. The route takes full advantage of the countryside and offers opportunities to enjoy the other summertime facilities here such as a miniature railway, boat trips on the lake and rowing boat hire. It's an ideal family day out.

Researched and written by: Neil Coates

Rudyard Lake

STAFFORDSHIRE

2 Return to the old railway and carry on cycling northwards. The **lake** is easily visible through the trees – some care is needed as parts of the bank are prone to collapse, so keep well away from the shoreline. Looking across the lake, you'll see some of the odd boathouses that so delighted their owners a century and more ago. The lake is a popular place with school groups and Sea Scouts, so may well be lively with dinghies and Canadian canoes.

3 Passing by an intermediate railway halt, our route reaches the terminus of the miniature railway at **Hunthouse Wood**. More of the shore remains to be followed, however, so continue northwards along the old track, shortly passing through a gateway and on to a wider base of potholed, compacted ballast and cinders. The lake gradually narrows to its northern tip where there is a small **car park** and turning area. You can turn around here and retrace the route back to the start for a total ride length of 4 miles (6.4km). Before doing so it is worth diverting left along the tarred access lane for 200yds (183m) to a viewpoint offering a panorama down the length of the lake. The bridge here is across the canal feeder leat, which gathers Dingle Brook beyond the reedy marsh to the north. American troops trained for the D-Day landings in 1944 in this area, while the cornfields and pastures beyond were once a popular golf course.

Rudyard Lake **STAFFORDSHIRE**

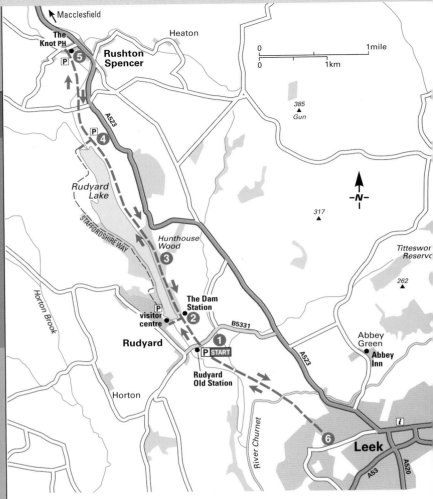

4 Back on the old railway continue to the village of **Rushton Spencer**. Look to the right of the car park for wooden bollards and the muddy railway track. Take this (not the wider potholed road) through the trees, initially a muddy stretch that soon becomes a strip of compacted gravel on a grassy trail. This leads to the old station at Rushton Spencer. There's a superb North Staffordshire Railway station house here, and also a village pub called **The Knot**.

5 This is the end of the line; from here retrace your outward route back to **Rudyard Old Station**.

6 As a final flourish it is possible to follow the old trackbed south to the outskirts of **Leek**, just short of an old tunnel. This trip is beside pastureland and partly follows the route of the canal feeder leat and the little **River Churnet**. Return the same way back to Rudyard.

The Abbey Inn

about the pub

The Abbey Inn
Abbey Green Road, Leek
Staffordshire ST13 8SA
Tel 01538 382865
www.abbeyinn.co.uk

DIRECTIONS: The Abbey Inn is 1.75 miles (2.8km) from Rudyard Old Station. Take the B5331 and turn right on to the A523. In 300yds (274m) turn left along Highup Road, signed for Meerbrook, and continue to a T-junction where you turn right. The Abbey Inn is 0.5 miles (800m) on the left

PARKING: 40

OPEN: all day, closed Tuesday

FOOD: daily, all day Saturday and Sunday May–September

BREWERY/COMPANY: free house

REAL ALE: Bass, guest beer

ROOMS: 3 bedrooms

Set in beautiful countryside on the Staffordshire moorlands on the outskirts of Leek, this magnificent building enjoys an elevated position overlooking the infant Churnet Valley. It was built with stones recovered from the ruins of the nearby Cistercian Abbey of Dieu la Cresse and looks far older than its 1702 year of construction. Inside, head for the non-smoking snug bar, a super little room with bare sandstone walls, pine tables, collections of gleaming brass and copper jugs and pans, and tip-top Bass on tap. The main bar is spacious and comfortable, with a brick fireplace, photographs of old Leek town on the walls and a good mix of furnishings. From the front patio you have views along an elm-lined lane to the sandstone tower of Leek's parish church, and glimpses of the high moorlands to the north of town.

Food

From an extensive printed bar menu you can order hot filled baps, filled jacket potatoes and local favourites like oatcakes filled with cheese, and steak and mushroom pudding. Limited daily specials may include sweet and sour pork, tarragon chicken in white wine with mushrooms, and a range of fish dishes.

Family facilities

The Abbey Inn has a children's licence so they are welcome anywhere in the pub and they have a standard menu to choose from. There's also a good play area (slides, climbing ropes) adjacent to the garden.

Alternative refreshment stops

The Rudyard Hotel and a café and snack bar in Rudyard village.

☛ Where to go from here

In Macclesfield, to the north, visit Paradise Mill and the Silk Museum which together bring to life the industry that dominated the area during the Victorian era (www.silk-macclesfield.org).

Along the Manifold

Follow England's oldest multi-user trail on an easy ride through woodland, deep gorges and past spectacular caves above part-time rivers.

Disappearing rivers

If you enjoy this ride in the summer months, then mention of rivers may strike you as a mistake. There's no water to be seen in the first 4.5 miles (7.2km) of the route, and then only intermittently thereafter. The reason is that the underlying rock is limestone and as this is extremely porous the water cannot, except in the wettest weather, maintain a flow at the surface. Instead, it trickles away down 'swallets' to carve a remarkable underground course through fissures, passages and caves which are not necessarily directly beneath the dry riverbeds.

Both the River Hamps and the Manifold exhibit this characteristic. Their combined waters eventually resurface in the National Trust's estate at Ilam, a few miles towards Ashbourne. In place of the water are rivers of green. These are the enormous leaves of butterbur, which thrive in damp places and can survive the occasional flood of water after a particularly heavy downpour. It's at Dafar Bridge, just before you reach Wettonmill, that the waters are seen permanently at the surface. At the series of swallets here, an eccentric Edwardian spent a fortune burying iron pipes into the river bed in an attempt to create real 'Water Music' by means of differing pressures as the water disappeared underground. Success was elusive!

the ride

1 The signal box at the old station is the starting point. The station itself was an interchange between the standard gauge line to Leek and the narrow gauge Leek and Manifold Light Railway. This 2ft 6in gauge line meandered through these remote valleys between 1904 and 1934, and this is the route we now follow. The ride soon joins a wide cycle-pavement beside the main road. On reaching the crossing point, carefully cross into the 'No Traffic' lane opposite. You'll immediately cross a bridge over the **River Hamps**, one of many such crossings in the next few miles. It's an easy trip along the tarred way, curving this way and that towards the enclosing valley sides.

2 Soon after **Lee House Farm** is passed (teas and meals here in season) the ash woods close in and the route becomes tunnel-like beneath these bird-rich boughs. In 2 miles (3.2km) the route curves gradually left to reveal **Beeston Tor**. In the caravan field on your right here, note the old green hut, the former refreshment room of Beeston Tor Station. Here, also, the Hamps meets with the River Manifold, flowing south beneath the Tor towards the distant River Dove. The route now runs parallel to an access road before reaching a gateway and a lane at **Weag's Bridge**.

3 Carefully cross straight over and ride through the car park to and through the gate at the end, regaining a non-trafficked

The imposing site of Thor's Cave

stretch. This is probably the most spectacular part of the valley, the river gyrating between immensely steep cliffs cloaked in some of England's finest ash woods. As the route leaves the trees around a left-hand curve, stop to look back to see the awesome location of **Thor's Cave**, high above the valley. An interpretation board tells its history; a steep path leads up to it.

4 The tortuous road between Wetton and Grindon is soon reached at a gated bridge. Beyond here, and for the next 3 miles (4.8km), you will share the road with other traffic, so care is needed. It's easier to continue ahead along the flatter route marking the old railway (the other road here loops back in after 0.5 miles/800m) to reach the popular tea rooms at **Wetton Mill**. Beware of traffic here at another minor junction. This is a good place to turn around if you are taking the shorter alternative route (9 miles/14.5km round trip).

5 Continuing north, the road keeps company with the river to reach **Swainsley Tunnel**. This is shared with vehicles, but is wide enough for bike and car and also well lit. At the far end go ahead back on to a segregated track, cycling north to pass beneath bald **Ecton Hill** and its sombre mining remains. Crossing another road here, the valley sides gradually pull back for the final approach to journey's end, the station at **Hulme End**.

6 Turn around here and retrace your route back to the start. Take care at **Weag's Bridge** to take the gated lane rather than the access road to the caravan site at Beeston Tor Farm.

4h30 — 17 MILES — 27.4 KM — LEVEL 123

SHORTER ALTERNATIVE ROUTE

3h00 — 9 MILES — 14.5 KM — LEVEL 123

MAP: OS Explorer OL24 White Peak
START/FINISH: Waterhouses Old Station, grid ref SK 085503
TRAILS/TRACKS: the entire route is tarred, some of it badly pitted, about 3 miles (4.8km) is shared with light road traffic, one tunnel
LANDSCAPE: limestone gorges, ash woods and good views towards the moorlands
PUBLIC TOILETS: Waterhouses and Hulme End stations
TOURIST INFORMATION: Leek, tel 01538 483741
CYCLE HIRE: Waterhouses Old Station, tel 01538 308609; also Brown End Farm, tel 01538 308313
THE PUB: Ye Olde Crown Hotel, Waterhouses, near Point **1** on route

Getting to the start

Waterhouses Old Station is in the village of Waterhouses, on the A523 about half-way between Leek and Ashbourne. Turn up the road beside Ye Olde Crown Hotel, pass beneath the railway overbridge and turn left into the car park, continuing to the cycle hire centre at the top end.

Why do this cycle ride?

The scenery of the Hamps and Manifold valleys should be enough to tempt anyone on to this trail which follows the trackbed of a former railway through lime-stone gorges, and passing by the remains of the old railway and the industries it served. The terminus at Hulme End has an excellent visitor centre.

Researched and written by: Neil Coates

Waterhouses STAFFORDSHIRE

400 ▲

B5053

**Manifold Valley
Visitor Centre**

Hulme
End

B5054

River Dove

**Greyhound
Inn**

P

6

**Manifold
Inn**

Warslow

Ecton

-N-

Warslow Brook

369 ▲
Ecton
Hill

367 ▲
Narrowdale
Hill

B5053

**Swainsley
Tunnel**

River Manifold

372 ▲

Wetton
Hill

PH

Butterton

P **Wetton
Mill**

5 **4**

Wetton

PH

Hope

PH

Grindon Moor

333 ▲
Ossoms
Hill

322 ▲

Ford

P Grindon

PH

P

**Thor's
Cave**

3

Beeston Tor

Stanshop

Weag's
Bridge

**Beeston Tor
Farm**

River Hamps

River Manifold

348 ▲

355 ▲
Soles
Hill

Leek

2 **Lee House**

349 ▲

Winkhill

A523

PH

Waterfall

Waterhouses

Calton

**Ye Olde
Crown Hotel**

1

P **START**
**Waterhouses
Old Station**

A523

Cauldon

PH

Ashbourne

0
0   1km

Ye Olde Crown Hotel

about the pub

Ye Olde Crown Hotel
Waterhouses, Stoke-on-Trent
Staffordshire ST10 3HL
Tel 01538 308204

DIRECTIONS: see Getting to the start
PARKING: 20
OPEN: daily
FOOD: daily
BREWERY/COMPANY: free house
REAL ALE: Tetley, Burton Ale
ROOMS: 7 bedrooms

A traditional village local on the banks of the River Hamps, Ye Olde Crown dates from around 1648 when it was built as a coaching inn. Inside are two bars, each sporting original stonework and solid beams, the latter adorned with old water jugs. Log fires are lit in cooler weather. The lounge bar with its Edwardian darkwood half-panelled walls, wall benches and a vast array of copper and brass pieces, provides a comfortable retreat for a traditional pub meal and a pint of Tetleys after a good walk. Homely accommodation includes an adjacent cottage.

Food

Offering a traditional range of pub food, dishes are freshly prepared and take in cod and chips, steak and kidney pie, ham, egg and chips and home-made curries. Daily dishes may include cottage pie, chicken and ham pasta and a good roast lunch.

Family facilities

Families will find a friendly welcome towards children who have their own good-value menu to choose from. Unfortunately, summer alfresco seating and eating is limited to a few tables by the car park.

Alternative refreshment stops

There are tea rooms at Lee House Farm and Wetton Mill along the route. The Yew Tree pub at Cauldon, just 1 mile (1.6km) from the cycle hire centre and along the same road, has a remarkable collection of polyphons, automatic pianos and curios, a great favourite with children.

☛ Where to go from here

The Churnet Valley Railway, based at Cheddleton near Leek, operates steam trains into the beautiful Churnet Valley (www.churnet-valley-railway.co.uk).

Thor's Cave in the Manifold Valley

Waterhouses   STAFFORDSHIRE

Osmaston and Shirley

Follow challenging gravel roads and peaceful back lanes between charming medieval and estate villages near Ashbourne.

Shirley village

Shirley is the oldest of a gaggle of peaceful little villages visited on this ride. The village is recorded in the Domesday book; St Michael's Church originates from this period although it was rebuilt in Victorian times when the renowned Edwardian novelists, brothers John Cowper and Theodore Francis Powys, were born in the vicarage here. Note the enormous yew tree in the churchyard. At the edge of the village is Shirley Hall, family home to the Earls Ferrers.

The valley of Shirley Brook was dammed to power mills, of which the most spectacular is the glorious Osmaston Saw Mill. This is on your left at the foot of the first long, rough descent. The vast,

landscaped lake powered the overshot wheel that still survives beneath its imposing gable. The mill itself is a rather eccentric building built in 1845 for the owners of Osmaston Hall. The cedar-tree dotted parkland still contains the walled gardens, but the hall itself is no more. Osmaston village, built largely to house workers on the estate, is a charming mix of thatched cottages and picturesque houses and farms surrounding a village duck pond.

the ride

1 Ride uphill from the **Saracen's Head**, shortly passing by the gates to **St Michael's Church** at the heart of the village of Shirley. At the bend, fork left along the level lane, singposted '**No Through Road**'. This starts a very gradual climb away from the village. Beyond the sports ground, the lane becomes a rough track.

2 Keep left at the fork by the **brick barn**, starting a hill which courses along the

edge of a largely fir tree plantation. At the top a cross-track runs along the lip of a steep slope. Go ahead here down a very steep and loose gravel descent through beech woods into the valley of **Shirley Brook**. It levels off between a huge mill pond and the old **saw mill**, before commencing an equally challenging ascent through landscaped **Osmaston Park**. Keep ahead as the surface changes to tar and then back again, before reaching the valley crest above a spinney. Ride ahead from here to reach the village of **Osmaston**.

3 It's worth exploring this charming little village before returning to the duck pond and green. Put this on your left and take the road for **Wyaston** and **Yeaveley**. A level 0.5 miles (800m) follows, the typical higher hedges with banks of wild flowers lining the route. A descent into a shallow valley means a lengthy uphill stretch before the quiet, winding lane reaches the **Shire Horse Inn** at the edge of **Wyaston**. Keep on the main lane, soon entering this straggling hamlet. Pass by the first left turn and continue beyond the village to a second left turn (Shirley and Rodsley), also signed as **National Cycle Trail 68**. Turn left here and trace the lane all the way through to the cross lanes at the heart of **Rodsley**.

4 You have a choice of routes here. To cut the full route short, turn left at this crossroads and cycle the lane back to Shirley. It's an undulating lane with a long but gradual hill after **Shirley Mill Farm** as the final flourish into **Shirley** itself. For the

Top: Village green pond in Osmaston
Left: Osmaston Saw Mill

— 3h30 — 10 MILES — 16.1 KM — LEVEL 1 2 3 —

SHORTER ALTERNATIVE ROUTE

— 2h30 — 6.75 MILES — 10.9 KM — LEVEL 1 2 3 —

MAP: OS Explorer 259 Derby
START/FINISH: Saracen's Head in Shirley (check with landlord beforehand for parking), grid ref SK 220416
TRAILS/TRACKS: back lanes and rough tracks, one section of busier road on the longer option
LANDSCAPE: mixed arable and pasture farmland, country estates
PUBLIC TOILETS: none on route
TOURIST INFORMATION: Ashbourne, tel 01335 343666
CYCLE HIRE: nearest is on the Tissington Trail at Mapleton Lane, north of Ashbourne town centre, tel 01335 343156
THE PUB: The Saracen's Head, Shirley, see Point 1 on route

🛈 Some short, steep ascents and descents and high hedges along some roads. Some very challenging short hills, which will not suit younger children or less-fit cyclists. The longer option has a section of busier road, with good sight lines. Suitable for experienced family groups.

Getting to the start
Shirley is signposted off the A52 about 6 miles (9.6km) south east of Ashbourne.

Why do this cycle ride?
This peaceful area has quiet by-roads and single-track lanes. The result is rewarding cycling in woods and fields, with good views.

Researched and written by: Neil Coates

Shirley

DERBYSHIRE

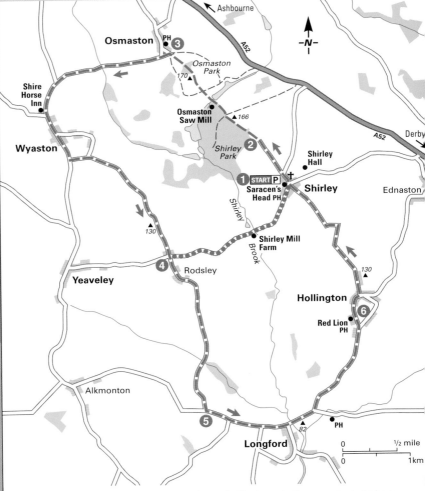

longer route, keep ahead at the crossroads, rising up through the hamlet along a narrowing lane to trace a winding course through to a T-junction with a busier road.

5 Turn left here along **Long Lane**. The road is easy riding, but take care as traffic is faster and much more common. Great views open out across south Derbyshire as you drop gradually into the valley of **Longford Brook**. In a mile (1.6km) turn left at a sign for

Hollington, starting a gradual climb up **Hoargate Lane**. At a junction with Back Lane, keep left up along **Main Street** and past the strand of houses and farms of **Hollington**.

6 Pass by the **Red Lion** and bend right to reach a cross lanes. Turn left along **Shirley Lane** (also Marsh Hollow), following this single track, partially green-centred lane through to **Shirley** village.

The Saracen's Head

Pub and church stand close together at the heart of this tiny, picturesque village. The pub (dated 1791) is an attractive white-painted brick building, with plants clambering up the walls and a tiny front garden filled with delphiniums. To the rear, outbuildings have been converted into letting cottages. Inside you'll find a single, L-shaped bar with a mix of tiled and carpeted floors, comfortable upholstered bench seating, and lovely views of rose-bedecked cottages and the churchyard. On tap you'll find a decent pint of Black Sheep Bitter and the menu lists some good, home-cooked food. A great village pub with few pretensions, an affable landlord and an easy-going atmosphere.

Food

The bar menu offers a good choice of home-cooked food, for example game pie, haddock and chips, steak and kidney pie, chicken, bacon and mushroom pie and decent filled rolls. Blackboard specials might highlight a range of curries including Thai green chicken.

Family facilities

Small children have a standard menu to select from. They can tuck into their meal in the pub or on fine days they can enjoy the flower-filled garden and the village views.

Alternative refreshment stops

Pubs at Osmaston (Shoulder of Mutton) and Wyaston (The Shire Horse).

☛ Where to go from here

Kedleston Hall is one of England's greatest country houses, built in 1765 when the entire village was moved to improve the owner's views (www.nationaltrust.org.uk).

about the pub

The Saracen's Head
Shirley, Ashbourne
Derbyshire DE6 3AS
Tel 01335 360330

DIRECTIONS: see Getting to the start
PARKING: 20. Please check beforehand with landlord before leaving your car in the car park
OPEN: closed Sunday evenings and all day Monday
FOOD: daily
BREWERY/COMPANY: free house
REAL ALE: Black Sheep Bitter, Bass, Marston's Pedigree
ROOMS: 1 en suite

Shirley

DERBYSHIRE

The Five Pits Trail

Follow an undulating off-road route between former coal mines transformed into peaceful lakes and parks.

Former Coalfield

Sparse remnants of the Derbyshire section of the old Yorks, Notts and Derby Coalfield are now a delightful string of picnic areas, fisheries, country parks and nature reserves interlinked by the Five Pits Trail. Reclamation and conservation efforts over the past 30 years have seen spoil tips and wasteland replaced by rich hay meadows and maturing woodland, while the areas of water have attracted upwards of 200 species of birds. The former collieries had a long death, with deep mines gradually being replaced by huge opencast workings, which had a lifespan of less than 20 years.

Today's landscape holds only the barest scars of these workings, and these are slowly being disguised. The cornfields and pastures, meadows and woodland are probably the greenest this area has been for 150 years. Mining still plays its part, however. The fine bird reserves at Williamthorpe Ponds are partially filled by water pumped up from old workings from miles around. This is at a constant 10°C, and in winter attracts countless water birds to a frost- and ice-free home.

the ride

1 The **Tibshelf Ponds picnic site**, a popular place with locals and fishermen, is a picturesque mix of wooded glades, meadows and ponds where Tibshelf Colliery stood. The route is known as the Five Pits Trail, recalling busier days in this part of Derbyshire. Turn left from the car park, passing between ponds and up a short incline to a cross track. A **Five Pits Trail** board indicates the way back left, an initially rough path that soon meets a graded path, which you follow right. In a short distance you'll reach the rear of the **Wheatsheaf pub** and a descent beneath a road through an underpass. Rising again, turn right on to the compacted track. Crossing a rough lane, the way drops steeply down; don't speed, as the surface is badly rutted. This descent is matched by a long gradual climb and, soon, **Hardstoft Lane** picnic site.

2 Cross the road here, continuing along the firm track to reach **Locko Plantation**, planted in 1970, a mix of spruce, sweet chestnut and other strong growing species that clothe the remnants of the old spoil heaps at Pilsley Colliery. A very steep descent ends at a gate; carefully cross and pick up the trail opposite, rising again to cross **Timber Lane** into another picnic area. The track leaves left from the rear of this, rising gently to a junction. Here keep left, heading for **Grassmoor**. The next road crossing at the edge of **Williamthorpe** is rather busier, so take care here.

3h30 · 11.5 MILES · 18.4 KM · LEVEL 2

MAP: OS Explorer 269 Chesterfield & Alfreton

START/FINISH: Tibshelf Ponds picnic area, grid ref SK 441600

TRAILS/TRACKS: old railway and hard-surfaced tracks

LANDSCAPE: mixed immature woodland, hay meadows and cornfields, with views across Derbyshire to the Peak District

PUBLIC TOILETS: none on route

TOURIST INFORMATION: Chesterfield, tel 01246 345777

CYCLE HIRE: none near by

THE PUB: Weeping Ash Country Inn, Hardstoft, see Directions to pub, page 175

Care to be taken at the road crossings. There are some short, steep climbs and some longer, gentler inclines

Getting to the start

From Chesterfield head south on the A61 through Clay Cross, turning on to the B6014 eastbound at Stretton (signed Tibshelf). At the edge of Tibshelf turn right on to the B6025, then very shortly left on the B6026 for Newton. In 300yds (274m) turn left into Shetland Road. In 500yds (457m) turn right into Sunny Bank. The car park is at the end of this road.

Why do this cycle ride?

This is a lovely ride along old railways and colliery tracks, long since reclaimed and now a green corridor between the resurgent pit villages of this part of Derbyshire. Excellent countryside and a fascinating heritage offer a moderately challenging route within sight of the edge of the Peak District.

Researched and written by: Neil Coates

Five Pits Trail

DERBYSHIRE

3 The next junction is at **Wolfie Pond**. Here, keep left for **Grassmoor** before forking right just before a gate. The open meadows here are typical of the reclaimed areas; more await you at **Grassmoor Country Park**, the end of the line. Spend time exploring the thickets, hay meadows and ponds before returning to an overbridge to commence the return journey.

4 A long, gradual climb returns you to **Wolfie Pond**, where you turn left for **Williamthorpe**. After a while pass through the outskirts of an industrial estate built on the site of another old colliery. A steep descent brings you to a wide bridge across a brook. Turn right along the wheelchair route, passing the large ponds before, at the far end, turning sharp left up an incline for **Holmewood**. Pause at the crossways at the top and look left to spot the distant, crooked spire of Chesterfield's parish church. Your way is right, soon reaching **Holmewood Bridge**. Dismount here, cross the bridge and rejoin the **Five Pits Trail** on the left, shortly crossing a busy road.

5 Pleasant woodland is superceded by cornfields and meadows before the outward route is rejoined at a junction. Follow signs for **Tibshelf** from here, crossing lanes with care.

6 Excellent views to the right (west) encompass the distant edge of the Peak District and the war memorial above **Crich**. Beyond the Wheatsheaf underpass, follow the trail back to **Tibshelf Ponds**, turning left at the lane to the car park.

Along the Five Pits Trail near Tibshelf

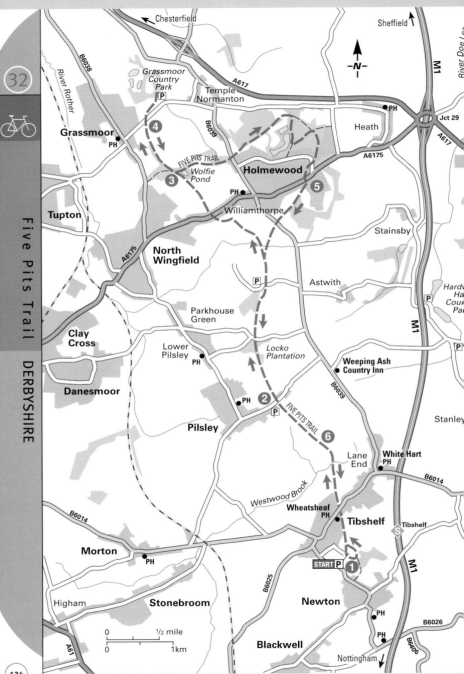

Chesterfield

Sheffield ↑

River Doe Lea

M1

–N–

B6038

River Rother

Grassmoor Country Park

P

Temple Normanton

A617

B6039

PH

Heath

Jct 29

A617

Grassmoor

PH

4

FIVE PITS TRAIL

3

Wolfie Pond

Holmewood

A6175

5

Tupton

PH

Williamthorpe

Stainsby

A6175

North Wingfield

P

Astwith

Hardwick Hall Country Park

P

Parkhouse Green

Locko Plantation

P

M1

Clay Cross

Lower Pilsley

PH

Weeping Ash Country Inn

P

Danesmoor

PH

2

B6039

Stanley

P

Pilsley

FIVE PITS TRAIL

6

Lane End

White Hart

PH

B6014

B6014

Westwood Brook

Wheatsheaf

PH

Tibshelf

Tibshelf

S

Morton

PH

START P

1

M1

Higham

B6025

Newton

PH

B6026

Stonebroom

PH

Blackwell

B6406

Nottingham ↓

0   ½ mile
0   1km

Weeping Ash Country Inn

about the pub

Weeping Ash Country Inn
Hardstoft, Chesterfield
Derbyshire S45 8AE
Tel 01246 850276

DIRECTIONS: from the Tibshelf Ponds
car park return to the B6026 and the mini-
roundabout accessing Tibshelf High Street.
Turn right up the High Street and go through
the village to a mini-roundabout at the White
Hart pub. Turn left for Chesterfield (B6039)
and drive for a mile (1.6km); the pub is on
the right at a junction

PARKING: 50

OPEN: daily

FOOD: no food Sunday evening

BREWERY/COMPANY: free house

REAL ALE: Hardys & Hansons Best, Old Trip,
Mild, seasonal beers

ROOMS: 7 bedrooms

The Weeping Ash is a very comfortable
and well-appointed country inn, catering
for loyal local drinkers, a good passing
trade and guests using the inn as a
base for exploring this peaceful part
of Derbyshire. As you would expect,
weeping ash trees surround this
rambling stone-built inn which stands in
the heart of Hardstoft. Country sporting
paraphernalia (gin traps, fishing rods,
gun cases), local photographs, and a
collection of porcelain adorn the walls
and window sills within the comfortably
furnished interior, which comprises a

'locals' bar, two lounge bars and two
neatly laid-up dining areas. You'll find
winter log fires, decent ale and a genuine
warm welcome for walkers and cyclists.
Bedrooms are housed in tastefully
converted outbuildings.

Food
From a wide ranging bar menu, opt for
the traditional chilli, liver and onions,
bangers and mash or hot filled rolls or look
to the specials board for something more
imaginative, perhaps loin of venison with
red wine and rosemary *jus* or pork loin
on buttered mash with smoked bacon
and cream sauce. There is a separate
restaurant menu.

Family facilities
Children can let off steam in the play area
by the car park and on fine days families
can make good use of the small patio
areas. Children are very welcome indoors
where younger family members have their
own menu.

Alternative refreshment stops
There are plenty of pubs and shops
in Tibshelf.

☛ Where to go from here
Hardwick Hall, one of the most magnificent
Elizabethan mansions in England, houses
remarkable tapestries, furniture and
woodwork (www.nationaltrust.org.uk).

Five Pits Trail DERBYSHIRE

Through Delamere Forest

Discover the wildlife of leafy Delamere Forest and its many trails.

Delamere Forest

Take time to have a look at Blakemere Moss, the largest of the peatlands in Delamere Forest Park, covering an area of roughly 82 acres (33ha). Peatlands are unique habitats lying somewhere between open water and dry land. The Moss started out as a water-filled hollow following the last ice age, about 11,000 years ago, created as the glacier, which covered this part of Cheshire, receded. The hollow was later colonised by plants which, as they died, sank to the bottom. However, because of the low levels of oxygen they did not decompose as plants normally do, but gradually built up layers of peat until they completely filled the hollow and created what we see today, a low-lying mire.

A gravel road through the Scots and Corsican pine trees in Delamere Forest Park

Delamere Forest woodland trail

1h30 | **7 MILES** | **11 KM** | **LEVEL 1 2 3**

MAP: OS Explorer 267 Northwich and Delamere Forest

START/FINISH: near the visitor centre at Linmere; grid ref: SJ 549705

TRAILS/TRACKS: good, stony, bumpy in places, generally dry

LANDSCAPE: woodland trails and tracks, waymarked throughout

PUBLIC TOILETS: at start

TOURIST INFORMATION: At start, and in Chester, tel 01244 402111

CYCLE HIRE: Eureka Cyclists cycle hire at the Visitor Centre, tel 0151 339 5629; www.eurekacyclists.co.uk

THE PUB: Abbey Arms, Oakmere

◑ The route is undulating and some of the tracks are stony and uneven

Delamere Forest CHESHIRE

The range of wildlife in the forest is exceptional. So, keep an eye open for a hunting fox, or a badger – though you'll be lucky to see either in broad daylight. But grey squirrels are plentiful. At dusk, you may spot noctule bats, darting among the trees. In daytime, see if you can pick out the call of the great tit – it sounds like it is calling 'Teacher, Teacher'. Patience may reward you with the sight of a treecreeper or a nuthatch. From a distance, they seem similar, but treecreepers invariably start at the bottom of trees and work their way up, while nuthatches often seem to hang upside down, and work their way down the tree.

the ride

1 Leave Linmere car park by riding left along the access road and shortly going left over a **railway bridge** onto a broad trail to a barrier. Beyond, continue along the trail. At the first major junction, near a **bench**, keep forward on the **white trail** – you follow the white trail throughout this ride. At the next junction, go left onto the

Getting to the start

The nearest village is Hatchmere, about 4 miles (6.4km) south east of Frodsham. Head south from Hatchmere to Delamere Station, and there turn right to the Linmere car park. From the south, use the A49 from Tarporley, and then branch left onto the B5152 for Delamere.

Why do this cycle ride?

The ride provides an opportunity to explore a changing woodland landscape, one that is among the foremost places in Cheshire for birds and wildlife as it is far from major urban areas.

Researched and written by: Terry Marsh

White Moor Trail, shortly bearing right. Cross a railway bridge onto a sandy track, and at the next junction, bear right again. The trail loops around and re-crosses the railway track to a junction. Go right to follow an undulating route through to a T-junction. Turn left, following the trail, which finally emerges at a roadway (**Ashton Road**).

2 Cross with care, and at the next two junctions, follow the **white trail**. At the next junction, stay with it, as it wheels right to follow another undulating stretch to a T-junction. Turn right, and then go through a dip at the bottom of which, when the trail forks, keep forward, climbing very steeply for a few moments to another junction.

3 Go forward, as the trail now twists and turns, and finally comes out to a T-junction, not far from Ashton Road.

4 Turn left, linking up with the **blue trail**. The route continues and once more crosses Ashton Road, on the other side heading down a **straight drive** through the forest. At the next junction, bear right, having now acquired the **red trail**. Keep on, with **Blakemere Moss** in view through the trees on the left. Before long the red trail diverts so continue with the blue and white trail to a T-junction, immediately at the edge of Blakemere Moss.

5 Turn right, and follow the trail as it bends around the end of the **lake**. At the next junction, keep forward for Linmere car park. Take the next track on the right to meet the outward trail at the **bench**. Bear left for the **visitor centre**, and retrace the outward route.

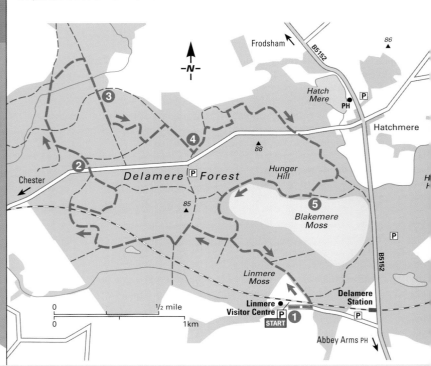

Abbey Arms

about the pub

Abbey Arms
Chester Road, Oakmere
Northwich, Cheshire CW8 2HB
Tel: 01606 882747

DIRECTIONS: return to Delamere Station and the B5152 and turn right. The pub is at the crossroads with the A556 in 2 miles (3.2km)
PARKING: 100
OPEN: daily; all day
FOOD: daily; all day
BREWERY/COMPANY: Greene King
REAL ALE: Greene King IPA & Abbot Ale, Ruddles, John Smiths Cask

Children will love the Abbey Arms, so it's well worth loading up the bikes after this woodland ride for the 2 mile (3.2km) drive to Oakmere. Owners Greene King have invested heavily in providing attractions for families, so much so that kids won't want to leave. While dad and mum savour a well-earned drink, children will be content to explore the huge adventure play area or have fun at the crazy golf (free). If you're lucky, your visit may coincide with the balloon modeller and face-painting activity, both monthly and free. At weekends there's a tuck shop for children. This may be a big, bright and breezy pub, but it has a friendly, bustling atmosphere and children will have a great time here.

Food

A wide-ranging menu lists straightforward pub food, from sandwiches to Tex-Mex dishes, lamb kebabs, steak pie, curries, roast chicken and a range of steaks and grills.

Family facilities

In addition to the above, there are high chairs, baby-changing facilities, a children's menu, and plenty of outdoor seating.

Alternative refreshment stops

None on the route. Kelsall has a range of restaurants.

☛ Where to go from here

Spend some time exploring Chester. The cathedral, founded as a Benedictine monastery in 1092, dates from 1541 and is a fine example of a medieval monastic complex (www.chestercathedral.com). At the Dewa Roman Experience discover what life was like in Roman Britain through a reconstructed street and the sights, sounds and smells of Roman Chester. Alternatively, you can visit Mouldsworth Motor Museum.

Delamere Forest   CHESHIRE

Around Willington, Utkinton and Kelsall

Vistas of the lush Cheshire countryside.

Deer sheltering from the bright sunshine in a field at Willington

Fruity traditions

The village of Willington has a long tradition of fruit growing, so keep an eye open for fields of rhubarb or strawberries, as well as apple orchards and wild damson trees in the hedgerows. Damsons, normally associated with pies and jams, were also used to provide a dye for clothing and to add to whitewash to create pastel colours for room decoration. You may also spot some deer in a large park beside the route.

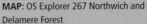

1h30 — **7 MILES** — **11 KM** — **LEVEL 123**

MAP: OS Explorer 267 Northwich and Delamere Forest

START/FINISH: Chapel Lane, Willington; grid ref: SJ 531667

TRAILS/TRACKS: entirely on quiet country lanes, but with numerous ascents and descents

LANDSCAPE: mainly farmland

PUBLIC TOILETS: none on route

TOURIST INFORMATION: Chester, tel 01244 402111

CYCLE HIRE: Eureka Cyclists Cycle Hire, Woodbank, Chester, tel 0151 339 5629; www.eurekacyclists.co.uk

THE PUB: The Boot Inn, Boothsdale

❶ Although fairly short this is an undulating ride on twisting and sometimes steep narrow lanes. Good road sense required

Getting to the start

Willington is one of many small villages in this part of rural Cheshire. The easiest approach is along the A54 Winsford to Tarvin road, or along the A556 from Northwich. An alternative is to head for Kelsall, and then by rural lanes to Willington. There is a small car park in Chapel Lane.

Why do this cycle ride?

This is a splendid exploration of pastoral Cheshire, following undulating and twisting lanes — care needed at all times against approaching traffic — and linking three charming villages. Cameo vistas of the lush Cheshire countryside come and go, seen through hedgerow gaps and from the top of country lanes.

Researched and written by: Terry Marsh

the ride

1 Leave the parking area in Chapel Lane and go left to **Willington Road**, turn left again. Follow the lane as it bends through a dip, and climbs gently flanked by hedgerows and woodland. At **Willington Hall Hotel**, turn left on a side road for **Utkinton**, climbing steeply. Soon you

start to pass through **farmland**, bound for the village of Utkinton.

2 On reaching Utkinton, turn left into **Quarrybank**, now tackling a long, steep climb with good views on the right to distract from the effort. At the top of the climb, at the entrance to **Rowley Farm**, the road swings left. Keep following Quarrybank, still climbing, now more easily, and then beginning a long descent.

3 At a T-junction, go left, signed for **Kelsall**. Pass along the edge of **Primrosehill Wood**, a detachment from Delamere Forest mainly of Scots and Corsican pine, and continue towards Kelsall, before breaking out into farmland once more. Continue past the **Summer Trees Tea Shop**, and then take the next

turning on the right into **Waste Lane**. A long, steady descent leads round a bend, and then go forward to the edge of Kelsall. At a crossroads, turn left, by **Th'ouse at Top pub**, and follow the road round towards the centre of Kelsall.

4 Opposite the church, as the road bends to the right, turn left into **Church Street**. The road now descends to a T-junction. Go left into **Common Lane**, and then take the next left, signed for Willington and Utkinton. Now climb once more, past **farms** and large houses.

5 At the next junction turn right, for **Utkinton**. Go through a dip, passing the turning to **The Boot Inn**, and keep forward to complete the ride at Chapel Lane.

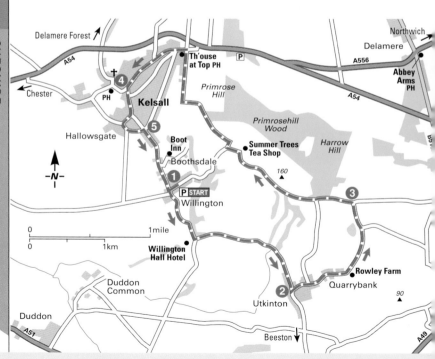

The Boot Inn

A real hidden gem in a superb setting on a wooded hillside, with views across the Cheshire plain to the Cllwydian hill, this quiet dining pub, originally a small ale house, has been converted from a charming row of sandstone cottages. Inside, it has been opened up, but you will find quarry-tiled floors, old beams, crackling log fires, and plenty of cosy alcoves around the central bar. An extension with French windows overlooks the small, sun-trap garden. The Boot offers tip-top ales – try the local Weetwood brews – decent wines and freshly prepared food.

Food

You're spoiled for choice if you fancy a hearty snack, as there are home-made soups with crusty bread, hot paninis, sandwiches (beef and horseradish), salad platters and hot baguettes filled with pork and peppers with hoisin sauce. Main meals take in braised shoulder of lamb with root vegetables and red wine, breast of duck with orange and cranberry, and smoked haddock with rarebit topping.

Family facilities

Although there are no special facilities for children, there is a family dining area and smaller portions of the main menu dishes can be ordered.

Alternative refreshment stops

Summer Trees Tea Shop on the route. Pubs and restaurants in Kelsall.

☛ Where to go from here

Children will enjoy a visit to Chester Zoo, the largest zoological gardens in Britain, with 7,000 animals and 500 species. Look for the penguin pool, the Bat Cave for endangered bat species, the National Elephant Centre, and the children's Fun Ark (www.chesterzoo.org). At Beeston Castle there are 4,000 years of history to be discovered and breathtaking views from the Pennines to the mountains of Wales (www.english-heritage.org.uk).

Utkinton CHESHIRE

Middlewood Way

Bollington

CHESHIRE

Leafy railway trackbed and canal tow path combine in this ancient transport circuit.

Poynton Coppice

Poynton Coppice is classed as ancient semi-natural woodland, and as such is a rarity. It has never been ploughed up or used for any purpose other than the production of timber. Only one-fifth of British woodland, has this select status, and Poynton Coppice has not been disturbed since 1945, when the trees were cut off at ground level and left to grow back from the base. As a result, the wood contains trees that are all of the same age. In the coppice, you get plants such as wood sorrel, woodruff and yellow archangel, all ancient woodland indicators, which demonstrate that the woodland has been established for a long time.

Coppicing used to be the most common form of woodland management, and relied upon the rotational cutting of regrowth to produce both underwood (the coppice) and large timber (standards). This not only provided medieval man with a continuous supply of wood in different sizes, but also produced woodland species with continuous woodland conditions in suitably different stages, and particularly a balance between light and shade.

the ride

1 Leave the car park by locating the path (near the play area) that leads up wide-spaced steps on the nearside of the viaduct to reach the **old railway trackbed**. You will need to carry or push bicycles up this short section. Once at the top, set off northwards along a delightful route, flanked by mixed woodland.

Above: The Macclesfield Canal

2h00 — **8 MILES** — **12.7 KM** — **LEVEL 1**23

MAP: OS Explorer 268 Wilmslow, Macclesfield and Congleton

START/FINISH: Adlington Road, Bollington; grid ref: SJ 930780

TRAILS/TRACKS: old railway trackbed in good condition and canal towpath

LANDSCAPE: rural Cheshire, farmland rising to minor hills to the east

PUBLIC TOILETS: at the start and at Nelson Pit visitor centre

TOURIST INFORMATION: Macclesfield, tel 01625 504114

CYCLE HIRE: none locally

THE PUB: The Miners' Arms, Adlington

🛈 One steep downhill section, towpath is narrow in places with some seasonal overhanging vegetation. Steps to negotiate

Getting to the start

Bollington lies about 2.5 miles (4km) north east of Macclesfield. Leave the A523 for the B5090 and travel through the centre of Bollington. Look for signs to 'Middlewood Way', one of which directs you into Adlington Road. The car park, and an adjacent children's adventure play area, is about 200 yards (180m) down the road.

Why do this cycle ride?

This is a ride of contrasts. On the one hand, there is the pleasure of cycling along a renovated railway trackbed – the Middlewood Way – through light mixed woodland, and on the other, a delightful return along the towpath of the Macclesfield Canal, which has glorious views over the foothills of the Peak District National Park.

Researched and written by: Terry Marsh

2 **Poynton Coppice** is worth a brief detour on foot (see below). After that, as before, the on-going route description is easy, as the ride simply follows the trackbed as far as **Bridge 15**. Here, leave the trackbed, and go up (dismount here) to cross a minor road and reach the **Nelson Pit visitor centre**.

3 From the visitor centre, cycle up towards the car park, and there go through a narrow gap to join the tow path of the **Macclesfield Canal**. Turn right, and immediately cross a large, cobbled humpback bridge, and go beneath Bridge 15 to continue along the tow path. There are a couple of short sections between **Bridges 18 and 19** where the tow path dips briefly to the water's edge, and, with young children, it may be safer to dismount.

4 Leave the tow path at **Bridge 26**, by climbing up steps on the right to meet a minor road. Turn right, and follow the road as it drops very steeply to the northern edge of **Bollington**, and back to the Adlington Road car park.

Right: A sign made from a wheel on the Middlewood Way

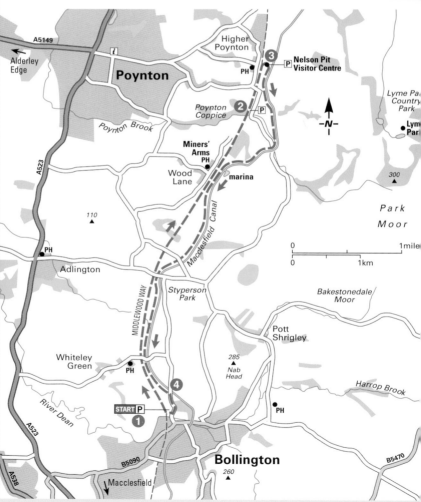

MACCLESFIELD 4 MILES · MARPLE 6 MILES
MIDDLEWOOD WAY

A5149

← Alderley Edge

Poynton

Higher Poynton

PH

3 ● P ▶ **Nelson Pit Visitor Centre**

Lyme Pa Country Park

Lym Par

Poynton Coppice

2 ● P

-N-

Poynton Brook

Miners' Arms PH ●

Wood Lane

marina

Park Moor

A523

Macclesfield Canal

300 ▲

110 ▲

PH ●

Adlington

Styperson Park

0 ——————— 1 mile
0 ——————— 1km

Bakestonedale Moor

MIDDLEWOOD WAY

Pott Shrigley

Whiteley Green

PH ●

285 ▲ Nab Head

Harrop Brook

4

River Dean

START P ● 1

PH ●

B5090

↓ Macclesfield

260 ▲

Bollington

B5470

A523

A538

The Miners' Arms

A big, bright and modern village pub that is well organised and set up to attract and entertain families. The spacious and airy bars and dining area are adorned with old farming memorabilia. Open fires add warmth and character to the place, and the friendly welcome to families extends to organising family fun days with children's entertainers. The pub is also popular with walkers and cyclists, and there are bike racks in the car park.

about the pub

The Miners' Arms
Wood Lane North, Adlington
Macclesfield, Cheshire SK10 4PF
Tel: 01625 872731
www.minersarms.info

DIRECTIONS: Wood Lane is located east off the A523 between Adlington and Poynton, just 150 yds (135m) off the cycle route

OPEN: daily; all day

FOOD: daily; all day

BREWERY/COMPANY: Spirit Group

REAL ALE: Boddingtons, guest beers

Bollington

CHESHIRE

Food

Traditional pub menus include a wide range of light meals, beef and ale pie, lamb shoulder, lasagne, oven bakes (lamb navarin and beef and beer casserole), and sweet and sour chicken.

Family facilities

In addition to the above, you'll find a children's menu, high chairs, family quiz nights, and a large garden with an adventure play area.

Alternative refreshment stops

Picnic sites along the Middlewood Way.

park (www.nationaltrust.org.uk). Nether Alderley Mill near Alderley Edge dates from the 15th-century and features original Elizabethan timberwork and Victorian machinery, and is in full working order.

☛ Where to go from here

Magnificent Lyme Park, the largest house in Cheshire, has been the home of the Legh family for 600 years and famously featured as Pemberley in the BBC's production of *Pride and Prejudice*. Visit the house and explore the historic gardens and 1,400 acre

Gisburn Forest

Gisburn Forest

LANCASHIRE

Explore Lancashire's biggest forest and discover its flora and fauna.

Gisburn Forest

Gisburn Forest is Lancashire's biggest, covering 3,000 acres (1,215ha). It was opened in 1932, around the same time as Stocks Reservoir, alongside it. The reservoir is huge, formed by damming the River Hodder and submerging the village of Stocks in the process of providing drinking water for the towns of central Lancashire. When it's full it can hold 2.6 billion gallons. Gisburn Forest and Stocks Reservoir are favoured places for birdwatchers. In springtime, keep an eye open for visiting osprey, which quite often use the reservoir for on-the-wing food supplies on their way northwards to Scotland at breeding time.

You will almost certainly spot members of the tit family, notably great, blue and coal tits, and may be lucky to see a greatspotted woodpecker. This is a good time, too, to look for orchids: Gisburn is renowned for its common spotted orchid, which flourishes in the damp conditions.

the ride

1 Set off along a narrow path from the car park, to a sharp left-hand bend, then descend, before climbing gently to pass a barrier, and reach a **broad forest trail**. Turn right, and about 100 yards (110m) later, when the track forks, keep forward. Before reaching a group of buildings (**Stephen Park**), leave the broad trail and turn right at a waymark onto a very narrow path that follows the edge of an open area, and finally heads back towards the buildings.

36

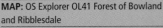

1h00 **6 MILES** **9.7 KM** **LEVEL 2**

2 On reaching **Stephen Park**, turn right on a broad trail, which immediately forks. Keep left, climbing gently, and then heading downhill. Continue following the main trail as it weaves a way through the forest to a **barrier** coming up to a T-junction, where the three main forest cycle trails divide. Here turn left, pursuing the **Purple Trail**.

3 Continue to the access to **Hesbert Hall Farm**, and there branch right, passing a barrier into a short stretch of dense woodland with a clearing ahead. Now make a long descent to cross a **stream**, beyond which the track rises to a T-junction, where the Red and Green route rejoin. Turn left.

Top: Picnic tables in Gisburn Forest
Below: A view from the Gisburn Forest Trail

MAP: OS Explorer OL41 Forest of Bowland and Ribblesdale

START/FINISH: Cocklet Hill car park; grid ref: SD 746550

TRAILS/TRACKS: mainly broad forest trails, some narrow paths and stony, bumpy trails

LANDSCAPE: forest

PUBLIC TOILETS: none on route

TOURIST INFORMATION: Clitheroe, tel 01200 425566

CYCLE HIRE: Pedal Power, Waddington Road, Clitheroe, Lancashire BB7 2HJ, tel 01200 422066

THE PUB: The Hark to Bounty, Slaidburn

🛈 Maps are useless in Gisburn - follow the Purple Trail. Stony trails and overhanging vegetation

Getting to the start

Gisburn Forest is well signed across the surrounding countryside, but the start is best reached along the B6478 from Slaidburn (south west) or Long Preston (north east).

Why do this cycle ride?

Forests like Gisburn are known for mile after mile of conifers with scarcely a decent view. But at Gisburn, more and more broadleaved trees are being planted, and areas are being cleared to allow for good views. The trails in Gisburn are waymarked; this route follows the shortest, the Purple Trail. Maps can't keep up-to-date with what is happening on the ground, so waymark chasing is the best way.

Researched and written by: Terry Marsh

Gisburn Forest

LANCASHIRE

4 The broad trail eventually leads on, after winding through the forest, to another T-junction. Here, turn left, descending, and following a bumpy route that brings **Stocks Reservoir** into view. Eventually, just before reaching a road, turn left at a **waymark post** onto a narrow path through mixed woodland to reach the **road**, which now crosses an arm of the reservoir.

5 On the other side, leave the road by turning left up a steep and narrow path – you may have to dismount here. Follow this through **woodland**, steep in places, and finally emerge at a broad forest track at a bend. Keep left and then forward, and climb to another **barrier** giving on to a T-junction. Turn right, and 100yds (110m) later turn left, having now rejoined the outward route, which is retraced to the start.

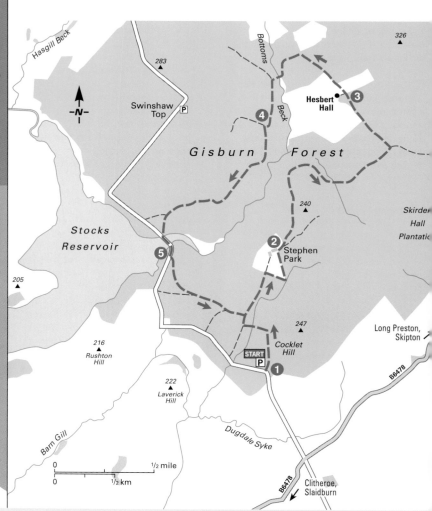

The Hark to Bounty

The setting – a beautiful village on the moors above Clitheroe – is one of the attractions of this historic stone pub. It dates from the 13th century and was known as the The Dog until 1875 when Bounty, the local squire's favourite hound, disturbed a post-inn drinking session with its loud baying. View the original first floor courtroom, for many years the main court between Lancaster and York, and still in use until 1937. It's now a function room, complete with old jury benches and a witness box. Downstairs, the atmospheric old bar has old-fashioned settles, exposed beams, a roaring log fire, plenty of brass ornaments and old pictures on the walls.

Food

Traditional favourites include home-made fish, steak and kidney pies, vegetable and cheese crumble, and grilled haddock topped with tomatoes and Lancashire cheese, supplemented by pasta and curries from the chalkboards. Snacks take in filled jacket potatoes and ploughman's lunches.

Family facilities

Children are very welcome throughout and there's a children's menu, high chairs, smaller portions and changing facilities.

Alternative refreshment stops

None on the route. Refreshments in Slaidburn and Clitheroe.

☛ Where to go from here

Developed on the site of former 17th-century cottages, Slaidburn Heritage Centre provides a site for exhibitions and information relating to the history of this fascinating area. South of Clitheroe are the 14th-century ruins of Whalley Abbey, originally a medieval monastery, set in the grounds of a 17th-century manor house, now a retreat and conference centre. Guided tours, visitor centre and coffee shop.

Gisburn Forest

LANCASHIRE

about the pub

The Hark to Bounty
Slaidburn, Clitheroe
Lancashire BB7 3EP
Tel: 01200 446246
www.harktobounty.co.uk

DIRECTIONS: from Gisburn Forest return to the B6478 and turn right for 3 miles (4.8km) to reach Slaidburn. Cross the river and take the second turning right for the pub

OPEN: daily; all day

FOOD: daily; all day Sunday

BREWERY/COMPANY: free house

REAL ALE: Courage Directors, Theakston Old Peculier, guest ales

ROOMS: 9 en suite

Green ways of Wensleydale

A glorious green terrace above one of the grandest of the Dales.

Bolton Castle

You hardly need to look for Bolton Castle. It dominates the landscape as you follow the road east of Carperby and towers over you as you toil up the lane of the main climb. The bulk of the castle dates back to 1399; it was established by Richard le Scrope, 1st Lord Scrope of Bolton and Lord Chancellor of England, and is still owned by his descendants. Much of the fabric is intact and there are rooms on five floors with furnishings and tableaux that give a vivid impression of what life in the castle was like. Mary Queen of Scots was imprisoned here for a time, though she was probably not too uncomfortable as she is said to have had 51 servants at her disposal! The castle grounds include a medieval garden, a herb garden and England's highest vineyard.

The old lead-mine site that is so conspicuous near the end of the off-road section is only one of many in the area, with the highest concentration being in nearby Swaledale. There is little to see in the way of buildings, shafts or levels here, just the large areas of bare spoil. The lack of vegetation colonising the ground indicates that there are significant residual concentrations of lead.

the ride

1 Cross the footbridge and follow a narrow tarmac path out to a wider, roughly surfaced lane. Bear right, cycle up to a road and turn right. About 2 miles (3.2km) beyond Carperby is a left turn signed for **Castle Bolton**, and the main climb of the route. Pass close under the corner of one of the **towers** and then at the top turn left, following signs for the car park and toilets.

2 Where the lane swings up into the car park, keep straight ahead through a gate and along an easy track. Follow the track through several gates and skirt to the left of some large **wooden farm sheds**; there can be muddy splashes here. After the next gate, the track becomes a little rougher, wiggling left through another gate and then right again. The track beyond is distinctly rougher, especially where it

14th-century Castle Bolton is visible on parts of the route

dips at a small **ford**; many people may prefer to walk this short section.

3 At the next gate bear left above the wall, on easy grassy going with some wheel ruts and a few avoidable rocky patches. After some perfect, almost lawn-like grass, dip to a ford, sometimes dry but still quite rough. More good grassy going follows. At the next gate bear half left on a smooth green track, following signs to Askrigg and Carperby, which gives delightful easy riding for the next 0.5 mile (800m) to **Low Gate**.

4 At Low Gate go straight ahead up the hill on more smooth green track, signed for Askrigg. Level out and descend to a gate where a rougher track (**Peatmoor Lane**) crosses. Follow the green track ahead, across a level grassy plateau, until it descends to **Oxclose Gate**. From here the track skirts to the left of the conspicuous bare ground and spoil heaps on the site of the **old lead mine**.

5 Opposite this the track acquires a good gritty surface, and soon swings down to a gate, with a **ford** just beyond. Wheel the bikes across this and beware the drop just below. Follow the stony track through another gate. Beyond this a short section is sometimes wet but can be avoided by skirting to the right, crossing ruined walls. Go up to another gate, swing left through it and down 50yds (45.7m) to a signpost.

6 For the shorter loop, descend the steep, twisting track to the little village of **Woodhall**. The surface is loose in places, and inexperienced riders should walk

| 2h00 | 12.5 MILES | 20.1 KM | LEVEL 1 2 3 |

SHORTER ALTERNATIVE ROUTE

| 1h30 | 9.75 MILES | 15.7 KM | LEVEL 1 2 3 |

MAP: OS Explorer OL30 Yorkshire Dales – Northern & Central

START/FINISH: small car park on A684 at Aysgarth; grid ref: SD 995889

TRAILS/TRACKS: good grassy tracks; a few short rough sections to be walked; return on lanes which are muddy after rain

LANDSCAPE: high pasture and moorland with views of broad pastoral dale

PUBLIC TOILETS: at Bolton Castle car park

TOURIST INFORMATION: Aysgarth Falls National Park Centre, tel 01969 663424

CYCLE HIRE: none locally

THE PUB: The Wheatsheaf Hotel, Carperby

🛑 Basic loop: steep climb on road, short sections of rough track, steep descent – mountain bike recommended. Off-road sections on longer loop are considerably rougher and only for older, experienced children – mountain bike essential

Getting to the start

Aysgarth is on the main A684 road through Wensleydale. Parking by arched footbridge about 0.5 mile (800m) west of the village.

Why do this cycle ride?

Persevere as far as Low Gate and the real worth of this ride becomes apparent. From here, you follow a magical green ribbon of a bridleway along a terrace high above the valley. You crest another slight rise and more smooth, grassy trails unfurl ahead. At the tarmac, it's downhill nearly all the way.

Researched and written by: Jon Sparks

Wensleydale

NORTH YORKSHIRE

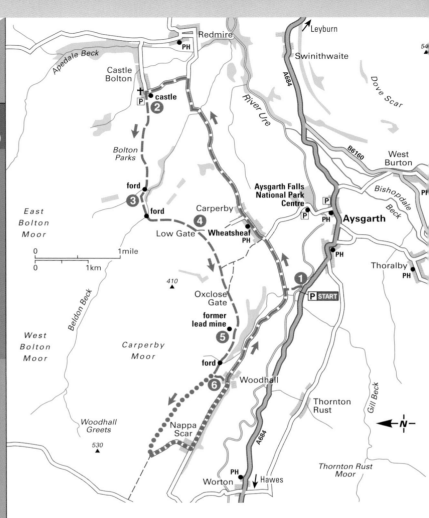

down. Turn left on the wider road for an easy run, almost entirely downhill, back to the start.

For the optional extension, turn right and climb the steep rough track. After two gates the gradient eases and the track winds through hummocks. Go through a gate alongside a **small plantation**. Beyond is the final climb, very tricky in places with bare rock and large loose stones; only experts will ride it all. Over the top there's

smooth friendly grass, then a final section of rutted track leads to a gate by a barn. The track beyond soon begins to descend, getting steeper and rougher. At a junction turn sharp left, almost immediately meeting tarmac. Follow the steep lane, which can have an overlay of loose grit in places, down into the hamlet of **Nappa Scar** and turn left on to the wider road.

The Wheatsheaf Hotel

The Wheatsheaf is quietly proud of a couple of its more famous guests. In 1941 it was the honeymoon location for Alf Wight – rather better known as 'James

Herriot' of All Creatures Great and Small fame. The following year it played host to an even more famous visitor in the shape of Greta Garbo, then performing a few miles away at Catterick Garrison. Garbo's legendary wish of 'I want to be alone' might be satisfied on the expansive moors above rather than in the sociable bar or the adjoining snug – which truly lives up to its name.

There is also a panelled dining room, and while you're there, do take a peek into the residents' lounge with its magnificent 17th-century fireplace. When the weather permits, there is outside seating at the front (south-facing) and there are more tables tucked in among shrubs and conifers behind the car park.

Food

Home-made dishes on the bar menu include giant Yorkshire puddings with various fillings, leek and parsnip hotpot, steak and bacon pie, Kilnsey trout with almonds, in addition to sandwiches and ploughman's lunches.

about the pub

The Wheatsheaf Hotel
Carperby, Leyburn
North Yorkshire DL8 4DF
Tel: 01969 663216
www.wheatsheafinwensleydale.co.uk

DIRECTIONS: village signposted off the A684 at Aysgarth
PARKING: 20
OPEN: daily; all day Saturday and Sunday; closed Monday lunchtime in winter
FOOD: daily
BREWERY/COMPANY: Black Sheep Brewery
REAL ALE: Black Sheep Best & Special, Websters Yorkshire Bitter
ROOMS: 8 en suite

Family facilities

Children are welcome in the pub and overnight (one family room), and there's a children's menu.

Alternative refreshment stops

The George & Dragon in Aysgarth village and a café at Aysgarth Falls National Park Visitor Centre.

☞ Where to go from here

Stop off at Bolton Castle (www.boltoncastle.co.uk); head for Hawes to visit the fascinating Dales Countryside Museum (www.destinationdales.org.uk); watch traditional ropemaking at the Hawes Ropemaker (www.ropemakers.co.uk); or learn about cheese-making at the Wensleydale Cheese Experience (www.wensleydale-creamery.co.uk).

Wensleydale   NORTH YORKSHIRE

The Hambleton Hills

An exciting ride on the top of the moors.

Hambleton Hills

The long tarmac lane that takes you north from Sutton Bank seems unremarkable in itself, but there's a history, dating back to the Iron Age tribes who settled here around 400BC. They would have used this road long before the Romans followed in their footsteps. Evidence of the tribes' existence is all around you, from the burial tumuli near the escarpment's edge to a 60 acre (24.3ha) fort on Roulston Scar. Strangely, there are no traces of any hut circles within the fort's huge ramparts. It is possible that this was a temporary bastion in times of war, but it could also have been a huge cattle corral for neighbouring settlements.

Hambleton has many connections with beasts of burden. When the Great North Road became a turnpike the Scottish cattle drovers turned to the hills to avoid the tolls. The previously mentioned road became known as the Hambleton Drove Road, a busy highway with several drovers' inns along the way. Hereabouts there were two – one, Dialstone House, is now a farm, but the other, the Hambleton Hotel, remains an inn.

Hambleton has long been associated with racehorses. In 1740 an Act of Parliament decreed that racing could only take place at Hambleton, York and Newmarket. Fifteen years later, however, the racecourse was closed, but nearby Hambleton House is to this day a well-known training stable for thoroughbreds.

the ride

1 Before you leave the centre, take a look at the panoramas to the south and west, for you can see for miles across the flat fields of the Vales of Mowbray and York. Alf Wight, alias the fictional vet James Herriot, believed this view to be the finest in England. Apparently, both York Minster and Lincoln Cathedral are discernible on a clear day. From the visitor centre car park, turn left up

the lane signed to Cold Kirby and Old Byland. Take the left fork past **Dialstone Farm** and its tall **communications mast**, before heading north on an ever-so-straight lane through cornfields and pastures.

2 The lane comes to a T-junction by a triangular wood, the **Snack Yate Plantation**. This is a popular starting point for serious mountain bikers who will swoop down on rough tracks through Boltby Forest. Your route turns left down the lane. It's a gentle downhill for a short distance. Just before the road dives off the edge, turn left through a gate on to a grassy bridleway along the escarpment's edge. You're riding on the Hambleton Hills. The first stretch is slightly uphill, but the track is firm and the views wide-sweeping. You'll see a small **reservoir** surrounded by forestry and the village of **Boltby** huddled under a pastured hill.

3 The bridleway climbs to the top of the hill at **High Barn**, an old stone ruin shaded by a fine stand of sycamore. The going eases and the cliffs of an **old quarry** appear ahead. Here the bridleway goes through a gate on to a walled track for a short way. Ignore the bridleway on the left, which goes back to the Hambleton Road, and stay with the edge path to the hill above the rocks of **Boltby Scar**. This is the highest point of the ride. Note the wind-warped larch trees around here – they add to the views over the edge and across the expansive Vale of Mowbray.

4 The trees of the **Boltby Forest** now cover the west slopes, almost to the summit.

A view near Boltby Forest

2h00	7.4 MILES	12 KM	LEVEL 1 2 3

MAP: OS Explorer OL26 North York Moors – Western

START/FINISH: Sutton Bank Visitor Centre; grid ref: SE 516831

TRAILS/TRACKS: good level lanes followed by undulating bridleways on the escarpment's edge

LANDSCAPE: pastoral plateau and moorland ridge

PUBLIC TOILETS: Sutton Bank Visitor Centre

TOURIST INFORMATION: Sutton Bank Visitor Centre, tel 01845 597426 (weekends only Jan– Feb)

CYCLE HIRE: none locally

THE PUB: The Hambleton Inn, Sutton Bank

 A short section near Point 5 becomes narrower and with a few rocks in places. Inexperienced cyclists should dismount

Getting to the start

Sutton Bank is 6 miles (9.7km) east of Thirsk. Take the A170 Scarborough turn-off from the A19 at Thirsk. This climbs the difficult road to Sutton Bank (caravans prohibited). The centre and car park are on the left at the top.

Why do this cycle ride?

You can enjoy some of the north of England's best views and experience a bit of adventure with a ride on the 'edge'.

Researched and written by: John Gillham

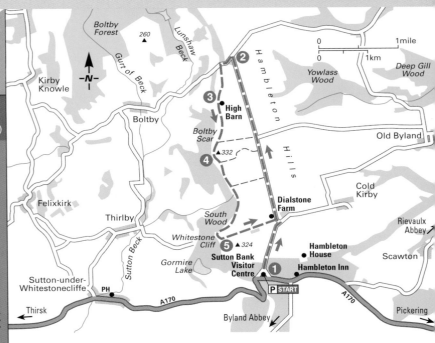

Beyond the next offshoot bridleway, which you should ignore, the path becomes narrower with a few embedded rocks in places. The difficulties are short-lived, but the younger and less experienced riders might prefer to dismount. The riding gets easier again as the bridleway arcs right above **South Wood**. At the end of this arc you turn left to a sign that tells you that the continuing edge path is for walkers only. This is a fine spot to linger and admire the views. To the south the half-moon-shaped **Gormire Lake** lies in a nest of broad-leaved woodland and beneath the sandy-coloured **Whitestone Cliff**.

5 When you've rested, turn left on a bridleway to **Dialstone Farm**. This heads east across large prairie-like fields. Beyond a wood, the **High Quarry Plantation**, you'll see the hurdles of the **equestrian centre**.

Past the large **farm** turn right along the tarred lane, then right again, back to the visitor centre car park.

On a track near Boltby Forest

The Hambleton Inn

about the pub

The Hambleton Inn
Sutton Bank, Thirsk
North Yorkshire YO7 2HA
Tel: 01845 597202

DIRECTIONS: beside the A170 Thirsk to Scarborough road, at the top of Sutton Bank	
PARKING: 50	
OPEN: all day Sunday; closed Monday except Bank Holidays	
FOOD: daily; all day Sunday	
BREWERY/COMPANY: free house	
REAL ALE: local Hambleton ales	

Just a few hundred yards from the Sutton Bank edge and those famous James Herriot views, The Hambleton Inn is backed up by sprucewoods. It's an extremely popular pub with walkers and cyclists. The whitewashed Georgian building was once frequented by cattle drovers, who herded their beasts across the high Hambleton Drove Road. The inn has a large lawned garden to the rear, and flagged patios to the front and sides. Expect an enthusiastic and extremely friendly service, imaginative pub food, summer hog roasts and live entertainment.

Food
Food is freshly prepared and a cut above the pub norm. Snacks include a traditional ploughman's lunch and baked baguettes (crab and lemon mayonnaise, roast ham and pickle), while more substantial bar meals range from beef burger and chips and deep-fried Whitby haddock and chips to liver and bacon with onion gravy, and pasta with poached salmon and lemon and watercress sauce. Separate evening menu.

Family facilities
The pub is really geared up for families. Children are very welcome inside the pub where an above-average children's menu is available for younger family members, as well as smaller portions of adult dishes. When the weather's fine there's good patio seating and a large lawned area with play area to keep children amused.

Alternative refreshment stops
Café at Sutton Bank Visitor Centre.

☛ Where to go from here
Visit nearby Rievaulx Abbey (www.english-heritage.org.uk), once the most important Cistercian abbey in Britain; the soaring ruins are powerfully atmospheric in the beautiful Rye valley. Another evocative ruin to explore is Byland Abbey at the base of the Hambleton Hills, or head east to Pickering to take a steam railway journey through stunning scenery on the North Yorkshire Moors Railway (www.northyorkshiremoorsrailway.com).

Hambleton Hills

NORTH YORKSHIRE

Terrington and Castle Howard

Terrington

NORTH YORKSHIRE

A ride through Yorkshire's most magnificent estate.

Castle Howard

Six years after Henderskelfe Castle burned down in 1693, Charles Howard, the 3rd Earl of Carlisle, asked his friend, Sir John Vanbrugh, to design its replacement, Castle Howard. Vanbrugh at this time was a complete novice, though he would later design Blenheim Palace. However, he formed a successful team with Christopher Wren's clerk, Nicholas Hawksmoor. The building programme would last 100 years, the lifetime of three earls, but the legacy left Yorkshire with one of Britain's most elegant palaces, set among magnificent and colourful gardens, complete with lakes, fountains, classical statues and temples.

In the house itself, the marble entrance hall is lit subtly by a dome. Explore further and you'll see treasures built up over centuries, including antique sculptures, fine porcelain, and paintings by Rubens, Reynolds and Gainsborough. In 1940 fire came to haunt the Howards once more. A devastating blaze destroyed the dome and twenty of the rooms, leaving the palace open to the elements and in need of extremely costly renovation. That it was done so successfully is all down to George Howard, who inherited the estate after the death of his two brothers in World War Two.

the ride

1 Terrington is a peaceful little village with fine sloping greens either side of the main street, giving the place a spacious feel. The cottages, which are largely Victorian, are built with local limestone. Above them, just off the main street, stands the church, a square-towered building that dates back to Saxon times – there's an

Castle Howard is set amongst 1,000 acres (405ha) of grounds and gardens

2h00	9.3 MILES	15 KM	LEVEL 123

Anglo-Saxon window in the south aisle. Much of the structure is 13th-century but was modernised around 1860.

Heading east past the ivy-clad **Bay Horse Inn** towards Castle Howard is slightly downhill, a nice start – the tea rooms tempt you straight away. If it's hot, a splendid avenue of trees on the way out of the village will offer some welcome shade.

2 Take the right fork, signed 'to Ganthorpe, York', 0.5 mile (800m) out of the village. Now you pay for your downhill as the road climbs to the top of **Cross Hill**, where there's a good view back to Terrington. The lane levels out as it passes through the stone cottages and farms of **Ganthorpe**. This hamlet was the birthplace of the historian, Arthur Toynbee (1886–1975) and the botanist, Richard Spruce (1817–93), who travelled to places like the Andes and the Amazon in search of specimens for scientific research. There's another short downhill section as the lane bends right by **Sata Wood**, then it's uphill again.

3 Turn left at the T-junction, where you get glimpses of a couple of the **Castle Howard domes**, then left at the crossroads following the directions to Slingsby and Castle Howard. The road, known as the **Stray**, is straight and madly undulating like a Roman road, with wide verges and avenues of trees lining the way. Some of the traffic is speedy so take care! Soon you pass beneath the extremely narrow stone arch of the Castle Howard estate's **Carrmire Gate**, which is flanked by castellated walls, then you come upon the gate house with its pyramidal roof. There's a roundabout next to a 100ft (91m) **obelisk** of 1714 dedicated

MAP: OS Explorer 300 Howardian Hills and Malton

START/FINISH: roadside parking in the main street, Terrington; grid ref: SE 670706

TRAILS/TRACKS: country lanes with some hills

LANDSCAPE: rolling pastoral hills and parkland

PUBLIC TOILETS: at Castle Howard

TOURIST INFORMATION: Malton, tel: 01653 600048

CYCLE HIRE: none locally

THE PUB: Bay Horse Inn, Terrington

🛑 The hilly terrain might be a little tiring for younger children. Take care on the Stray (Point 3) – some of the traffic here is faster than it should be

Getting to the start
From the A64 north east of York, follow the signs for Castle Howard and take the first left after the castle entrance. Alternatively, from Helmsley follow the B1257 signed 'Malton' to Slingsby and turn right for Castle Howard. Turn right by the castle's Great Lake.

Why do this cycle ride?
This pleasant ride combines the sophistication of the Castle Howard Estate and the simple beauty and rural charm of the Howardian Hills.

Researched and written by: John Gillham

Terrington

NORTH YORKSHIRE

to Lady Cecilia Howard. Here you need to decide whether or not to visit the palace (highly recommended).

4 Continuing down the Stray you'll pass the **Obelisk Ponds**, which are enshrouded by woodland, then the **Great Lake**, across which you get a great view of the palace and its many domes.

5 Turn left for 'Terrington' at the crossroads just beyond the lake. The lane soon swings right and climbs through the trees of **Shaw Wood**. If you have mountain bikes and

Neatly lawned houses at Terrington at the end of your ride

are experienced riders you could take the bridleway at the next bend (**South Bell Bottom**) then double back on the track over Husket and Ling Hills to meet the lane further west. If not, continue with the lane, which winds downhill across **Ganthorpe Moor** to meet the outward route by the first T-junction east of Terrington. Though you've still got the trees for shade, the downhill is now an uphill so you'll probably deserve that refreshment at the **Bay Horse Inn**.

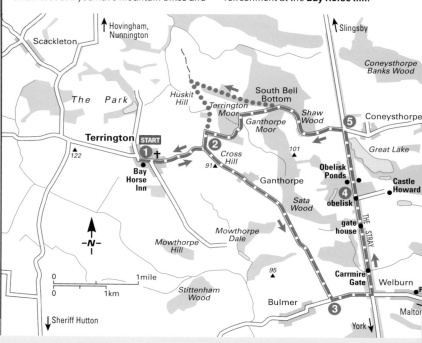

Bay Horse Inn

about the pub

Bay Horse Inn
Main Street, Terrington
Malton, North Yorkshire YO60 6PP
Tel: 01653 648416

DIRECTIONS: see Getting to the Start; pub in the village centre	
PARKING: 30	
OPEN: daily; all day	
FOOD: daily; all day	
BREWERY/COMPANY: free house	
REAL ALE: Theakston Best, Black Sheep Riggwelter, John Smith's Cask, guest beers	
ROOMS: 4 en suite	

Terrington is an idyllic peaceful little village with stone cottages and greens, surrounded by the rolling Howardian Hills. The homely and friendly 400-year-old Bay Horse Inn, formerly a tailor's shop, reflects this rural charm from the outside to the interior. An archway of ivy surrounds the door of this whitewashed stone-built pub. Inside there's a welcoming log fire in the cosy lounge, while the public bar offers time-honoured pub games in the form of darts, dominoes, shove ha'penny and cribbage. At the back there's a conservatory adorned with old farm tools, and a small but attractively planted garden.

Food
Well-liked bar food takes in sandwiches, salads and sausage and mash and more substantial offerings like lambs' liver and onions, loin of pork in cider and apple cream sauce, steak and ale pie, and lamb shank with mash and fresh vegetables.

Family facilities
Families are very welcome inside the pub, especially in the conservatory. There's a typical children's menu and the garden is sheltered and safe for children.

Alternative refreshment stops
Tea Rooms, Terrington (by the post office); Hayloft and Lakeside Cafés at Castle Howard; The Malt Shovel, Hovingham – a fine pub just north of Terrington.

🖝 Where to go from here
Don't miss out on exploring Castle Howard and its wonderful gardens and landscaped grounds (www.castlehoward.co.uk). Near Malton is the Eden Camp Modern History Theme Museum (www.edencamp.co.uk) which tells the story of civilian life in World War Two. Within reach is Nunnington Hall (www.nationaltrust.org.uk), Sherriff Hutton Castle and Yorkshire Lavender in Terrington.

Terrington

NORTH YORKSHIRE

Dalby Forest

Dalby Forest

NORTH YORKSHIRE

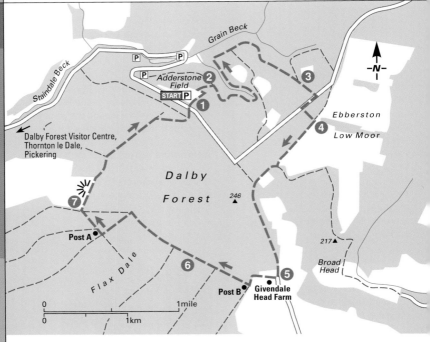

A short ride through the forest where you seek the wildlife that's watching you.

The Forest

In 1919, when the Forestry Commission was founded, Britain's woodland cover had shrunk to around 5 per cent, which meant we had to import large quantities of timber to meet the increasing needs of industry. In Yorkshire they turned to Dalby on the south east corner of the North York Moors. The area, once part of the Royal Hunting Forest of Pickering, had degenerated into boggy heathland, poverty-stricken upland farms and a huge rabbit warren that provided fur for a felt hat industry. Several streams drained the moorland plateau and flowed south west into Dalby Beck, forming a rigg and dale landscape. Scrub oak and birch clustered around these streams, but in general the ground was only suitable for conifers. By 1921 the planting began and within years over 8,500 acres (3,442ha) of Sitka Spruce and Scots Pine had covered the ground.

Conservationists hated these new forests, complaining that wildlife had been decimated, but today, if you stay quiet and look hard enough, you'll see that it's really quite abundant. In quieter corners you may stumble upon the Bambi-like roe deer. Many of the mammals, such as the pygmy shrew and the otter, stay clear of humans and it's bird-life you're more likely to spot. Besides the common blue tits, you're quite likely to see a wading heron, or a tiny warbler such as that summer visitor, the chiffchaf, so called because of its birdsong.

the ride

1 The **green cycle route** begins beyond the trees at the south east end of the large **Adderstone Field** (the furthest from the visitor centre). Here you turn left along a narrow slightly downhill track. Though still easy, it's the most difficult section of the route – use gentle braking if you're a little unsure. Ignore two lesser, unsigned left fork tracks.

2 Turn right along a much wider forestry track which takes a winding course round the afforested valley of **Worry Gill**. Where the more demanding red route goes off on a rough track to the right, your green route goes straight on, still using a well-graded track.

3 Where a track doubles back, go straight on up a steady hill before meeting the **forest drive** again. Cross this with care – it can be quite busy on summer weekends – before turning right along it for 200yds (183m). Turn left along a narrow path signed with red and green waymarkers and just before a 30 mile per hour speed limit sign (hope you were not speeding!). If you're early and it's summer, you may be able to dally and eat some of the bilberries that grow beside the path.

| 2h00 | 6 MILES | 9.7 KM | LEVEL 1 2 3 |

MAP: OS Explorer OL27 North York Moors Eastern Area

START/FINISH: car park at Adderstone Field, Dalby Forest; grid ref: SE 883897

TRAILS/TRACKS: forestry roads and a few narrow paths, mostly well graded

LANDSCAPE: conifer forest

PUBLIC TOILETS: Visitor Centre, Lower Dalby (not on route)

TOURIST INFORMATION: Dalby Forest Visitor Centre, tel 01751 460295

CYCLE HIRE: Cycle Hire Kiosk next to Visitor Centre, Low Dalby, tel 01751 460400

THE PUB: New Inn, Thornton le Dale, off the route

🚴 There's a short, rough and slightly downhill section of track at the start. The forest drive road needs to be crossed with care twice

Getting to the start

From the A170 at Thornton le Dale head north on a minor road signed the Dalby Forest, then turn off right on the Dalby Forest Drive, where you'll come to the tollbooths. Adderstone Field, the start of the ride, lies about 5 miles (8km) beyond the visitor centre.

Why do this cycle ride?

It's a good introduction to forest tracks, with just a few hilly bits to get your pulse racing, but nothing frightening to put off the inexperienced. There's lots of wildlife for the observant cyclist.

Researched and written by: John Gillham

Dalby Forest

NORTH YORKSHIRE

4 The path reaches a **flinted road** at the south east edge of the forest. Turn right along this then left at the next junction. Looking left, you'll see the rougher high pastures of **Ebberston Low Moor** decline to the greener, more fertile fields of the **Vale of Pickering**.

5 Turn right just before reaching **Givendale Head Farm** along a rutted farm track with a grassy island in the middle. Turn right at the next junction (**Post B**) on a downhill section, followed by an uphill one where you're joined by a **farm track** from the left.

6 A long hill follows to a wide junction where you go straight on along a tarred lane. A sign tells you that you're now at the head of **Flaxdale**. Stay with the tarred lane at the next bend and junction. Turn right at the crossroads along a long sandy track (**Post A**), then right again at the next junction. Note the **linear earthwork** to both left and right – nobody seems to know the exact origins of these.

7 After going straight on at the next junction past a fine stand of **Scots pines,** you get fine views over the farm pastures of High Rigg to **Levisham Moor**. There's another downhill section followed by an uphill one. Take a right fork at **Newclose Rigg**. Where the red route goes straight on, your green route veers right along the main track. There's a downhill left curve beyond which you take the **upper right fork**, which brings the route back to the forest drive opposite Adderstone Field.

Top: A track in Dalby Forest

New Inn

A Georgian coaching inn in the centre of a picturesque village complete with beck running beside the main street, and village stocks and market cross. The inn retains its old-world charm, with log fires, low beamed ceiling, traditional furniture and hand-pulled ales.

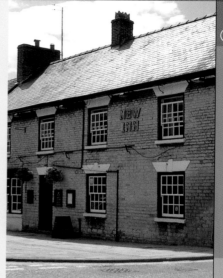

Food

Freshly cooked food is one of the pub's attractions, with many tempting choices on the interesting menu and specials board: medallions of beef fillet, pan-fried chicken supreme, grilled halibut steak, rack of lamb, and salmon fillet with baby cucumber show the range of main courses.

Family facilities

Children are welcome in the dining area if eating and they have their own menu.

about the pub

New Inn

Maltongate, Thornton le Dale
Pickering, North Yorkshire YO18 7LF
Tel: 01751 474226

DIRECTIONS: beside the A170 in the centre of the village
PARKING: 15
OPEN: daily; all day in summer
FOOD: daily
BREWERY/COMPANY: Scottish & Newcastle
REAL ALE: Theakston Black Bull, John Smith's, Greene King Old Speckled Hen
ROOMS: 6 en suite

Alternative refreshment stops

There's a café and kiosk at the Dalby Forest Visitor Centre.

☛ Where to go from here

The Beck Isle Museum at Pickering houses many photos and artefacts that will show you the local customs. The museum follows the historical developments in social and domestic life of the last two centuries (www.beckislemuseum.co.uk). Re-live the golden age of steam with a ride on the North Yorkshire Moors Railway, Britain's most popular heritage railway, through 18 miles (29km) of stunning scenery (www.northyorkshiremoorsrailway.com).

Dalby Forest

NORTH YORKSHIRE

Warter Wold

A pleasant countryside ride discovering the rolling Yorkshire Wolds and some charming villages.

uninhabitable swamps. These settlers made clearings and left much evidence of their existence in the form of burial mounds (tumuli) and earthwork dykes – you'll see one of those from the bridleway south of Huggate.

The Yorkshire Wolds

The Yorkshire Wolds form the most northerly outcrop of chalk in Britain. Here, smooth, rounded hills top shallow valleys with streams trickling through grass and woodlands. Chalk makes rich fertile ground for farming and the prehistoric settlers did just that. In those days the hills were tree-covered, good for providing cover from wild animals, while the valleys were

The Romans conquered the region but settled quite peaceably here; you'll be riding along one of their roads into Warter. But the Normans were a little more brutal – William the Conqueror, angered by the resistance of the locals, set about his 'harrying of the North'. The whole area was sacked and set ablaze. Gone were the trees. The Wolds people never replanted them – some say it is because they believed that witches could hide behind them.

The Enclosure Acts of the late 1700s brought more significant changes. The large, straight-edged fields with long hawthorn hedges were set up then, allowing the patchwork of pasture and cornfields you see today. Villages like Warter and North Dalton had popped up in the valleys to be near the water table – look out for the dewponds and the water pumps.

the ride

1 From the car park, cycle back to the village green and turn right past the old **church**. Take the first right, a narrow road climbing steeply at first with a shallow grassy vale to the left.

2 There's a T-junction at the top of the hill, where you turn left signed '**Market Weighton & Dalton**', on the level, at first, then, beyond a left-hand bend, an easy descent. By a red-bricked house and a narrow wood turn right, highlighted by a **Middleton signpost**. After the first bend the road passes some high manicured hedges then beneath magnificent beech trees near **Middleton Lodge**.

3 The lane comes to a junction on the northern edge of **Middleton-on-the-Wolds**. Turn right if you want to have a look around then return to the same spot, or left past a **post box** and the last houses to continue the journey. From the top of the first hill there are fine views northwards across the rolling Wolds. There's a small

Looking across Warter Wold from the Bridleway

5h00	**15 MILES**	**24 KM**	**LEVEL 123**

41

MAP: OS Explorer 294 Market Weighton & Yorkshire Wolds Central

START/FINISH: Warter village car park; grid ref: SE868502

TRAILS/TRACKS: country lanes, some hilly and an easy section of grass-track bridleway

LANDSCAPE: rolling hills

PUBLIC TOILETS: none on route

TOURIST INFORMATION: York, tel 01904 621756

CYCLE HIRE: none locally

THE PUB: Wolds Inn, Huggate

🛑 A long route with some hills. Not suitable for young children

Getting to the start

Leave the York ring road on the A1079, then at Barmby Moor take the Pocklington turn-off (B1246) to the left. Warter lies 5 miles (8km) along this road. Turn right at the village green to the signed village car park.

Why do this cycle ride?

If you want a good summer's day ride and would like to sample the Yorkshire Wolds without taking to mountain biking, this is your route.

Researched and written by: John Gillham

Warter Wold

EAST YORKSHIRE

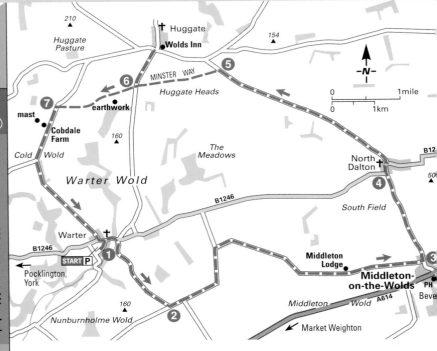

dip preceding a steady climb into Dalton village, where you meet the B road at the apex of a bend.

4 Go straight on towards the village centre where there's a splendid duck pond, then go left by the **Methodist chapel**. The road climbs steadily and is pleasant with flower-decked verges.

5 After 3 miles (4.8km) turn left by a large **ash tree** on to a wide, rutted, grassy bridleway, part of the Minster Way. This firm track, lined by thorn bushes to the right and thistles to the left, eases across **Huggate Heads**. To the south the fields fall away into a shallow wooded vale. After 1.5 miles (2.4km) the bridleway comes to another lane.

6 Turn right to reach **Huggate**, and the **Wolds Inn**. Return along the lane to the bridleway. This time turn right on a similar

grass track, which winds around hillsides above two steep-sided grassy vales so typical of the Yorkshire Wolds.

7 Just beyond the second the track comes to the road. Climb left, past the communications mast and **Cobdale Farm**, then take the left fork, signed 'Warter'. It's the course of a Roman road, which, beyond **Lings Plantation**, makes a long steady descent. Brake gently here to control your speed. At the bottom of the hill lies **Warter** and an old building with a clock, dated 1868. Turn left here, then right at the green to pass a charming terrace of **whitewashed cottages** with thatched roofs and porches fronted by the quaint cast-iron street lamps from the Victorian era. The road leads back to the car park.

Wolds Inn

about the pub

Wolds Inn
Driffield Road, Huggate
Pocklington, East Yorkshire YO42 1YH
Tel: 01377 288217

DIRECTIONS: village signposted south off A166 between York and Driffield. Pub in village centre
PARKING: 45
OPEN: closed all day Monday and Friday lunch (except Bank Holidays)
FOOD: daily
BREWERY/COMPANY: free house
REAL ALE: Tetley, Timothy Taylor Landlord, summer guest beer
ROOMS: 3 en suite

Probably the highest inn on the Yorkshire Wolds, this venerable village local, close to the parish church, also claims 16th-century origins. Beneath a huddle of tiled roofs and white-painted chimneys, it sports an interior of wood panelling, gleaming brassware and open fires. Separate locals' games room and good real ale on tap. Pleasant rear garden with views of the surrounding Wolds. A great favourite with cyclists.

Food
Baguettes and sandwiches line up alongside bar main dishes of gammon and egg, home-made steak pie, grilled fillet of plaice, pork chops and mushrooms, and a weekly changing curry. A typical restaurant meal may feature cod and pancetta fishcakes, followed by rack of lamb cooked in garlic, or decent steaks with all the trimmings. Sunday roast lunches.

Family facilities
Children are very welcome inside the pub. There's a children's menu, smaller portions of adult dishes are also available, notably good-value Sunday lunches, and there are high chairs.

Alternative refreshment stops
The Star Inn at North Dalton.

☛ Where to go from here
Head off to see Burnby Hall Gardens and Stuart Collection in Pocklington, where there are 9 acres (3.6ha) of beautiful gardens with lakes, woodland walks and a Victorian garden to explore. In Beverley, the Museum of Army Transport tells the story of army transport from horse-drawn wagons to the present.

Warter Wold

EAST YORKSHIRE

Hudson Way

Hudson Way

EAST YORKSHIRE

Gentle riding through rich, rolling farmland.

The Hudson Way

The route takes its name from George Hudson (1800–71), originally from Howsham, about 20 miles (32km) away, who became known as the 'Railway King'. Hudson was a financier (and sometimes a less than scrupulous one) rather than an engineer, who masterminded many of the great railway projects in the boom years of the middle 19th century. The line from York,

Cycling out of South Dalton

via Market Weighton to Beverley, was a relatively small part of his empire.

There are abundant opportunities for wildlife-spotting all along the railway route, but Kiplingcotes Chalk Pit is of particular interest. First worked in the 1860s to provide chalk for the railway, the pit closed in 1902 and is now managed as a Nature Reserve by Yorkshire Wildlife Trust. It features several distinct habitats: the quarry floor, the steep chalk faces, and the original grassland above, making it home to a wide variety of wild flowers. These in turn support a great range of butterflies, at their best in July, when more than 20 species may be seen.

Among the various crops farmed locally, one of the most distinctive yet least familiar is borage. At a distance you may think that the purple-blue fields are growing lavender but at closer range the two plants are quite different. Borage is a sturdy plant, which produces star-shaped flowers. The young leaves were traditionally used in salads and the flowers are also edible, but it is principally grown as a source of oil, and has many uses in aromatherapy and herbal medicine; ancient wisdom has it that it will cheer you up and give you courage. It is not recommended to handle borage plants without gloves as they are covered in stiff, prickly hairs.

the ride

1 With your back to the road, turn right along the **railway track**. The actual riding surface is quite narrow, flanked by lush grass and then flowery banks, with lots of willowherb and scabious. Soon pass an access gate for **Kiplingcotes Chalk Pit** (the crumbling chalk faces can be seen by simply continuing along the track). Dip down through staggered barriers to cross a farm track where a bridge is missing, and up the other side to resume. The track soon leads out into a car park at the former Kiplingcotes station. There is an information board here and the **old signal box** is sometimes open as an information centre.

2 Keep straight on past the old platforms. Negotiate another set of barriers and dip, and shortly after cross the tarmac lane to **Wold Farm**. The views open out briefly but then it's back into a cutting – watch out for nettles and brambles. Go up a slight rise

| 2h00 | 10.75 MILES | 17.3 KM | LEVEL 1 2 3 |

SHORTER ALTERNATIVE ROUTE

| 1h30 | 10 MILES | 16.1 KM | LEVEL 1 2 3 |

MAP: OS Explorer 294 Market Weighton and Yorkshire Wolds Central
START/FINISH: Car park near Kiplingcotes Chalk Pit; grid ref: SE 909430
TRAILS/TRACKS: Old railway track, narrow in places; optional return on lanes
LANDSCAPE: rolling farmland with scattered woods
PUBLIC TOILETS: none on route
TOURIST INFORMATION: Beverley, tel 01482 867430
CYCLE HIRE: none locally
THE PUB: Light Dragoon, Etton

Getting to the start
Follow A1079 east from York, skirt round Market Weighton and climb up on to the Wolds. Turn left at the first cross-roads and follow the road down to a junction just before a bridge. Turn left then go for about 1.25 miles (2km) to a small car park on the right.

Why do this cycle ride?
To many people a rolling landscape of chalk hills, broad fields and scattered woods, is quintessentially English. The Yorkshire Wolds produces gentle scenery, most of it given over to farming. The route follows the trackbed of a former railway line, which you can follow for the full 11 miles (18km) from Market Weighton to Beverley. Those who want to avoid road riding entirely can ride it as an out-and-back route, but the return through the lanes is very pleasant.

Researched and written by: Jon Sparks

to cross a lane and dip back down on to the **railway track**. Continue until it becomes necessary to drop down right, quite steeply, to a lane.

3 Cross and climb back up the other side on to the embankment. Soon there's a view ahead towards the village of Etton. Cross the track to **Etton Fields Farm**, and another field track shortly after. The following section can be quite muddy. (Those who are planning an out-and-back ride could turn round before the muddy section.) Where the shrouding trees fall back and the surroundings open out, look out for the stump of a **windmill** on the left. Just before a bridge over the track ahead, go right up a narrower track to a road.

4 Turn left, go over the bridge and follow the road straight down into the village

of **Etton**. At the T-junction turn left. **The Light Dragoon** is almost opposite.

5 Continue along the village street. Just after the **last houses** turn right, signposted for South Dalton, and up a short climb. Dead ahead as the gradient eases is the tall prominent spire of **St Mary's Church**, South Dalton. As the road begins to descend, turn left at a crossroads, signposted to Kiplingcotes and Market Weighton.

6 The road rolls along the crest of a broad ridge before a steeper descent leads down to an **angled crossroads**. Go left, signposted for Market Weighton, Kiplingcotes station and the Hudson Way. Just after passing a right turn to **Middleton-on-the-Wold**, turn left up the tarmac track that leads to Kiplingcotes station. Bear right back along the **railway track** to the start.

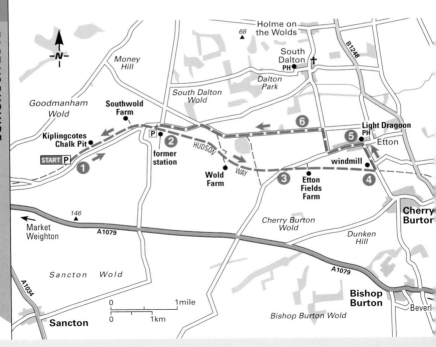

The Light Dragoon

is more extensive and may include Etton salad (black pudding, bacon and feta cheese), home-made steak pie with shortcrust pastry top, lasagne and prime steaks with sauces.

Family facilities
Children are made very welcome here. Youngsters have their own menu and some play equipment in the garden.

Alternative refreshment stops
None on route. Options in Cherry Burton.

☛ Where to go from here
Beverley and Market Weighton are both historic market towns and well worth exploring on foot. Visit the impressive Minster and enjoy a drink in the utterly unspoilt and candlelit White Horse Inn (Nellies) in Beverley.

Even if you don't plan on making the return through the lanes, it's not a problem to include this fine pub in your ride, as it's only about 0.5 mile (800m) from the nearest point on the railway track. It sits firmly at the centre of the charming village of Etton, which is not much more than one long street. The lounge bar is cosy and comfortable and some old wagon wheels incorporated into partitions are a notable feature. There's a separate dining room behind, housed in a modern extension that harmonises reasonably well with the original building. There's also a very pleasant garden, well away from road and car park, with swings and slide for the youngsters. On a summer evening the sky can be alive with swifts and swallows.

Food
At lunchtime tuck into various sandwiches, salads, pies and steak. The evening menu

Hudson Way

EAST YORKSHIRE

about the pub

The Light Dragoon
Main Street, Etton
Beverley, East Yorkshire HU17 7PQ
Tel: 01430 810282

DIRECTIONS: Etton is located 1 mile (1.6km) off the B1248 north west of Beverley. Pub is on the right in the village centre opposite a road junction

PARKING: 30

OPEN: daily

FOOD: daily, except Sunday evening

BREWERY/COMPANY: Scottish Courage

REAL ALE: Theakston XB & Black Bull

From Ravenscar to Robin Hood's Bay

Fabulous views and a unique industrial heritage.

Alum Quarries

Just after the start of the railway track proper, you pass through an area of partly overgrown spoil heaps with quarried faces above. For around two centuries, up to the Victorian era, this was an internationally important source of alum (potassium aluminium sulphate). This chemical, known since at least Roman times, had many uses, notably in the fixing of dyes. The shale rock in the cliffs was rich in aluminium sulphate and it is reckoned that over a million tons of rock were removed. The manufacturing process was centred on the alum works. The best source of potassium was seaweed; however, to complete the reaction, ammonia was required, and

the best source of this was human urine! Much of this was shipped all the way from London and off-loaded on the rocky shores directly below – a trade with some unique hazards. It is said that proud sea-captains were reluctant to admit that they carried this undignified cargo, but if they were found out the cry would go up, 'You're taking the piss!' It's as good an explanation as any for the origins of the phrase. You can find out more about the alum industry at the Coastal Centre in Ravenscar.

the ride

1 Descend the road until it bends sharply right. Turn left, past the **National Trust Coastal Centre**, on to an obvious descending concrete track. A rougher section needs care, but lasts less than

A collection of red-roofed stone cottages stand on the cliffs above Robin Hood's Bay

2h00 | 11.25 MILES | 18.1 KM | LEVEL 1 2 3

MAP: OS Explorer OL27 North York Moors – Eastern

START/FINISH: roadside parking on way into Ravenscar; grid ref: NZ 980015

TRAILS/TRACKS: almost entirely on well-surfaced old railway track; short street sections at Ravenscar and Robin Hood's Bay

LANDSCAPE: steep cliffs and coastal slopes, woodland and farmland, sea views

PUBLIC TOILETS: at start

TOURIST INFORMATION: Whitby, tel 01947 602674

CYCLE HIRE: Trailways, Hawsker (about 3 miles from Robin Hood's Bay, on the railway route), tel 01947 820207

THE PUB: The Laurel Inn, Robin Hood's Bay

🛈 Busy roads and car park in Robin Hood's Bay village (possible to turn round before this)

Getting to the start

Turn off the A171 about midway between Whitby and Scarborough – signed for Ravenscar. Turn left at a T-junction, then right near an old windmill. The road descends into Ravenscar and there is extensive roadside parking as the descent gets steeper.

Why do this cycle ride?

The former railway line between Whitby and Scarborough can now be followed, in its entirety, on two wheels. The full distance is 20 miles (32.2km) one way, so this ride picks out probably the finest section, looping around Robin Hood's Bay. It is a little confusing that the name of the bay and the much-photographed village are exactly the same, but the ride gives great views of the former and a chance to visit the latter.

Researched and written by: Jon Sparks

100yds (91m). Swing left through a gate on to the old **railway trackbed** and a much easier surface.

2 The track now runs below the scarred face of the **alum workings**, with some ups and downs that clearly don't match the original rail contours exactly. After this, take care crossing a **steep concrete track** that runs down to a farm.

3 Pass under an **arched bridge**. Note more quarried cliffs up on the left, while looking down to the right – if the tide is not too high – there are extensive rocky platforms in the bay, with conspicuous parallel strata. There's a short cutting and the sea views are blocked by tall gorse and broom, then it becomes more open again as the track swings gradually inland. A tall embankment

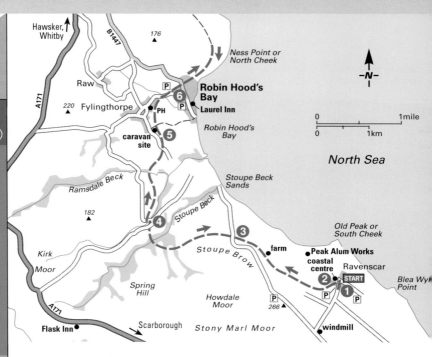

crosses a **steep wooded valley**. Go under a bridge and make a sharp left turn on to a lane.

4 Go up 2oyds (18m) and then sharp right to the continuation of the track. Keep right at a fork and the track resumes its steady gentle descent, then starts to turn uphill for the first time. As you come into the open after a **tunnel of trees**, the direct way ahead is again blocked (unless you're Evel Knievel!). Slant down left, cross a lane, and then climb back up on to the continuing trackbed.

5 Pass a **cricket ground**, the back of a caravan site, then a farm. Cross the rough farm track and keep straight on, through a gate where the surface changes to tarmac, on the outskirts of Robin Hood's Bay. Go through another gate and drop down to a road. Turn right down this for 1ooyds (91m) then left on a lane signposted to **Station Workshops**. At the top of the rise is the old

station building and just beyond it a large car park. (It is, of course, possible to descend the road all the way into the village of Robin Hood's Bay, but it's a very steep climb back. An alternative is to lock the bikes at the car park and go down on foot.)

6 Continue alongside the car park, drop down to a road, turn left and almost instantly right (very nearly straight across) on to **Mount Pleasant**. Follow this to its end then bear left up a short gravelled ride to regain the railway path. Continue for about 0.5 mile (8oom). There are good views back now over Robin Hood's Bay to the cliffs near Ravenscar. Look for a National Trust sign for **Ness Bay**. There is open access on foot so you could leave the bikes and walk down to the headland, a great picnic spot. This makes as good a turn-round point as any, though the track continues into Hawsker and on to Whitby.

The Laurel Inn

about the pub

The Laurel Inn
New Road, Robin Hood's Bay
North Yorkshire YO22 4SE
Tel: 01947 880400

DIRECTIONS: bottom of the village
PARKING: use village car park
OPEN: daily; all day (2pm–11pm Monday to Friday November to February)
FOOD: daily
BREWERY/COMPANY: free house
REAL ALE: Adnams Broadside, Tetley, Jennings Cumberland

The picturesque fishing village of Robin Hood's Bay is the setting for this delightful little pub. Tucked away in a row of fishermen's cottages at the bottom of the village overlooking the sea, the pub retains lots of character features, including beams and an open fire. The traditional bar is decorated with old photographs of the area, Victorian prints and brasses and an international collection of lager bottles. This coastal village was once the haunt of smugglers who used a network of underground tunnels and secret passages to bring the booty ashore.

Food
Bar food is limited to a simple and straightforward menu offering wholesome sandwiches and soups.

Family facilities
Due to its size there are few facilities for family groups although children are very welcome in the snug bar until 9pm.

Alternative refreshment stops
Various pubs and cafés in Robin Hood's Bay including The Victoria Hotel at the top of the village.

☛ Where to go from here
Locally, learn more about alum mining at the Peak Alum Works in Ravenscar and this fascinating coastline at the Ravenscar Coastal Centre. Children will enjoy visiting the Old Coastguard Station in Robin Hood's Bay. Head north to Whitby to see the moody and magnificent ruins of Whitby Abbey (www.english-heritage.org.uk) and visit the Captain Cook Memorial Museum

(www.cookmuseumwhitby.co.uk). High on the list for children may be the Sea Life and Marine Sanctuary in Scarborough, home to seahorses, otters, sharks, a seal hospital and convalescing sea turtles.

Wild Ennerdale

44

Ennerdale

CUMBRIA

A ride through the forest beyond Ennerdale Water.

Ennerdale

Pillar Rock, south east of the lake end, stands proud of the mountainside in a way that few other crags do, and has a distinct summit of its own. This was first reached in 1826 by a local shepherd, John Atkinson. If conditions are good there may well be climbers on the Rock – binoculars will help you spot them. Today the easiest routes to the top are considered as hard scrambling rather than rock-climbing, but over the years climbers have added many routes on the various faces, some of them very challenging.

Some forty years ago the legendary fellwalker Alfred Wainwright wrote, 'Afforestation in Ennerdale has cloaked the lower slopes...in a dark and funereal shroud of foreign trees'. But things are changing. The Forestry Commission now plants a wider diversity of trees in many of its forests, and in the upper reaches of Ennerdale things have gone much further.

The Wild Ennerdale project is slowly restoring much more natural woodland. It's worth reflecting that the bare slopes of rough grass are not entirely 'natural' either, but the result of centuries of farming, most notably overgrazing by sheep.

the ride

1 Turn left from the **car park**, rolling down to the shores of **Ennerdale Water**. The track runs beside the lake for about 1 mile (1.6km), then continues through the forest above the river, here called **Char Dub**. Dub is a common dialect word for a pool, and the char is a species of fish. Continue past **Low Gillerthwaite Field Centre** and then the youth hostel at **High Gillerthwaite**.

2 Just past the youth hostel the track forks. Keep right (really straight ahead). The track goes up and down more than you might expect. Take care on fast downhill bends where the surface is loose. Above all don't grab at the brakes. At the next fork 1 mile (1.6km) further on, a sign to the right

points to Pillar. Save the Pillar road for the return and keep straight on – in fact, this track straight ahead gives the best views of the **Pillar Rock**. The way climbs gradually to a more level stretch with open views across the valley to Pillar directly opposite. Pillar Rock is the centrepiece of a mass of crags strewn across the north face of the mountain. This is a worthy objective in itself and makes a reasonable turnaround point for those who feel they've gone far enough.

3 As Pillar falls behind, the valley head opens up. There's a space where you may find some vehicles and then the main track curves down right.

4 Straight ahead through a gate is a much rougher track leading 400yds (366m) to **Black Sail Hut Youth Hostel** – many people may prefer to walk for some or all of it. You can make yourselves tea or coffee in the members' kitchen, but don't forget to leave a suitable donation. Return to the gate. The bridleway going up right climbs to Scarth Gap Pass and then descends to Buttermere. Ignore it, and go back through the gate and down left to the **River Liza**.

5 Splash through the concrete ford and swing round right. Now keep straight along the track, mostly downhill, ignoring branches up and left until it swings down to the **river**.

6 Cross the bridge and go up to the 'Pillar' signpost. Rejoin the main track of the outward route to return to the **car park**.

Top: Walkers beside Ennerdale Water
Left: Above Ennerdale Water

MAP: OS Explorer OL 4 The English Lakes (NW)

START/FINISH: Bowness Knott car park; grid ref: NY 109153

TRAILS/TRACKS: good forest roads, occasionally bumpy

LANDSCAPE: lake, forest, wild valley ringed by high fells

PUBLIC TOILETS: none on route

TOURIST INFORMATION: Egremont, tel 01946 820693

CYCLE HIRE: Ainfield Cycle Centre, Cleator, tel 01946 812427; Mark Taylor Cycles, Whitehaven, tel 01946 692252

THE PUB: Shepherds Arms Hotel, Ennerdale Bridge, near the route

🛈 Rough track on the last short section (400yds/366m) to Black Sail Hut – mountain bike and some skill required, or walk. Suitability: children 10+. Younger children will enjoy a shorter version

Getting to the start

The car park is half way along the north shore of Ennerdale Water, at a dead-end. Access is via minor roads east from Ennerdale Bridge or south from Lamplugh.

Why do this cycle ride?

Although relatively gentle in itself, this route joins the world of the mountaineer, the fell-runner and the long-distance walker, entering the heart of the high fells. At the head of the valley, lonely Black Sail Hut Youth Hostel makes a perfect place to stop. You can make yourself a cup of tea there and even stay the night – but make sure that you book in advance (tel 0411 108450, not open all year).

Researched and written by: Jon Sparks

Ennerdale CUMBRIA

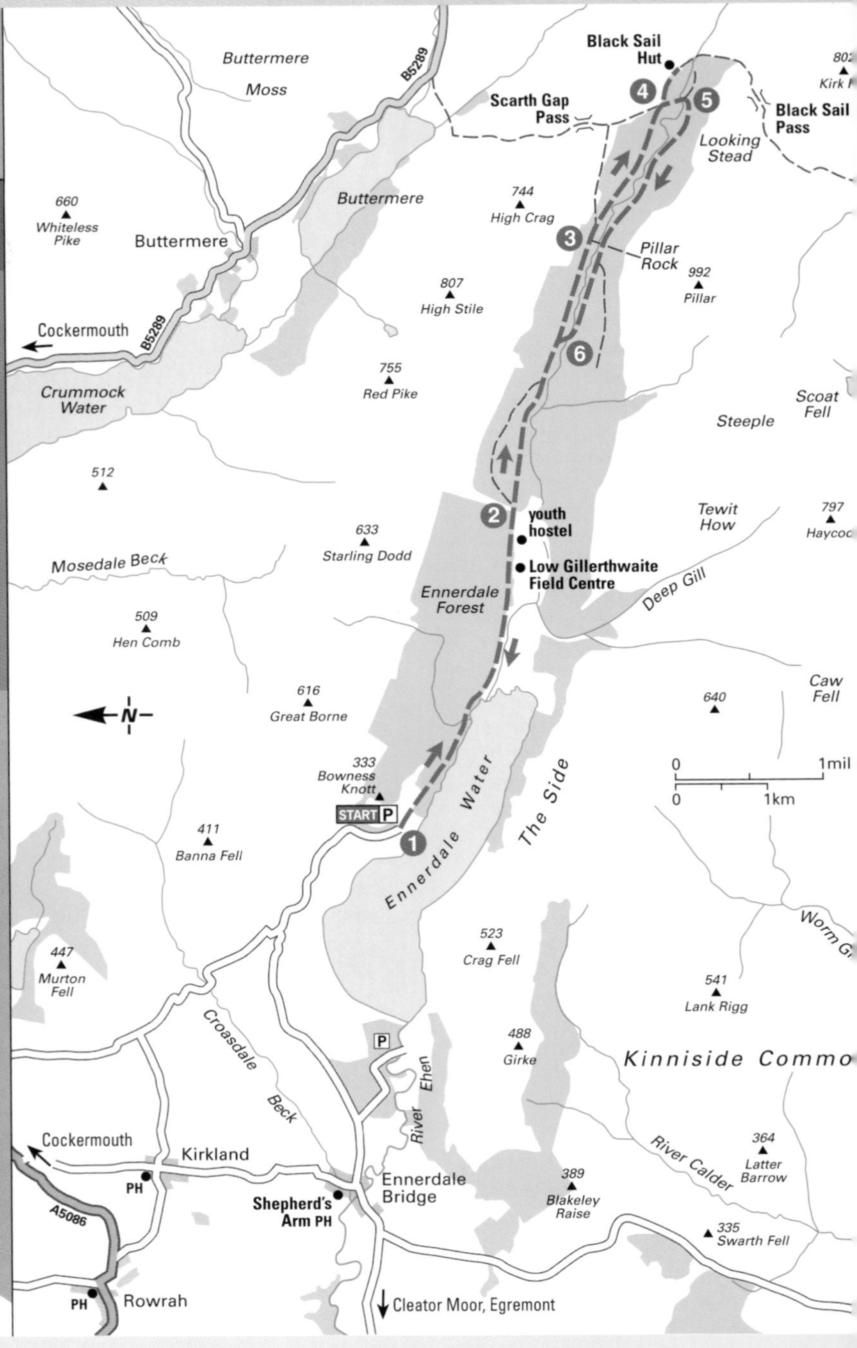

Ennerdale CUMBRIA

Buttermere
Moss

B5289

Black Sail
Hut

Scarth Gap
Pass

Black Sail
Pass

802
Kirk F

4

5

Buttermere

Looking
Stead

660
Whiteless
Pike

Buttermere

744
High Crag

3

Pillar
Rock

992
Pillar

Cockermouth

B5289

807
High Stile

6

Crummock
Water

755
Red Pike

Scoat
Fell

512

Steeple

Mosedale Beck

633
Starling Dodd

2   youth
hostel

Low Gillerthwaite
Field Centre

Tewit
How

797
Haycoc

509
Hen Comb

Ennerdale
Forest

Deep Gill

N

616
Great Borne

Caw
Fell

640

0   1mil
0   1km

333
Bowness
Knott

START P

1

Ennerdale Water

The Side

411
Banna Fell

Worm Gr

523
Crag Fell

541
Lank Rigg

447
Murton
Fell

Croasdale Beck

P

River Ehen

488
Girke

Kinniside Commo

Cockermouth

Kirkland

PH

A5086

Shepherd's
Arm PH

Ennerdale
Bridge

389
Blakeley
Raise

River Calder

364
Latter
Barrow

335
Swarth Fell

PH   Rowrah

Cleator Moor, Egremont

Shepherds Arms Hotel

The Shepherds Arms Hotel sits at the heart of the village of Ennerdale Bridge, smack on the Coast-to-Coast walk. This cream-washed country inn is welcoming and homely, its traditionally furnished bar (wood floors, bookcases, open log fires) dispense cracking real ales and hearty, home-cooked food to refuel the weariest of cyclists. In fact, walkers and cyclists are important here, evidenced by the maps posted in the bar, and the weather forecast chalked up daily on a blackboard. In addition, the en suite bedrooms are very comfortable, with period furnishings and pleasant views, and a restful night's sleep is guaranteed.

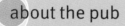

about the pub

Shepherds Arms Hotel
Ennerdale Bridge
Cumbria CA23 3AR
Tel 01946 861249
www.shepherdsarmshotel.co.uk

DIRECTIONS: in the centre of the village, 3.5 miles (5.7km) west of the start of the ride
PARKING: 6 (good street parking)
OPEN: daily, all day
FOOD: daily
BREWERY/COMPANY: free house
REAL ALE: Timothy Taylor Landlord, Coniston Bluebird, Jennings Bitter, guest beers
ROOMS: 8 bedrooms (6 en suite)

Food
From the bar menu, tuck into spinach and Wensleydale tart, local lamb chops, steak and ale pie with a suet crust, served with hand-cut chips or opt for something lighter like a warming bowl of soup, freshly made sandwiches and decent salads. Separate restaurant menu.

Family facilities
Children are welcome in the bars and overnight, with plenty of games and toys to keep them amused. There's a delightful garden, although it does border a fast-flowing stream, so supervision is necessary.

Alternative refreshment stops
None on route, although those venturing to Black Sail Youth Hostel (Point 4) can make themselves tea and coffee in the member's kitchen (donations).

☛ Where to go from here
The ruined 12th-century Egremont Castle is well worth a visit for its impressive red sandstone gatehouse. At the Florence Mine Heritage Centre just off the A595 you can tour the pit and see reconstructions of 19th-century pit life in the visitor centre.

Ennerdale CUMBRIA

Wast Water to Stanton Bridge

A pleasant rural ride with
a short option and a
magnificent scenic finale.

Wast Water

Wast Water is England's deepest lake,
reaching a maximum depth of almost
260ft (79m), which means that its bed is
well below sea level. The steep slope of
The Screes, which face you across the lake,
is continued deep underwater. The Screes,
below the two summits of Whin Rigg and
Illgill Head, are composed of decaying
crags and masses of loose rock and
boulders. This is landscape that is still
evolving. There is a path, which you may be
able to make out, running along the base of
The Screes just above the level of the lake.
It is no surprise to find that it is extremely
rough going in places.

Looking up to the head of the lake
and at the centre of the view (and of the
National Park logo) is the pyramidal peak of
Great Gable, 2,949ft (899m) high. High on
its slopes facing you are the Napes Crags,
beloved of the earliest rock-climbers and

Left: Cyclists on the route above Wast Water
Next page: Scafell and Great Gable

of generations since. But only with very
sharp eyes, or binoculars, and even then
only in favourable light, are you likely to
discern the natural obelisk called Napes
Needle. Its first ascent in 1886 is often
regarded as the birth of rock-climbing. It
features in a memorial window in the lovely
little church at Wasdale Head.

the ride

1 Head west along the road towards
Gosforth, climbing slightly and
passing close under the craggy slopes of
Buckbarrow. Climb a little more and then
descend to a junction.

2 For the shorter loop, go left here, signed
for Nether Wasdale. Follow the narrow
lane and descend to a junction. Keep left
and descend quite steeply into **Nether
Wasdale**, levelling out at the village green,
with **The Screes Inn** on the left and the
Strands Hotel on the right (Point 5). For the
longer ride, continue straight ahead at Point
2 and go straight on at the next junction.
The road is fairly level, with views over the
valley of the **River Irt** to the left and wooded
slopes on the right. A little over 1 mile
(1.6km) from the last junction, look for a
bridleway on the left, signed for Hall Bolton.

3 Turn left onto the bridleway. The initial
descent from the road is as rough as it
gets. Keep right where the track forks and
go straight ahead between the buildings at
Rainors. Wind down to an attractive bridge
over the **River Bleng**. Beyond this there's a
short grassy section, then join the surfaced

drive to **Hall Bolton**. Turn right and follow the drive out to a road. Turn left. Note, this track is rarely very muddy, but after wet weather you risk a soaking on the grassy section beyond the bridge. To avoid this, continue along the road at Point 3 over a small climb and then down steeply to **Wellington Bridge** and the outskirts of **Gosforth**. Bear left on a farm lane (bridleway) through **Row Farm** and on to **Rowend Bridge**. Turn left to follow the road to Santon Bridge. This adds about 1 mile (1.6km) to the total distance. Follow the road easily to **Santon Bridge**, past the pub and over the bridge.

4 Turn left on a narrow road past a campsite and soon begin a steeper climb at **Greengate Wood**. The gradient eases and the views ahead start to include the craggy outline of **The Screes**. Descend gently to **Forest Bridge**, then keep left, over **Cinderdale Bridge**, into **Nether Wasdale**. Follow the level road into the village and its twin pubs.

5 Retrace to **Cinderdale Bridge**, then keep left on the lane, signed to Wasdale Head. There are glimpses of The Screes and then of the lake, but trees screen them as you pass the youth hostel at **Wasdale Hall** and it's only when you cross a cattle grid to open fellside that the full panorama hits you. Follow the road down and then up a short climb to near a **cross-wall shelter** on the right, which commands a great view.

6 Continue down to cross **Countess Beck** and turn left. It's now little more than 0.25 mile (400m) back to the start.

| 2h00 | 11.25 MILES | 18.1 KM | LEVEL 1 2 3 |

SHORTER ALTERNATIVE ROUTE

| 1h00 | 5 MILES | 8 KM | LEVEL 1 2 3 |

MAP: OS Explorer OL 6 The English Lakes (SW)

START/FINISH: by Wast Water, roadside parking at Greendale; grid ref: NY 144057

TRAILS/TRACKS: lanes; longer route has a short section of grassy bridleway

LANDSCAPE: wooded farmland then open fellside with view of lake and high fells

PUBLIC TOILETS: Gosforth

TOURIST INFORMATION: Ravenglass, tel 01229 717278; Sellafield, tel 019467 76510

CYCLE HIRE: Ainfield Cycle Centre, Cleator, tel 01946 812427; Mark Taylor Cycles, Whitehaven, tel 01946 692252

THE PUB: The Screes Inn, Nether Wasdale, see Point 5 on route

🚫 Some ascents and descents on both routes. Shorter loop, suitability: children 8+. Longer loop, suitability: children 11+

Getting to the start

Head east from Gosforth, pass a car park, then keep left on the Wasdale road. Follow this for 3 miles (4.8km) then keep left, signed to Wasdale Head for 2.5 miles (4km). Park in a grassy area on the left just past Greendale.

Why do this cycle ride?

The magnificent view of high fells around the head of Wast Water inspired the Lake District National Park logo, and would win many votes for the finest view in England. The ride saves this until near the end, first exploring the gentler scenery around Nether Wasdale.

Researched and written by: Jon Sparks

Wast Water

CUMBRIA

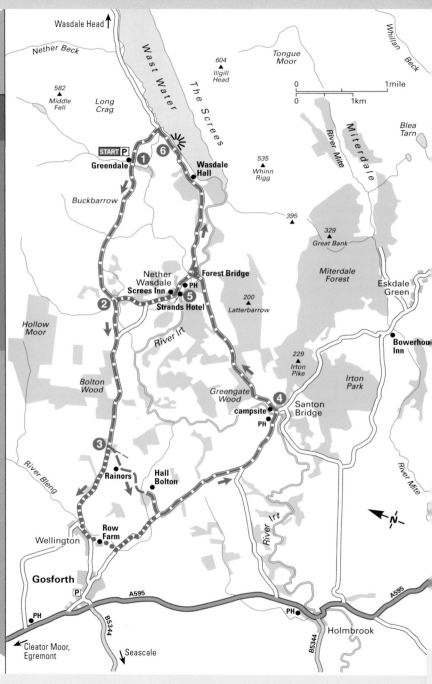

West Water CUMBRIA

Wasdale Head ↑

Nether Beck

West Water

The Screes

Whillan Beck

Tongue Moor

604
▲
Illgill Head

0   1mile
0   1km

Blea Tarn

582
▲
Middle Fell

Long Crag

Miterdale

River Mite

START P ① ⑥
Greendale

Wasdale Hall

535
▲
Whinn Rigg

Buckbarrow

395
▲

329
▲
Great Bank

Miterdale Forest

Eskdale Green

Nether Wasdale
Forest Bridge

Screes Inn PH
② ⑤
Strands Hotel

200
▲
Latterbarrow

Hollow Moor

River Irt

229
▲
Irton Pike

Irton Park

Bowerhou Inn

Bolton Wood

Greengate Wood
④
campsite PH

Santon Bridge

River Bleng

③
Rainors

Hall Bolton

River Irt

River Mite

Row Farm

N

Wellington

Gosforth

P

PH   A595   PH

B5344

Holmbrook

← Cleator Moor, Egremont   ↓ Seascale   B5344   A595

The Screes Inn

about the pub

The Screes Inn
Nether Wasdale, Seascale
Cumbria CA20 1ET
Tel 019467 26262
www.thescreesinnwasdale.com

DIRECTIONS: on the main road through the village, west of the church
PARKING: 20
OPEN: daily, all day
FOOD: daily
BREWERY/COMPANY: free house
REAL ALE: Black Sheep Bitter, Coniston Bluebird, Yates's Bitter, guest beer
ROOMS: 5 en suite

Two pubs face each other across the lane through Nether Wasdale, but both are owned by the same people. To pick one over the other may be invidious, but the 300-year-old Screes Inn does have one or two advantages: it's easy to park your bikes in sight of the outdoor tables, and it's open all day. Outside seating is separated from the road by an expanse of grass – a sort of village green – with a sunny aspect and glimpses of the fells lining Wasdale. Inside, it's a typically rambling Lakeland pub. The bars are partly slate-floored, and there's usually a log fire crackling in the grate – the perfect spot to savour a pint of Yates's bitter. Bike storage for overnight visitors.

Food

Specials from the blackboard might include smoked haddock, leek and potato pasties or Mexican wraps. Alternatively, try Woodall's Cumberland sausage with apple sauce, lasagne or home-baked steak and kidney pie. Vegetarians will always be well looked after as The Screes has a vegetarian chef.

Family facilities

Families will find a separate family room for the children to relax in. Small portions of main menu dishes are available (young children have their own menu), and there is plenty of good outdoor seating.

Alternative refreshment stops

The Strands Hotel in Nether Wasdale and, on the longer ride, the Bridge Inn at Stanton Bridge.

☛ Where to go from here

St Olaf's Church at Wasdale Head is one of England's smallest, and in its cemetery are the graves of several rock-climbers; this village became known as the birthplace of rock-climbing in Britain in the 1880s.

Bouth and Oxen Park

An action-packed short ride, with an exciting off-road option.

A wooded landscape

Magnificent woodland, dominated by sessile oak, is a major feature of this ride. Cyclists on the longer route who take the climb to Ickenthwaite will have plenty of time to appreciate this. In earlier times these woods were an industrial resource, providing raw materials for the bobbin industry and for charcoal-making to feed the many small iron makers in the area. Near the start of the ride, Moss Wood and the adjoining Height Springs Wood are now maintained by the

Woodland Trust. The track into Moss Wood is a bridleway so you could easily ride in a short way to get a closer look. You will see areas where the trees have been coppiced. This seemingly drastic operation involves cutting the tree back almost to ground level, but does not kill the plant. Instead it puts out many small shoots which in a few years provide thin timber ideal for both bobbin-making and charcoal-burning.

Just beyond the Manor House Inn in Oxen Park, you pass a grey barn-like building beside the road. Note the carved sign on the wall, which dates it to 1697, and portrays a selection of blacksmith's implements. Incidentally, a blacksmith is a general ironworker, who would largely have been involved in producing tools – one whose main job is shoeing horses is strictly called a farrier.

the ride

1 Follow the lane north, away from Bouth. Keep left at the first junction, signed to Oxen Park. The lane twists up through **woodland**, with a couple of quite sharp sections of climbing, passing the entrance to **Moss Wood**, before levelling out. At the next junction there is a triangle of grass.

Top: The Vale of Colton
Below left: On a track between traditional dry-stone walls

2 For the shorter ride go left here, signed to Oxen Park. The road twists and descends, crosses a little valley, then begins a steep twisting climb. As climbs go, this is not too long. Over the top, freewheel a short way to a T-junction on the outskirts of Oxen Park. Turn left to rejoin the longer loop shortly after Point 5.

For the longer route, keep right at Point 2, signposted 'Rusland: Gated Road'. Follow this lane until it drops to a T-junction. There's no need, but those with mountain-biking blood in their veins may not be able to resist splashing through the ford under the trees just before the junction. Turn right on the wider road, signed to **Grizedale**, and follow it for 0.75 mile (1.2km). Shortly after passing the elegant **Whitestock Hall**, look for a sharp left turn, signed to Ickenthwaite.

3 This leads immediately into a very steep climb, so engage low gear in advance. The gradient eventually eases and then the woods give way to fields.

2h00 — **7.75 MILES** — **12.5 KM** — **LEVEL 1 2 3**

SHORTER ALTERNATIVE ROUTE

1h00 — **4.5 MILES** — **7.2 KM** — **LEVEL 1 2**

MAP: OS Explorer OL 7 The English Lakes (SE)

START/FINISH: lane north of Bouth; grid ref: SD 328859

TRAILS/TRACKS: quiet lanes; rough tracks on longer ride, short challenging descents

LANDSCAPE: mix of woods and pasture, many small hills, views to higher fells

PUBLIC TOILETS: none on route

TOURIST INFORMATION: Ulverston, tel 01229 587120

CYCLE HIRE: South Lakeland Mountain Bike Sales & Hire, Lowick Bridge, Ulverston, tel 01229 885210; Wheelbase, Staveley, tel 01539 821443

THE PUB: White Hart Inn, Bouth, see Point **1** on route

🚴 Steep gradients on both loops. Shorter loop, suitability: children 7+. On longer loop, off-road descents require experience and skill, or walk short sections, suitability: children 12+. Mountain bike recommended

Getting to the start
Bouth is 1.25 miles (2km) north of the A590. Park in a grassy lay-by on the northern edge of the village, beyond the pub, or further along the lane on the first part of the ride.

Why do this cycle ride?
This short ride packs in a lot, in an area that's pure Lake District yet never inundated with visitors. For every climb there's a pleasant descent, and a new view to enjoy.

Researched and written by: Jon Sparks

Bouth **CUMBRIA**

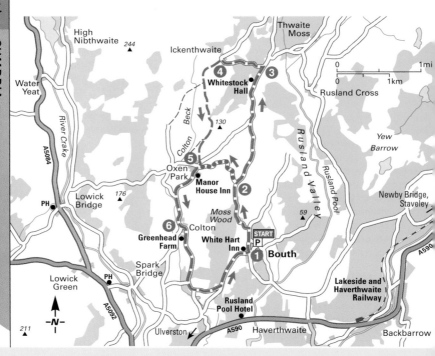

4 Just after **Low Ickenthwaite** turn left on to a bridleway signed to Oxen Park. The track is initially stony with a good ribbon of grass down the middle. After a second gate it becomes stonier but is still straightforward. Stay close to the wall on the left, ignoring a couple of branch tracks. The track then climbs a bit on to an open, bracken-covered area. The best riding is generally in the centre of the track as the sides are quite rough. Go through another gate, and a little more climbing leads to the crest. Keep straight ahead at another fork and the track levels off. A short steep section at the start of the descent calls for some skill. If in doubt, walk down this. Then descend more steeply to another gate. The twisting descent beyond this is steep and loose and requires great care. Again, walk down rather than risk a nasty fall. Just beyond its foot is another gate.

5 Emerge on to a road and turn right into **Oxen Park**. As you enter the village, the shorter ride joins in from the left. Keep straight ahead through the village. The road begins a sweeping descent into the soft green **Vale of Colton**.

6 Just after the **Old Vicarage** turn left, signposted 'Colton Church and Bouth', up a short steep climb. At the crest another sign to Colton Church and Bouth points left, up a further climb. But this is an off-road route, so continue straight on. Descend to pass **Greenhead Farm**, and the road is fairly level along the valley side. Keep left through two junctions. The road curves and makes a steep final drop to a T-junction (take care). Go left for an almost level run along a broader road back through **Bouth**.

White Hart Inn

about the pub

White Hart Inn
Bouth, Ulverston
Cumbria LA12 8JB
Tel 01229 861229
www.edirectory.co.uk/whitehartinn

DIRECTIONS: in the middle of the village
PARKING: 30
OPEN: closed Monday and Tuesday lunchtime; open all day Saturday and Sunday, July–September
FOOD: daily
BREWERY/COMPANY: free house
REAL ALE: Jennings Cumberland Ale, Black Sheep Bitter, Tetley, 3 guest beers
ROOMS: 4 en suite

A 16th-century former coaching inn, the White Hart is in a quiet village among woods, fields and fells. Sloping beamed ceilings and floors in the main bar show the building's age, while two log fires help create a cosy and welcoming atmosphere. Walls and ceilings are festooned with bric-a-brac and old photos – look out for the farm tools, stuffed animals and long-stemmed clay pipes. The landlord has a genuine passion for real ale, with six great ales, including brews from Cumbrian micro-breweries, to draw the customers in. He refuses to allow vinegar in the bar as it 'affects the quality of the beer'. A pub that has its priorities right!

Upstairs there's a more open feel to the restaurant, with a large window giving it a fine outlook, shared with the rear terrace. The terrace has heaters for those chillier days, and a pleasant view of pastures and the wooded flanks of Colton Fell.

Food

The menu offers fresh food cooked to order using beef, pork and lamb from Abbots Reading Farm, a few miles away. Typically, this might include steak and stout pie, lamb and apricot pie, and pork medallions in port and mushroom sauce. Expect also soups, salads, sandwiches and pizzas.

Family facilities

Children are welcome in the eating areas and games room, and there's a limited children's menu. Play area on the village green opposite.

Alternative refreshment stops

Manor House pub in Oxen Park (Point 5).

☞ Where to go from here

Lakeside is the steamer stop at the southern end of Lake Windermere and the starting point for the Lakeside and Haverthwaite Railway (www.windermere -lakecruises.co.uk). A short steam trip runs to Haverthwaite and there's a small collection of steam and diesel locomotives. Next door the fascinating Aquarium of the Lakes is well worth a visit (www.aquariumofthelakes.co.uk).

Bouth CUMBRIA

Grizedale Forest Park and Satterthwaite

A great circuit of the forest park.

Grizedale Forest

The speed and near-silence of a bike sometimes gives you some great wildlife encounters. We were privileged to see a family of foxes playing in the first few miles of this route. This may be exceptional, but deer – both red and roe – are widespread in the forest, and the sight of a buzzard overhead is almost guaranteed. (Buzzards are occasionally mistaken for eagles, but if you see a large bird of prey circling over this forest, it's a buzzard.) In spring the courtship flights of these big birds of prey are beautiful to watch, and you may also see them being mobbed or harassed by other birds.

In the second half of the route there are great views west to the Coniston Fells. The principal peak at the southern end of the range is the Coniston Old Man (originally Allt Maen, meaning a high stone or cairn). To its left you glimpse the rock buttresses of Dow Crag, one of the great rock-climbers' crags of England. The sides of the Coniston Fells are heavily scarred, most obviously by slate quarries, but also by the copper mines which worked for around 500 years, reaching their peak in the 19th century.

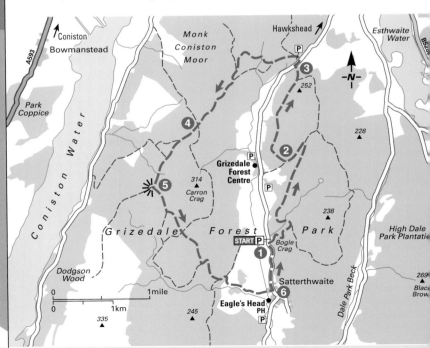

| 2h00 | 9.5 MILES | 15.3 KM | LEVEL 123 |

MAP: OS Explorer OL 7 The English Lakes (SE)

START/FINISH: Bogle Crag car park, Grizedale Forest; grid ref: SD 337933

TRAILS/TRACKS: forest tracks with mostly good surface, short sections of field track and lane

LANDSCAPE: forest, with views to the fells

PUBLIC TOILETS: Grizedale Forest Centre

TOURIST INFORMATION: Hawkshead, tel 015394 36525

CYCLE HIRE: Grizedale Mountain Bikes, Grizedale, tel 01229 860369

THE PUB: The Eagles Head, Satterthwaite, see Point **6** on route

🛑 Some moderately steep descents with loose surfaces so mountain bike recommended. Suitability: children 12+. There are other waymarked routes in the forest which are shorter and easier

Getting to the start

Grizedale Forest lies to the east of Coniston Water, with the village of Grizedale at its heart. Bogle Crag car park is 0.75 mile (1.2km) south of the village on the only road through the valley, and 0.5 mile (800m) north of Satterthwaite.

Why do this cycle ride?

Grizedale Forest Park has many waymarked cycle routes on the forest roads, as well as a pre-existing network of bridleways, some of which offer much tougher riding (strictly for hardened mountain-bikers). The route makes for a fine day out, and gives a fair sample of what the forest has to offer.

Researched and written by: Jon Sparks

Grizedale CUMBRIA

Cycling through Grizedale Forest

the ride

1 At the top of **Bogle Crag car park** go round the barrier and straight up the rocky track at a steady gradient. At a junction of tracks bear left, and enjoy a brief downhill respite and a fairly level section before some more steady climbing, sustained but never really steep. Where this eases off, turn left (**purple route marker**).

2 At the next fork keep right on the easy forest road, which sweeps round to the right (the left branch is a bridleway which makes a steep, rocky, experts-only descent direct to the Grizedale Forest visitor centre). After some undulations there's a longer downhill, then another substantial climb, quite steep to start. Just over the top, reach a junction of tracks. Go left and gently downhill to a **gate**. The most challenging part of the uphill section is now over.

3 Go round the gate on the left, with care as the ground is rocky. Come out to the road and turn right. After 200yds (183m) turn left at **Moor Top**. Go through the **car park** and immediately beyond the barrier fork left. Pass a small lake (**Juniper Tarn**) in the trees on the left and at the next fork go right. Curve round the head of a small valley and climb fairly gently, keeping straight on where another track joins from the right. At the next junction keep right. The next section is broadly level, past stands of **younger trees**. Pass an area of broadleaf planting (mostly birch) and get the first view of the **Coniston Fells** away to the right. Continue, to reach a double junction, almost a crossroads.

4 Bear left and then right to maintain the same general direction. Keep on along the **main track**, past several turnings descending to the right, until an obvious track forks off down to the right. There's a **bench** here, with a great view of the full length of the **Coniston Fells**. It's a perfect place to pause for a drink or snack, or just to enjoy the panorama.

5 Ignore the descending track and keep on along the level one. Soon there's a small rise and the track swings round to the left. A bridleway breaks off to the right here – another classic mountain bike route. Keep straight on and descend, passing another track that branches off to the right. At the next junction keep left (**green waymark**). This section is quite loose, so take care. Keep straight on at the next junction – a narrower track on the right makes it a crossroads. There's more fast descent through **mature forest** – the surface here is mostly good, but gets looser as you drop to a T-junction. Turn left and continue the descent, winding down through **broadleaf woods**. Keep left at the next junction, over a slight rise, then look out for a right turn (easy to miss) just before the track reaches fields on the right. Follow this slightly rougher track down to a gate and then through fields. It's bumpy in places as it descends to another gate, then continue across the level valley floor.

Sculpture of a man with an axe in Grizedale Forest

The village of **Satterthwaite** is ahead. There's a short rise, with bedrock visible, before you meet the road.

6 Turn left here for a direct return to **Bogle Crag car park**, or turn right for 400yds (366m) to **The Eagles Head** pub.

The Eagles Head

about the pub

The Eagles Head
Satterthwaite, Ulverston
Cumbria LA12 8LN
Tel 01229 860237

DIRECTIONS: in the centre of the village, just south of the church	
PARKING: 8	
OPEN: closed Monday lunchtime	
FOOD: no food Monday evening	
BREWERY/COMPANY: free house	
REAL ALE: Barngates Cracker Ale, Hawkshead Gold, guest beer	

'Walkers and cyclists are always welcome, however muddy.' That comment sums up the unpretentious Eagles Head. And on some of the rougher routes in Grizedale, it is understood that mountain-bikers can get very muddy indeed. This fine pub says it is 'In the Heart of the Grizedale Forest', and that seems to be true in more senses than the purely geographical. The interior is warm and cosy in a style typical of many a Lakeland hostelry, complete with slate floor, log fires and simple furnishings. On a fine day there is intense competition for tables in the small but delightful garden, with its sheltering trees and flower-decked walls. Additional attractions include tip-top local ales, in particular Barngates Cracker Ale.

Food

There are separate lunchtime and evening menus, with sandwiches (home-roast ham and cheese), filled jacket potatoes and leek and mushroom crumble at lunchtime. Some main courses like home-made steak and chicken or game pies, overlap on both menus. The evening menu has a good choice of curry dishes among others.

Family facilities

Families are made very welcome.

Alternative refreshment stops

Café at the Grizedale Forest visitor centre; pubs and cafés in nearby Hawkshead.

☛ Where to go from here

Admire an annually changing exhibition of Beatrix Potter's paintings used to illustrate her children's books, often incorporating local scenes, at the Beatrix Potter Gallery, Hawkshead.

Grizedale CUMBRIA

Around the Winster Valley from Bowland Bridge

A loop through a delightful secluded valley, with minimal traffic.

The Winster Valley

The valley floor and the hills to the west are of slate, the ridges to the east of limestone. The strata in both cases generally dip down towards the east, and the younger limestone actually lies on top of the older slate.

The slate is part of what geologists call the Windermere Group of rocks and is roughly 400 million years old. The limestone – carboniferous limestone, to be precise – is 300–350 million years old, and quite young by geological standards (the most ancient rocks in Britain are nearly ten times as old).

The woods on the western slopes of the valley are dominated by oak, while on the limestone ash trees are more common, with many gnarled yew trees on steeper slopes and where the soil is thin. You can see some fine examples where the lane climbs the steep flank of Yewbarrow. Yews are tough, slow-growing, long-lived trees and

able to survive where there seems to be hardly any soil. It is also worth knowing that yews are the best trees to shelter under when it rains, as their down-sloping leaves shed the water to the outside.

the ride

1 Follow the road, with the pub on your left, and cross the **bridge** that gives Bowland Bridge its name. Soon the road begins to climb quite steeply. Fortunately, you don't have to go too far up before you turn off to the left, signposted to Cartmel Fell and High Newton. There's a brief stretch of more level riding, then another short steep climb before you swoop down past the turning for **Cartmel Fell Church**. Continue straight on to meet a wider road at an angled junction.

2 Go straight across the junction on to a surfaced track over a cattle grid, signed to Ashes and Low Thorphinsty. Go through **Ashes farmyard**. After another 100yds (91m) the way ahead is blocked by

A cyclist negotiating a path lined with bushes and plants near Ashes in the Winster Valley

a gate. Turn left immediately before this, go through another gate and down a grassy track. After a second gate the grass gets longer, but it's only a short way further to a lane. While it's rarely muddy, the long grass will give you a good wetting after rain.

3 Turn right along the lane and follow it easily down the valley for 2 miles (3.2km) to a **crossroads** with an old-fashioned black-and-white **signpost**.

4 Turn left, signed to Witherslack. Climb slightly over the **Holme**, a slatey hump rising from the valley floor, then dip down again to **Bleacrag Bridge**. Bear left at the junction, at a triangle of grass, on to a narrow lane which has remnants of grass down the middle. This gradually draws closer to the rocky limestone flanks of Yewbarrow, climbing into a dark tunnel of yew trees. There are lots of exposed roots in the thin soil, and the first close glimpses of the limestone. Another lane joins in from the right.

Winster Valley

CUMBRIA

MAP: OS Explorer OL 7 The English Lakes (SE)
START/FINISH: Bowland Bridge; grid ref: SD 417896
TRAILS/TRACKS: quiet lanes, with a short optional section on grassy bridleway
LANDSCAPE: lush valley overlooked by limestone escarpment
PUBLIC TOILETS: none on route
TOURIST INFORMATION: Bowness-on-Windermere, tel 015394 42895
CYCLE HIRE: South Lakeland Mountain Bike Sales & Hire, Lowick Bridge, Ulverston, tel 01229 885210; Wheelbase, Staveley, tel 01539 821443
THE PUB: Hare & Hounds Country Inn, Bowland Bridge, see Point **1** on route
🚲 Undulating ride with a few steep hills. Suitability: children 8+

Getting to the start
Bowland Bridge is a tiny village 1.75 miles (2.8km) south west of Crossthwaite, on a minor road between the A5074 and the A592. Park in the small lay-by opposite the Hare & Hounds Country Inn, or in others scattered along the first part of the route.

Why do this cycle ride?
Although close to main roads and to tourist sights like Bowness, the Winster Valley is remarkably quiet. It's a great place for a relaxing ride, with few worries about traffic and a better than average chance of sunshine. Limestone crags overlook the lush valley floor with its outcrops of slate, a geological boundary between the earlier and later stages of the ride.

Researched and written by: Jon Sparks

The view south west across Winster Valley

5 Continue along the lane past **Strickland Hill** and **Askew Green** until the way kinks through the farmyard of **Low Low Wood**, with a fine barn. Go through a gate ahead on to a rougher section of lane, past **Middle Low Wood** and **High Low Wood**. Climb to a T-junction and turn left. As you come over the crest and twist down past the beautiful **Pool Bank farm**, there's the best view yet of the steep flanks of the **Whitbarrow ridge**. At another grass triangle turn left, signed to Bowland Bridge.

6 Keep right past **Cowmire Hall**, swing round and drop down to another junction. Keep left here and go along the valley bottom near the river to reach the junction at **Bowland Bridge**. The **Hare and Hounds** is just to the right.

Hare & Hounds Country Inn

In the beautiful Winster Valley, with stunning views over Cartmel Fell, this 17th-century coaching inn is just 10 minutes' drive from the southern tip of Windermere. It's a truly rural, attractive building that successfully blends ancient and modern, with its rough stone walls, farming memorabilia and simple wooden furniture. Crackling log fires warm you in winter. On fine days head outside with your drinks and sit and survey the terrain covered by the ride. It's easy to overlook the orchard garden to the side of the pub, south-facing and enjoying views down the valley dominated by the crag-fringed ridge of Whitbarrow Scar. What better place to savour a pint from the ever-changing selection of real ales.

about the pub

Hare & Hounds Country Inn
Bowland Bridge, Grange-over-Sands
Cumbria LA11 6NN
Tel 015395 68333

DIRECTIONS: on the main road through the village
PARKING: 50
OPEN: closed Tuesday, open all day Saturday and Sunday
FOOD: daily
BREWERY/COMPANY: free house
REAL ALE: 4 changing guest beers
ROOMS: 3 en suite

Food
Satisfying bar meals include filled baps (Brie, bacon and cranberry), speciality Thai mussels with lemon grass, lime, chilli and fresh coriander, ploughman's lunches, fish pie and warm salads. Look to the seasonal menu for roast duck, shank of lamb, poached salmon and chargrilled steaks.

Family facilities
Children are welcome, and on summer days they can play on the swings in the garden.

Alternative refreshment stops
The Mason's Arms (great beer and super views) at top of Strawberry Bank near the start.

☛ Where to go from here
South east of Crosthwaite, Levens Hall is a fascinating Elizabethan house, noted for its plasterwork, panelling and topiary garden.

Thornhill to Drumlanrig

Thornhill

On a route steeped in cycling history discover the original bicycle.

Above: Drumlanrig Castle
Below: The River Nith

The first bicycle ride

In 1840 Kirkpatrick Macmillan was working as a blacksmith at Drumlanrig Castle, four miles north of Thornhill. He built his one and only bicycle in his smithy at Courthill, which you pass on this circuit. It was not a chain driven bicycle as we know it today but was operated by treadles hanging from the front of the machine, which connected to driving cranks on the rear wheel by metal rods. Another 45 years passed before the first rear wheel driven safety bike was produced commercially. Macmillan cycled 60 miles to Glasgow but unfortunately knocked down a child in the Gorbals, for which he was imprisoned. It was alleged that the sheriff paid his fine because he was so impressed with Macmillan's invention.

The castle and local organisations have capitalised on this symbolic moment in the history of transport by creating some well marked on and off road cycle routes. Those

without bikes of their own might want to start this route from Drumlanrig, which has a bicycle hire shop. You could also try your hand at mountain biking, as the castle has recently played host to the Scottish cross country mountain biking championships.

The route follows some already marked trails, both on the public roads (KM 150 and Byway signs) and within the castle grounds. You should see red squirrels in any of the woodland areas and, around the castle pond, heron, little grebe and the occasional kingfisher have been spotted.

the ride

1 Leaving the **Thornhill Inn** turn left into Drumlanrig Street, go over the roundabout and take the next left into New Street. At the end bear right down **Boat Brae**, a moderately steep and narrow descent to the junction with the main A702. This is not a busy road, forming part of a marked cycle route (National Byway). Pass over the old humpback bridge, which has refuges for pedestrians (and bikes!). In 500 yards turn right at Byway sign.

2 You are now following the valley of the **River Nith**. After a mile you pass the red sandstone buildings of **Tibbers Farm** with the Lowther Hills in the distance. Once you have passed a walled garden cross over a cattle grid leading into the grounds of

Drumlanrig Castle, ahead to the left through the trees. Bear right (at Byway sign) and you will soon see the river below. After less than a mile you arrive at a bridge over the river, signed Sanquhar 9, Drumlanrig 1.

3 Bear left here onto the **red estate road**, up a slight hill past signs to workshops and estate office. Ahead of you, at the end of an avenue of trees lies the imposing frontage of **Drumlanrig Castle**. Ride up to the castle and if it's open (house May – August; grounds May – September) you could stop for refreshments at the café or snack bar and visit the cycle museum. This has an impressive selection of bicycles ancient and modern, including a replica of Kirkpatrick Macmillan's first pedal cycle – which still works.

4 Emerging from the castle turn left, following 'Cycle Routes' sign, through a **white gate** into woods (beware speed bumps!), where you should see red squirrels which are quite common in this area. Gently descending through mostly coniferous woodland you pass a large pond 0.5 mile (0.8km) from the castle. Grey herons can be seen here. In another 0.5 mile (0.8km) you come to a T-junction.

5 Turn left, over a bridge then between open fields for 0.25 mile (0.4km) before heading back into woodland, including recently planted rowan and other broad-leafed trees. Just past **Holmbank** the road rises gently until you exit the woods by a

2h30 — **14 MILES** — **22 KM** — **LEVEL 2**

MAP: OS Landranger 78 Nithsdale and Annandale

START/FINISH: Thornhill Inn, grid ref NX 878954

TRAILS/TRACKS: Minor roads with short section on quiet main road

LANDSCAPE: woodlands and river valley with views over farmland to moors and hills

PUBLIC TOILETS: Penpont and Thornhill

TOURIST INFORMATION: Dumfries, tel 01387 253862

CYCLE HIRE: Rik's Bike Shed, Drumlanrig, tel 01848 330080

THE PUB: Thornhill Inn, Thornhill, see Getting to the start

🚴 At start and finish some traffic sense required on Drumlanrig Street in Thornhill

Getting to the start

Thornhill is 15 miles north of Dumfries at the junction of the A702 and A76. The Thornhill Inn is on Drumlanrig Street, the main road through the village. If you need to hire bikes, head west on the A702 from Thornhill, cross over the humpback bridge then take the first right after 0.25 mile until you reach Drumlanrig Castle.

Why do this cycle ride?

Those interested in the history of the bicycle will appreciate the significance of this route. There is some adventurous off-road cycling, and a visit to one of the best stately homes in Scotland.

Researched and written by: Richard Love

Thornhill

DUMFRIES & GALLOWAY

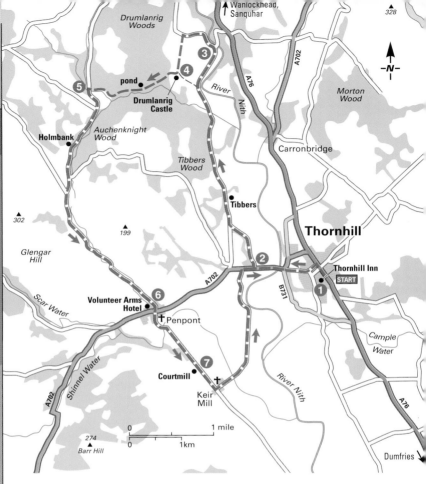

track on the left, giving views to distant moorland. After a sign to Penpont the route goes gently downhill following a stream and moss covered dry stone walls. You might see the spire of Penpont church ahead.

6 The village of **Penpont** consists of mostly whitewashed two storey houses. Public toilets are on the left just before the crossroads, where you will find the **Volunteer Arms Hotel** by turning right. Otherwise, taking care, continue straight across the main road. Three quarters of a mile after the bridge over the Scaur Water is

Courtmill smithy, the home of Kirkpatrick Macmillan, where a 1990 plaque commemorates 150 years since his invention of the bicycle.

7 Continue along this road and at **Keir Mill** turn right along Mortonholm Road (signed KM 150) then over a metal bridge, again following the Nith valley, until reaching a T junction at a converted church in 1.5 miles (2.4km). Turn right here onto the A702, past the turning you took earlier to Drumlanrig, and retrace the route back into **Thornhill**.

Thornhill Inn

This is a 19th-century coaching inn in the conservation village of Thornhill on the main road from Dumfries to Glasgow and Edinburgh. It reverted to its original name in 2004, having been known as the George Hotel for the past eighty years or so. It now caters for fishing folk, walkers and increasingly for cyclists, because of the popularity of the KM trail for road cycling and the Forest of Ae and Drumlanrig for mountain biking. Cycle lockups are available at the back of the pub. In the winter a log fire gives the inn a welcoming feel for visitors and locals alike. There is a gastro pub area as well as a non-smoking restaurant, and children are welcome in all areas. Belhaven Best and 60/- are hand-pumped beers available in the bar.

Food

The food is mainly standard pub-style cuisine which also includes steamed mussels, smoked salmon, pasta, haggis-stuffed chicken, venison casserole and steaks.

Family facilities

Children are welcome in the bar and restaurant, which offers a children's menu. There is no separate family area.

Alternative refreshment stops

There is a café and snack bar at Drumlanrig Castle and at Penpont the Volunteer Arms Hotel offers a beer garden, but only serves food on Saturday and Sunday.

about the pub

Thornhill Inn, 103-106 Drumlanrig Street, Thornhill, Dumfries and Galloway DG3 5LU
Tel: 01848 330326

PARKING:	10 spaces in front, 5 behind
OPEN:	Daily, all day
FOOD:	lunch 12-2 May to August, dinner 5-9
BREWERY COMPANY:	Belhaven
REAL ALE:	Belhaven Best and 60/-

☞ **Where to go from here**

About 15 miles north of Thornhill you can visit the Museum of Lead Mining at Wanlockhead, Scotland's highest village, and try your hand at panning for gold (www.leadminingmuseum.co.uk).

Thornhill

Gifford to Haddington

Between the coast and the hills of East Lothian.

Yester and Lennoxlove

The heartland of East Lothian consists largely of rolling countryside and gentle hills, ideal for cyclists. Set among an agricultural landscape is its most attractive feature, villages built from the local red and brown sandstone and characteristic pantiled roofs. One of these villages, Gifford, has grown up as a planned community, built to accommodate the estate workers associated with Yester Castle, now a ruin. Sir Hugo Giffard (sic) built the earliest castle in 1250 and, because of the sloping ground its base, the Goblin Ha' lies partly underground and survives to this day. The attractive 17th and 18th century village lies on its northern edge, linked to the Yester estate by an impressive avenue of lime trees.

Although there are cycle paths on disused railway lines in the area and you can link up with the national cycle network at Haddington, this route takes you exclusively through quiet country roads offering views towards the coast to the north and the Lammermuir Hills to the south. Half way round is Lennoxlove, dating from the 14th century, which is now the home of the Duke of Hamilton, Scotland's premier peer. Two hundred years ago this was the workplace of the poet Robert Burns' brother, who was the factor (agent) for the estate. His mother and sister also lived in a cottage nearby and you can follow some of their history around this route.

the ride

1 Turn right past the Goblin Ha', heading along Main Street (B6355) towards **Yester Church**, where you fork left onto the B6369 signed to Haddington. At this junction note the plaque (on the stone wall to your left) to the Rev John Witherspoon, the only clergyman to sign the American Declaration of Independence. The road rises gently, crossing a small stream, where herons and dippers can sometimes be seen, to **Myreside**.

2 You will have just passed a sign to the Chippendale International School of Furniture, which welcomes visitors. Looking back the way you have come you will see the Lammermuir Hills guarding East Lothian's southern flank. From here continue, mostly freewheeling, down the gentle incline. Ten miles (16km) ahead are the old volcanic plugs of North Berwick Law and the Bass Rock, while 4 miles (6.4km) to the right is Traprain Law, site of a prehistoric hill-fort where a hoard of Roman silver was found. At the next junction turn left, then right after 0.5 mile (0.8km).

Above: Nungate Bridge in Haddington

3 In 200 yards you pass the estate wall and woods of **Lennoxlove**, whose entrance is in a further 0.6 mile (1km). You may want to take a diversion into the grounds to view the trees and herbaceous borders or visit the house or Garden Café (restricted opening times). From the entrance gates continue for another 0.3 mile (0.5km) to the junction with the B6368.

4 If you want to sample the charms of **Haddington**, East Lothian's premier market town, turn right here. Otherwise turn left and in about 0.5 mile (0.8km) you will reach a further section of estate walls, with woods behind, on the left and views over fields to Haddington on your right.

5 In another 0.5 mile (0.8km) on the right is an off-road layby next to a **monument** to the family of Robert (Rabbie) Burns, Scotland's national poet. A hundred yards before this is the well his mother drew water from when she lived near here in the early 19th century. Continue along the road and soon bear left towards Bolton (just over

1h45 • **10 MILES** • **16 KM** • **LEVEL 1**23

MAP: OS Landranger 66 Edinburgh
START/FINISH: The Square, Gifford, grid ref NT 533680
TRAILS/TRACKS: Quiet B and minor roads
LANDSCAPE: Woods and agricultural land.
PUBLIC TOILETS: Gifford village
TOURIST INFORMATION: Haddington, tel 01620 827422
CYCLE HIRE: none near by
THE PUB: The Goblin Ha', Gifford
🛑 Watch out for occasional tractors and other farm vehicles

Getting to the start

From Edinburgh take the A1 east towards Berwick on Tweed, exiting on the B6471 into Haddington; turn right at the end of the main street onto the B6369 to Gifford, bearing left into Main Street to the car park in the Square in front of the Village Hall on the right.

Why do this cycle ride?

This gives an opportunity to experience good roads, usually fairly quiet, with views across rolling farmland and distant hills in one of the more English looking parts of Scotland. It also offers a chance to enjoy the house and grounds of one of the stately homes of Scotland.

Researched and written by: Richard Love

Gifford

EAST LOTHIAN

a mile away). Along this section are mixed woods in the estate and views ahead to the Lammermuirs.

6 **Bolton** is a small mostly 18th century village of attractive brown stone houses with traditional pantiled roofs. Note the cylindrical doocot (dovecot) with its little lantern tower next to the farm opposite the church on your left. In the churchyard you will find the Burns family burial plot. Just after leaving the village bear left up a gentle incline and take the left turn ahead. For the next mile there are farms to your left and woods to the right. Eaglescairnie Mains Farm does B&B.

7 At the next junction bear left onto the B6355, passing a striking thatched house, **Bolton Muir,** with tall chimneys and a wooden facing. Follow this undulating road with a final descent back to **Gifford** over the **Gifford Water** to the car park in the Square.

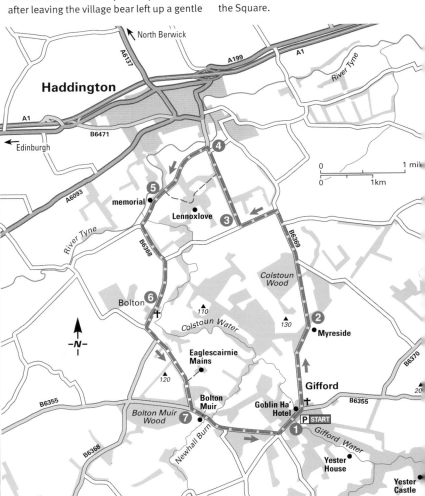

The Goblin Ha' Hotel

The Goblin Ha' has two bars: the public bar in a 17th-century pantiled building on the corner of the village square but the main lounge bar and dining areas only appeared in the attached 18th-century building on Main Street last century. The name derives from the partially underground Goblin Ha' (the Hall in nearby Yester Castle), dating from the 13th century. It is referred to in Sir Walter Scott's poem Marmion and earlier records state that 'ancient stories relate that it was built by magic arts'. The main bar and dining areas have recently been extensively modernised to create a conservatory and beer garden at the back. Beers from the local Belhaven Brewery are always on tap and it has a range of guest beers in both bars. In 2003 it won the CAMRA Best Pub of the Year award for Edinburgh and Southeast Scotland.

Food
The food includes traditional bar meals such as haddock and chips, burgers, steak pie and curry, as well as a wider dining room menu using local produce, including venison casserole, rack of lamb, salmon steak and a range of salads. Sunday roast lunches.

Family facilities
Children are welcome in all areas. There are separate children's menus and play areas next to the beer garden.

Alternative refreshment stops
The Tweeddale Arms Hotel in Gifford, the Garden Café at Lennoxlove or Peter Potter Gallery in Haddington are all good options.

☞ Where to go from here
Visit the Seabird Centre in North Berwick, featuring live camera links to the Bass Rock, which has the largest gannet colony in the northern hemisphere (www.seabird.org).

Gifford

EAST LOTHIAN

about the pub

The Goblin Ha'
Main Street, Gifford, East Lothian
EH41 4QH
Tel: 01620 810244

DIRECTIONS:	Gifford Village Square, see Getting to the start
PARKING:	10 spaces outside Village Hall or use Main Street
OPEN:	daily, all day
FOOD:	daily, 12-2, 6-9
BREWERY COMPANY:	Belhaven
REAL ALE:	Belhaven Best and guest beers

Acknowledgements

The Automobile Association wishes to thank the following establishments for their assistance in the preparation of this publication.
Royal Oak Inn, Winsford front cover inset; Shepherds Arms Hotel, Ennerdale 183; Trout Inn, Lower Wolvercote 75.

The remaining photographs are held in the Association's own photo library (AA World Travel Library) and were taken by the following photographers:
Martyn Adelman 114; Pat Aithie 77; Jeff Beazley 200; Pete Bennett 160; Malc Birkitt 116; E A Bowness 180, 181, 187b, 191, 195; Ian Burgum 76, 91; John O'Carroll 24/5; Neil Coates 120/1, 120, 123, 124, 128t, 129b, 131, 132, 135; Steve Day 29; Kenya Doran 68/9, 70, 72; Derek Forss 44, 45, 47; David Foster 43, 51; John Gillham 159, 167, 168; Paul Grogan 105, 106, 107, 108/9, 111, 112/3, 115; David Hancock 79, 80/1, 83, 119; Mike Haywood 88; Anthony Hopkins 127b; Debbie Ireland 31t; Richard Ireland 127t; Caroline Jones 8/9, 86; Dennis Kelsall 28, 31b, 33, 34, 35, 36, 39, 67, 71, 84, 87, 92/3, 92, 95, 96, 97, 99t, 99b, 100/1, 103; Andrew Lawson 110; Tim Locke 52, 53, 55, 56/7, 59, 60, 63; Richard Love 200/1, 203, 207; Tom Mackie 194; Terry Marsh 136, 137, 139, 140/1, 143, 144/5, 146, 147, 148/9, 149, 151; S&O Matthews 38, 116/7; John Morrison 156, 158, 162, 163, 166, 171, 172, 176/7; Graham Rowatt 179; Jon Sparks front cover, 155, 175, 184, 187t, 188, 188/9, 193, 196, 197, 199; Richard Surman 65, 66; David Tarn 152; Rupert Tenison 9; Martyn Trelawny 60/1; Sue Viccars 11, 12/3, 15, 17, 19, 20, 23, 27; Wyn Voysey 40, 41, 49, 50.

Every effort has been made to trace the copyright holders, and we apologise in advance for any unintentional omissions or errors. We would be pleased to apply any corrections in any following edition of this publication.